Studies in Regional and Local History

General Editor Nigel Goose

Previous titles in this series

Volume 1: *A Hertfordshire demesne of Westminster Abbey: Profits, productivity and weather*
by Derek Vincent Stern (edited and with an introduction by Christopher Thornton)
(ISBN 978-0-900458-92-7, £29.99 hb)

Volume 2: *From Hellgill to Bridge End: Aspects of economic and social change in the Upper Eden Valley, 1840–95*
by Margaret Shepherd
(ISBN 978-1-902806-27-3, £35.00 hb
ISBN 978-1-902806-32-7, £18.95 pb)

Volume 3: *Cambridge and its Economic Region, 1450–1560*
by John S. Lee
(ISBN 978-1-902806-47-1, £35.00 hb
ISBN 978-1-902806-52-5, £18.99 pb)

Volume 4: *Cultural Transition in the Chilterns and Essex Region, 350 AD to 650 AD*
by John T. Baker
(ISBN 978-1-902806-46-4, £35.00 hb
ISBN 978-1-902806-53-2, £18.99 pb)

Volume 5: *A Pleasing Prospect: Society and culture in eighteenth-century Colchester*
by Shani D'Cruze
(ISBN 978-1-902806-72-3, £35.00 hb
ISBN 978-1-902806-73-0, £18.99 pb)

Volume 6: *Agriculture and Rural Society after the Black Death: Common themes and regional variations*
by Benn Dodds and Richard Britnell
(ISBN 978-1-902806-78-5, £35.00 hb
ISBN 978-1-902806-79-2, £18.99 pb)

Volume 7: *A Lost Frontier Revealed: Regional separation in the East Midlands*
by Alan Fox
(ISBN 978-1-902806-96-9, £35.00 hb)

Land and Family

Trends and local variations in the
peasant land market on the Winchester
bishopric estates, 1263–1415

John Mullan and Richard Britnell

University of Hertfordshire Press
Studies in Regional and Local History

Volume 8

First published in Great Britain in 2010 by
University of Hertfordshire Press
Learning and Information Services
University of Hertfordshire
College Lane
Hatfield
Hertfordshire AL10 9AB

British Library Cataloguing in Publication Data
A catalogue record for this book is available from the British Library

ISBN 978-1-902806-94-5 hardback
ISBN 978-1-902806-95-2 paperback

Design by Geoff Green Book Design, CB4 5RA
Printed in Great Britain by Athenaeum Press Limited, Gateshead, NE11 0PZ

Publication grant

Publication has been made possible by a generous grant from the Marc Fitch Fund

Contents

Figures

Tables

Abbreviations

AHEW III	E. Miller (ed.), *The agrarian history of England and Wales, III: 1348–1500* (Cambridge, 1991)
AHR	*Agricultural History Review*
BL	British Library
HRO	Hampshire Record Office
Page, 'Estate'	M. Page, 'The peasant land market on the estate of the bishopric of Winchester before the Black Death', in R. H. Britnell (ed.), *The Winchester pipe rolls and medieval English society* (Woodbridge, 2003), pp. 61–80
Page, 'Farnham'	M. Page, 'The peasant land market on the bishop of Winchester's manor of Farnham, 1263–1349', *Surrey Archaeological Collections*, 90 (2003), pp. 163–79
Page, 'Southern England'	M. Page, 'The peasant land market in southern England: the estate of the bishops of Winchester, 1260–1350', in L. Feller and C. Whickham (eds), *Le marché de la terre au Moyen Âge* (Rome, 2005), pp. 315–40
PRBW 1301-2	*The pipe roll of the bishopric of Winchester, 1301–2*, ed. and trans. M. Page, Hampshire Record Series, 14 (Winchester, 1996)
PRBW 1409-10	*The pipe roll of the bishopric of Winchester 1409–10*, ed. and trans. M. Page, Hampshire Record Series, 16 (Winchester, 1999)

Studies in Regional and Local History

General Editor's preface

Volume eight in the *Studies in Regional and Local History* series is the product of research conducted between 1996 and 2003, now brought together in a single volume which throws important new light upon the peasant land market between the second half of the thirteenth and early fifteenth centuries. The existence of such a market was known to scholars in the earlier part of the twentieth century but, as it was then thought that it was restricted to the free tenantry rather than the mass of unfree tenants, it attracted little historical interest. It was only when an active land market among customary tenants who held land in villeinage was discovered by R.H. Hilton and M.M. Postan in the 1950s and early 1960s that the topic came to the fore. While the early evidence that excited Postan took the form of a cartulary for Peterborough Abbey, the detailed evidence of these transfers was subsequently found in manorial court rolls, which rarely survive before the last thirty years of the thirteenth century, and a number of detailed local and regional surveys were subsequently undertaken. The present study, however, is on a very different scale, and uses completely different sources.

The estates of the bishops of Winchester were extensive, including over fifty manors in all scattered across a number of southern counties – Berkshire, Buckinghamshire, Hampshire, Oxfordshire, Somerset, Surrey and Wiltshire. The manors that comprised these estates were also sometimes very large, and hence the bishop's Somerset manor of Taunton, and his Berkshire manor of Wargrave, each encompassed a number of villages. The widespread nature of these estates raised initially question marks over the suitability of this survey for inclusion in a series devoted to regional and local history, but after some discussion between Richard Britnell and the series' editor, it was agreed that – in the broadest sense – the bishops' estates could be taken to represent the heartland of southern England, that greater specificity was provided by the fact that roughly half of these manors were situated in the county of Hampshire, while the existence of more outlying manors, particularly those in Somerset, provided opportunities for inter-regional comparison with the central core of the estate. The extent and variety of the estate also makes possible comparison between manors of very different quality. In any case, the importance of this study was deemed to outweigh any semantic issues that might be raised in relation to the title of the series and the geographical extent of the bishop of Winchester's estates.

The records of the estates of the bishop of Winchester have been extensively used by medieval economic and social historians. Although no court rolls survive for Winchester, they provide the earliest surviving series of account rolls, the first extant account in the series covering the year 1208/9 and, although other series of account rolls can be found from the mid-thirteenth century, few provide such a regular and detailed series as do those for Winchester. They have been employed by a number of historians, including W.H. Beveridge, Postan and – perhaps most notably – J.Z. Titow, to examine a diverse range of features of medieval economy and society, including wage rates, the extent of demesne farming, lordship, rents, labour services, the size of holdings and death rates, while they provide the earliest evidence, dating from the first half of the thirteenth century, of yields of wheat, barley and oats. The accounts of the income and expenditure of individual manors were presented annually to the bishop by their respective reeves, were audited, and then copied in succession on to a file of parchment which was retained at Winchester, and it is these copies that form the pipe rolls upon which the present study is based. From 1262–3 the pipe rolls separately record entry fines and marriage fines, and it is this greater detail in the accounts that determined the date at which the survey should commence. A total of over 60,000 fines have been analysed, providing a far larger quantitative basis for examination of the medieval peasant land market than has ever been conducted before, while the quantitative data is supported by such qualitative evidence as is available. They provide insight into the timing of the development of a peasant land market, the influence of the existence of assart land and purpesture, changes in both the number and scale of transfers over time (notably before and after the Black Death), the changing nature of the bond between land and family, as well as the influence of both regional and local factors on all of these variables. While scope remains for further work on the local contexts that shaped the land market on the estates of the bishop of Winchester, this survey dramatically enhances our understanding of the subject in relation to one of the most extensive and wealthy estates of southern England.

Nigel Goose
University of Hertfordshire
August 2009

Preface

This study is the outcome of two three-year research projects directed by Paul Harvey and Richard Britnell with the aim of analysing material relating to the peasant land market in the Winchester pipe rolls. The first project, concerning the evidence from 1263 to 1350, was funded between 1996 and 1999 by the Economic and Social Research Council (grant R000236499), and the second, covering the period from 1350 to 1415, was funded by the Leverhulme Trust (grant F/100 128/E) between 2000 and 2003. Our thanks are owing to both these funds for making the research possible. Both projects benefited from the support of Hampshire County Council and the Hampshire Record Office, and we are pleased to have this opportunity to express our thanks for the excellent research environment that this co-operation made possible.

The material for the first of these two projects was collected by Mark Page, and that for the second by John Mullan. Studies resulting from the project by both these two authors have already been published, and are listed on p. 9 and in the bibliography to this volume, as well as being frequently cited during the course of its argument. It was always intended, however, that the results of the two projects should be integrated in a more extensive monograph. John Mullan wrote extensive and detailed drafts in preparation for such a publication in 2003, during the final year of his work on the project, but was then deflected into other duties when the research contract came to an end. The work of preparing a version for publication was then assumed by Richard Britnell. Paul Harvey has contributed a preliminary chapter to set the research into its historiographical context.

A large quantity of statistical evidence was made available by this research, but inevitably the database does not include all the material to be found in the Winchester pipe rolls, nor all the supplementary evidence that might be brought to bear on the numerous manors of this great estate. There is ample room for additional comparative research into many of the phenomena that our data have brought to light. However, we believe that our conclusions are sufficiently interesting to justify this overview of the evidence. The large number of different manors, and the many separate transactions recorded, make it possible both to survey general tendencies in southern England, and to identify a range of local variations, with an exceptional degree of confidence.

Richard Britnell
30 July, 2008

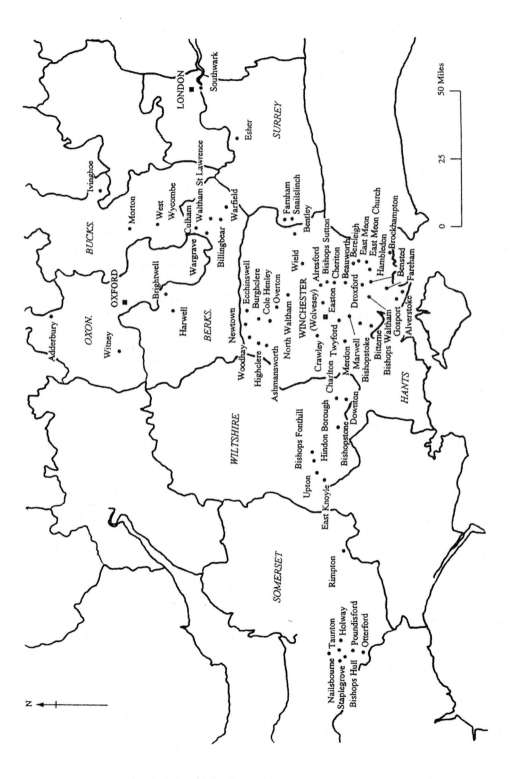

The estate of the bishopric of Winchester, c.1410. Reproduced courtesy of Hampshire County Council.

Chapter 1

The peasant land market and the Winchester pipe rolls

P.D.A. Harvey

The peasant land market – the buying and selling of properties by smallholding tenants – attracted little interest among historians before the middle of the twentieth century. That there was such a market was well known to archivists, editors, antiquaries, to anyone who examined the content of any cartulary or any medieval archive, for documents that it produced were there in their thousands, charters recording gifts, sales and leases of often tiny pieces of arable or meadow, minutely defined. As F.M. Stenton put it in 1920, in the introduction to his important edition of Danelaw charters, 'In and after the time of Henry II the charter evidence is copious. And as time goes on we obtain … an increasing body of charters which prove that people are selling parcels of land to one another.'[1] These people would all be freeholders, for villein tenants, once they had been classed as servile in the early thirteenth century, could not be party to a charter that would be accepted in a royal court of law. This perhaps explains historians' lack of interest: while no one could question the existence of freeholding peasants, they were seen as of little significance, an almost anomalous strand in a social structure of manorial lords and unfree tenants, a rural economy dominated by the demesnes that were worked by these tenants' labour services.

In an article in 1938 F.M. Powicke questioned this view. He suggested that free tenants, often of quite small holdings, were more numerous and a far more important part of rural society than had been supposed. He looked at their position in general, then in detail at charters from Weston Underwood in Buckinghamshire that recorded free tenants' transactions, and he concluded that 'Under the cover of the manorial system, a network of free tenant rights, becoming ever more complicated and constantly changing, was spread over rural England.'[2] Underlying Powicke's argument was the work of E.A. Kosminsky, published in Russian in 1935 and made known to Powicke, who did not read Russian, by M.M. Postan. From a statistical analysis of the 1279 Hundred Rolls that covered a swathe of counties across midland England, from Cambridgeshire to Warwickshire, Kosminsky showed that free tenants were far from being few and unimportant; in some areas they were more numerous and held more land than the villeins, and, indeed, villages could be found where there were no villeins at all, but only free tenants.

An English translation of Kosminsky's work was published in 1956,[3] and the

---

1. F.M. Stenton (ed.), *Documents illustrative of the social and economic history of the Danelaw*, Records of the Social and Economic History of England and Wales, 1st series, 5 (London, 1920), p. xlix.

2. F.M. Powicke, 'Observations on the English freeholder in the thirteenth century', in *Wirtschaft und Kultur: Festschrift zum 70. Geburtstag von Alfons Dopsch* (Baden bei Wien, 1938), p. 392.

3. E.A. Kosminsky, *Studies in the agrarian history of England in the thirteenth century*, trans. R. Kisch, ed. R.H. Hilton (Oxford, 1956).

following year a book by W.G. Hoskins brought home many of its lessons. This was his study of Wigston Magna in Leicestershire, a village where free tenants probably outnumbered the unfree in the later Middle Ages and where they certainly predominated in the historical record.[4] Hoskins's account of medieval Wigston was drawn not from the records of manorial lords and their demesnes – surveys, account rolls, court rolls – but from the free tenants' charters that recorded how lands passed between them and to others. A picture emerged that bore no relation to the classical manor of lord, demesne and villeins. At the same time, by implication Hoskins demonstrated the limitations of these charters as evidence even for these transactions and for those who took part in them. At best they present a patchy record, seldom comprehensive even when many survive; at Wigston they relate only to 'a good sample of families and tenements in one part of the village'.[5] There they survive in the records of the early-sixteenth-century hospital or almshouse: grants of land to the hospital and the earlier documents relating to the same properties, inevitably a very partial picture. Moreover, charters can be tantalisingly uninformative. Until the later thirteenth century it was unusual for them to give the date of the transaction; this can be assessed only from what can be discovered elsewhere of the parties and witnesses or, where we have the original charter and not just a cartulary copy, by the handwriting and any endorsements. Then, just at the point when charters begin to be dated, they stop telling us how much money changed hands: in the fourteenth and fifteenth centuries we are told only that the property was sold for 'a certain sum of money' or some such phrase.[6]

It was against this background that in 1960 the Northamptonshire Record Society published a mid-fourteenth-century cartulary, edited by C.N.L. Brooke and M.M. Postan and entitled *Carte nativorum*, the charters of the villeins. This was a turning point in our understanding of the peasant land market in England. The manuscript was in the archives of Peterborough Abbey, its title copied on the cover in an eighteenth-century hand from its first page of text. Postan tells how, on first seeing it in 1938, he thought that 'an antiquary should have known better than to perpetuate on the cover the title of *Carte nativorum*. Was it not a commonplace of legal history that villeins could not acquire or transfer property by charter?'[7] But he looked further and found that this title was entirely accurate: the manuscript was a register of charters recording the acquisition of lands by the abbey's unfree tenants, supplementary to the lands they held of the abbey in villeinage. Whether these charters would stand up to scrutiny in a court of law was beside the point. Peterborough's villeins were buying and selling lands, mostly probably free land but sometimes specifically land held in villeinage, and were recording these transactions in sealed charters; and the abbey,

4. W.G. Hoskins, *The Midland peasant: the economic and social history of a Leicestershire village* (London, 1957), pp. 28–30, 62.

5. *Ibid.*, p. 30; also p. 9.

6. P.D.A. Harvey, 'The peasant land market in medieval England – and beyond', in Z. Razi and R.M. Smith (eds), *Medieval society and the manor court* (Oxford, 1996), pp. 405–6.

7. C.N.L. Brooke and M.M. Postan (eds), *Carte nativorum: a Peterborough Abbey cartulary of the fourteenth century*, Northamptonshire Record Society, 20 (Northampton, 1960), p. xxviii.

instead of trying to stop this traffic by confiscating the lands or annulling the purchases, merely set about regulating it by keeping copies of the documents.[8]

No parallel has been found to Peterborough Abbey's register of its villeins' charters, but there is no reason to suppose that such charters were peculiar to this one estate. We can now accept that customary tenants – villeins – were a significant proportion of those transferring small amounts of land by charter, probably in the thirteenth and fourteenth centuries, and certainly in the fifteenth century, when the distinction between customary and other tenants, between unfree and free, was breaking down. What proportion, however, we do not know. It was a happy chance that Postan, working on Peterborough surveys, recognised in the charters names already familiar to him as villein tenants. Charters do not normally reveal a smallholder's status, free or unfree; this can be discovered only from manorial surveys and court rolls, and their survival along with relevant charters is unusual. However, in 1953 R.H. Hilton had already found that villeins were leasing lands from Gloucester Abbey in the thirteenth and fourteenth centuries by means of documents sealed with their own seals.[9] Systematic research would almost certainly discover that what was happening at Peterborough and Gloucester was happening on many other estates as well.

Hilton thus anticipated Postan in showing that unfree villeins might be parties to sealed charters. But there were other facets as well to Postan's historical introduction to *Carte nativorum*, making it seminal work, one of the more important of his contributions to knowledge. In 1889 F.W. Maitland, editing the court rolls of Ramsey Abbey's manor of King's Ripton in Huntingdonshire, had noted that the villeins' frequent surrenders of property into the hands of the manorial lord showed that 'a brisk traffic was done in small parcels of land'.[10] A.E. Levett, in work published in 1938, found that on the estates of St Albans Abbey villeins were regularly leasing parts of their holdings to one another, but no one had followed up Maitland's suggestion that villeins were effectively buying and selling unfree lands through the manorial court. Now, however, Postan set it beside the villeins' transfer of land by charter. In law the only way a villein could divest himself of his holding, or any part of it, was to surrender it – hand it back in the manorial court to the lord of the manor, who would then let it out to a new tenant in villeinage. The surrender and the entry of the new tenant would be recorded on the manor's court rolls. Sometimes the land would be surrendered specifically to the use (*ad opus*) of a named person who would then be admitted as the new tenant, and Postan saw these as instances of sales of land; the new tenant will have paid some form of purchase price to the old, and both will have

8. *Ibid.*, pp. xix, xxxii.

9. R.H. Hilton, 'Gloucester Abbey leases of the late thirteenth century', *University of Birmingham Historical Journal*, 4 (1953–4), pp. 11–13; reprinted in *idem, The English peasantry in the later Middle Ages* (Oxford, 1975), pp. 153–5.

10. F.W. Maitland (ed.), *Select pleas in manorial and other seignorial courts*, Selden Society, 2 (London, 1889), p. 105.

paid fees to the lord for effecting the transfer.[11] Taking these transfers in the manorial court along with conveyances by charter, whether by free or by unfree tenants, we have substantial evidence for what Postan called 'the village land market'.[12]

From some manors significant series of court rolls survive complete or nearly complete over many decades. Where this is the case they provide a better record of the transfers of customary, unfree, land than any but the fullest series of charters can give us of transfers of free land, whether by free or by unfree tenants. Partly this is because it is such a full record; in theory, and mostly in practice, every change in the tenure of unfree land had to be made in the manorial court and entered on the court roll. There is a gap in the record only if a court roll is lost from the sequence, and — as is *not* the case in a series of charters — we can nearly always tell if this has occurred, when one or more court rolls are missing. Unlike charters, all court rolls are dated. Then again, the court rolls record every change of tenure: not only what we assume to be sales and purchases, but changes when a tenant died or became too infirm to manage the holding, so that it passed to a widow, a son or another relative whose relationship to the former tenant is often revealed in the record. However, we are more likely to find a piece of property fully described and defined in a charter than on a court roll, and court rolls are far scarcer than charters; they survive in twos and threes from many places, but the full series that tell us most have seldom survived. Moreover, while we have charters relating to small pieces of land from the mid-twelfth century onwards, the earliest known original court roll dates from 1246 and very few survive from before the 1270s.[13]

There were growing signs of interest in the peasant land market before Postan wrote in 1960; Rosamond Faith, for example, was already at work on the fourteenth- and fifteenth-century land market on nine manors in Berkshire and one in Wiltshire. Even so, Postan's introduction to *Carte nativorum* was a huge stimulus to further investigation; this was the first publication to look at the land market as a whole, and the evidence of the court rolls along with the evidence of the charters showed that the buying and selling of small areas of land, customary as well as free, was a normal feature of rural life from the early thirteenth century.[14] Historians working on a

---

11. *Ibid.,* p. 106; Brooke and Postan (eds), *Carte nativorum,* p. xlvi. C. Howell, *Land, family and inheritance in transition: Kibworth Harcourt, 1280–1700* (Cambridge 1983), pp. 245–8, sees transfers *ad opus* as giving the incomer customary hereditary rights that would not pass if the holding had been transferred without this phrase: it meant that there was no break in tenure, for the holding was theoretically held by the original tenant, but to the use of the incomer. This interpretation may have arisen from *Select Pleas,* p. 106, and note, where Maitland, with less than his customary lucidity, comments that 'the idea of one man being seised of land to the use (*ad opus*) of another was a familiar idea enough in the manorial sphere long centuries before the Court of Chancery began to coerce the "feoffee to uses" with a writ of subpoena'. My understanding is that he is suggesting that villein tenure in general was in effect a form of tenure to use from the lord of the manor who was in law the freehold owner of all property held in villeinage. While we must always allow for local variation in custom and in phraseology, there seems no reason to doubt that '*ad opus*' means no more than the agreed transfer of the holding, probably normally against payment, from the current villein tenant to the other who is named.

12. Brooke and Postan (eds), *Carte nativorum,* p. xlix.

13. P.D.A. Harvey, *Manorial records,* 2nd edn (London, 1999), p. 41.

14. Brooke and Postan (eds), *Carte nativorum,* pp. xxxvii–xxxix.

particular area, a particular estate or a particular place now examined the land market as an integral part of the local economy and society: David Roden on the Chiltern Hills in 1969, Barbara Harvey on the estates of Westminster Abbey in 1977 and Zvi Razi on family structure at Halesowen in Worcestershire are examples.[15] But the peasant land market of itself now attracted research. P.R. Hyams argued in 1970 that it first developed in East Anglia and Kent in the early thirteenth century, and that it was the middle of the century before it became widespread in the rest of England,[16] and in 1988 L.A. Slota looked at the way manorial courts of St Albans Abbey accommodated, willingly or unwillingly, the growing number of land transfers.[17]

Others followed the lead of Rosamond Faith and investigated the way the land market worked on a single manor or a small group. They found that some phenomena recurred in many places: the fragmentation of virgates and other standard holdings through the agency of the land market; the tendency of holdings to polarise so that a range of uniform holdings would be replaced by some large, some small; a few tenants who would build up substantial holdings only to reduce them again years later; participation of townsmen in the land market in nearby manors; and so on. But they also found that there was no universal pattern. A few broad regional differences emerged: for instance, standard holdings disappeared much earlier in Norfolk than in County Durham. Otherwise there was enormous variety of experience between one place and another. On neighbouring manors the land market might be quite different in its form and in its effects for no apparent reason: different lordship, different topography, different agrarian history, different traditions may, any or all, have been responsible, but none could be pinpointed.

This came out clearly in four regional studies of the peasant land market that were published together in 1984, each an abridged version of a doctoral thesis. Rosamond Faith, with her work on Berkshire and Wiltshire, was joined by Janet Williamson on three manors in Norfolk, Andrew Jones on five places in Bedfordshire and Tim Lomas on the south-east corner of County Durham, while P.D.A. Harvey contributed general discussion on the chronology of the land market and the forms of the peasant holding.[18] But while the focus of the book was the peasant land market, its chronology and the way it worked in all these places, the authors inevitably looked at other questions too. The inheritance of holdings, the provision for non-inheriting children, the position of widows, migration to or from the manor, the whole structure of the peasant family – all these were relevant to the land market which, indeed, could not be viewed in isolation, and it is the peculiar merit of manorial court rolls that they

---

15. D. Roden, 'Fragmentation of farms and fields in the Chiltern Hills: thirteenth century and later', *Mediaeval Studies*, 31 (1969), pp. 231–7; B. Harvey, *Westminster Abbey and its estates in the Middle Ages* (Oxford, 1977), pp. 294–330; Z. Razi, *Life, marriage and death in a medieval parish: economy, society and demography in Halesowen 1270–1400* (Cambridge, 1980), pp. 76–97.

16. P.R. Hyams, 'The origins of a peasant land market in England', *Economic History Review*, 2nd series, 23 (1970), pp. 18–31.

17. L.A. Slota, 'Law, land transfer, and lordship on the estates of St. Albans Abbey in the thirteenth and fourteenth centuries', *Law and History Review*, 6 (1988), pp. 121–38.

18. P.D.A. Harvey (ed.), *The peasant land market in medieval England* (Oxford, 1984).

throw light on all these matters in a way that the charters recording the market in free land do not. It was in just this context, a detailed and ground-breaking demographic study of the village, that Zvi Razi in 1980 had looked at the land market in Halesowen. Now, in 1984, a second collection of essays edited by Richard Smith, entitled *Land, kinship and life-cycle* and not confined to the Middle Ages, explored this rather broader theme.[19] But the medieval land market was part of this picture, and the book included essays on its working, along with inheritance, on single manors in Norfolk by B.M.S. Campbell, in Suffolk by Smith himself, in Cambridgeshire by Jack Ravensdale and – a postscript to his earlier work – at Halesowen by Zvi Razi. In the same volume Ian Blanchard looked at groups of manors in Derbyshire and east Somerset with special reference to the effect of local industries on the land market, and two essays by Christopher Dyer examined peasant families and their holdings more generally in the late medieval west Midlands.

All these studies showed how much we depend on the chance survival of particularly complete series of manorial court rolls; the fewer gaps there are in a series, the more likely we are to gain an accurate picture of the manor's peasantry and their transactions, and for work on this topic we are as likely to be misled as enlightened if no more than a few stray rolls survive.[20] It was thus as a natural corollary to their work on medieval peasant families and their land that in 1996 Zvi Razi and Richard Smith edited another collection of essays, this time focused specifically on these documents as an historical source: *Medieval society and the manor court.*[21] It included a complete catalogue, by Judith Cripps, Rodney Hilton and Janet Williamson, of court rolls that survive in significant series. For the rest, one contribution, by P.D.A. Harvey, looked at the current state of research on the land market and at possible ways forward, and some of the other essays were also concerned with peasant families and their holdings. But the land market is only one of the areas of work that depend on court-roll evidence, and the essays covered a number of other topics, among them the law applied in manorial courts and its relation to the common law, an interesting question of current debate.

By the end of 1996, however, the research published in the present volume – an investigation of peasant families and the land market on the estates of the medieval bishops of Winchester – was already under way. It is on a far larger scale than any earlier work on this topic and, paradoxically, it owes nothing to court rolls – indeed, few medieval court rolls survive from the bishopric manors. Instead it is based on the bishops' estate accounts, the Winchester pipe rolls. For every one of the fifty-odd manors of the estate an account was drawn up every Michaelmas showing what money the bishop's local official, the reeve, had received and how it had been spent, drawing a balance owing either to the reeve or to the bishop; along with this cash account were accounts of the manor's corn and livestock. After the accounts for all the manors had been audited they were copied, one after the other, on a single file of

19. R.M. Smith (ed.), *Land, kinship and life-cycle* (Cambridge, 1984).
20. Z. Razi, 'The Toronto school's reconstitution of medieval peasant society: a critical view', *Past and Present*, 85 (1979), pp. 142–6.
21. Razi and Smith (eds), *Medieval society and the manor court.*

parchment that was the year's pipe roll. This was kept at Winchester, while the original accounts were probably returned to the manors to be referred to over the next few years but then subsequently discarded.

Other owners of large estates dealt with their accounts in the same way in the first few decades after demesne farming – running manors through the owner's own officials – replaced a general policy of leasing manors out in the late twelfth century. We have accounts copied out for entire estates – enrolled accounts like the Winchester pipe rolls – for Winchester Cathedral Priory, the archbishopric of Canterbury, Peterborough Abbey and a few others. But in several crucial ways the Winchester pipe rolls are unique. For one thing, they survive from a very early date, 1208–9, and are, indeed, all but the earliest manorial accounts that we have. For another, the bishops of Winchester continued this system, laboriously copying out all these accounts every year, long after other estates had changed to more efficient methods. Even Crowland Abbey, which continued enrolled accounts much longer than most, abandoned them between 1315 and 1319, whereas at Winchester the system persisted down to 1711, although in books, not rolls, from 1456.[22] Moreover, the series is amazingly complete, with very few gaps.[23] As a source of information on the administration and economy of a large medieval estate it is unparalleled in England, or, indeed, anywhere in Europe.

However, it is another peculiarity of the Winchester pipe rolls that makes them a source of information on the peasant land market. Manorial accounts in general tell us little or nothing of what happened in the manorial court. This was set out in detail on the court roll, which served as the permanent record of proceedings for future reference. Many of the transactions in the court produced money for the manorial lord: penal payments for greater or lesser offences, payments to have the judgment of the court, payment on taking over a villein holding – the so-called entry fine – and so on. For these sums the reeve would be answerable to the lord, and their total amount would be entered among his liabilities on the annual account as profits of the court, or 'Pleas and perquisites'. Exceptionally, on the Winchester pipe rolls, as also on manorial accounts from two other Winchester estates, the Cathedral Priory and St Mary's Abbey, the profits of the courts were entered not as single totals but as lists of the individual payments, explaining how each had come about.[24] At first this may have been done because no court rolls were kept, so that the pipe roll was the only written record of proceedings, but we can ascribe its continuance only to the same extraordinary conservatism that continued to produce the pipe rolls themselves. Certainly it is good fortune for the historian. Not only do the Winchester pipe rolls give us an incredibly full record of the agriculture, the buildings, the general economy, everything we would expect of manorial accounts, but for work on the land market

22. Harvey, *Manorial records*, pp. 25, 29–30.

23. For a printed list, see R.H. Britnell (ed.), *The Winchester pipe rolls and medieval English society* (Woodbridge, 2003), pp. 183–7.

24. P.D.A. Harvey (ed.), *Manorial records of Cuxham, Oxfordshire, circa 1200–1359*, Historical Manuscripts Commission Joint Publications, 23 and Oxfordshire Record Society, 50 (London, 1976), p. 79.

and for many other purposes they are all but equivalent to manorial court rolls, in a nearly complete series for the whole of the later Middle Ages, from the whole of a large estate scattered throughout southern England.

Until 1858 the pipe rolls and the other records of the estate, medieval and modern, were kept in Wolvesey Palace at Winchester. They then passed into the possession of the Ecclesiastical Commissioners in London, who in 1889 deposited them in the Public Record Office. In 1959 the Church Commissioners, who had become their legal owners in 1948, transferred them from the Public Record Office to the Hampshire Record Office at Winchester, where they remain. The 133 pipe rolls that were used for the present study, from 1263 to 1415, now have the reference 11M59/29–161.[25] In 1992 Hampshire County Council, keenly aware of the historical value of these records, hosted a meeting of medieval specialists to look at ways of making them more widely accessible and of initiating research based on them. The first result was the appointment of Mark Page to edit in translation the full texts of two sample rolls, for 1301–2 and 1409–10;[26] the Latin text of the first two surviving rolls, for 1208–9 and 1210–11, had been published long before, in 1903 and 1964 respectively.[27] Then, in 1995, seeking to extend the programme into research, it was agreed that the peasant land market would be a particularly appropriate subject: a topic of current interest and debate that in the Winchester pipe rolls could be explored more comprehensively and on a far larger scale than ever before. An application for funding to the Economic and Social Research Council was successful, and in 1996 Mark Page began three years' work on the rolls from 1263 to 1350. A relational database was the only possible way of dealing with such a mass of material and he entered on it, from every manor on each year's account in turn, every item under the separate paragraph of entry fines and marriages that now first appeared in the accounts to hive them off in the record from the rest of the courts' business.[28] They produced some 42,000 entries on the database, and from the information that emerged it was clear that the period following the Black Death would well repay similar investigation. The Leverhulme Trust awarded funding that would enable the project to be continued to 1415, as well as giving time for a preliminary analysis and report on the data from the whole project. John Mullan

---

25. A full account of their archival history is given by R.H. Britnell, 'The Winchester pipe rolls and their historians', in *idem* (ed.), *Winchester pipe rolls*, pp. 1–6.

26. M. Page (ed.), *The pipe roll of the bishopric of Winchester 1301–2*, Hampshire Record Series, 14 (Winchester, 1996), hereafter *PRBW 1301–2*; *idem* (ed.), *The pipe roll of the bishopric of Winchester 1409–10*, Hampshire Record Series, 16 (Winchester, 1999), hereafter *PRBW 1409–10*.

27. H. Hall (ed.), *The pipe roll of the bishopric of Winchester for the fourth year of the pontificate of Peter des Roches, 1208–1209* (London, 1903); N.R. Holt (ed.), *The pipe roll of the bishopric of Winchester 1210–1211* (Manchester, 1964).

28. This underlay the decision to begin the project in 1263 instead of 1209, the date of the earliest roll, as explained below (p. 14). The 54,000 entries of all profits from the manorial courts on the earlier rolls had been entered on another database by Katharine Stocks in research for 'Manorial courts in England before 1250' (unpublished PhD thesis, University of Durham, 1998); a brief account is K. Stocks, 'Payments to manorial courts in the early Winchester accounts', in Britnell (ed.), *Winchester pipe rolls*, pp. 45–59.

took over from Mark Page and began work in 2000, using a similar database modified in the light of experience, and adding a further 23,000 entries. While the present book is the definitive outcome of the project, both Mark Page and John Mullan have elsewhere published reports on particular aspects of the work.[29]

Latterly, interest in the peasant land market in England has been paralleled by work on the medieval land market in other parts of Europe. Two international milestones may be mentioned. The first was a conference at the École française in Rome in 1986, the proceedings of which were published in Italian in the following year.[30] While it was concerned with the land market at all periods, it included four medieval contributions, two on England, one on Castile and one on Tuscany. A more comprehensive survey is offered in the proceedings of two conferences organised by the Laboratoire de médiévistique occidentale de Paris specifically on the medieval land market; they were published together in 2005, partly in French, partly in English,[31] and presented a wide range of work from many parts of Europe: the period covered, the type of property and the sources of evidence all vary greatly from one contribution to another. In two ways we see how typical the English experience is. Everywhere our knowledge depends on the chance survival of records that show more or less clearly what happened in a particular place, often for quite a short period, but no more; there is no widespread or consistent source of information. And where we can compare one place with another we find differences that are not easy to explain. There will always be many gaps in our knowledge of the land market in medieval England, but there is probably no other region of Europe where we can hope to gain a fuller picture.

One study among those published in 2005 is perhaps especially relevant to what we can discover of the English land market. Antoni Furió and Antonio José Mirar Jódar, looking at fifteenth-century notarial registers from Valencia in Spain, show that alongside the land market, and closely linked to it, was a system of buying and selling

---

29. M. Page, *The medieval bishops of Winchester: estate, archive and administration*, Hampshire Papers, 24 (Winchester, 2002), pp. 16–20; idem, 'The peasant land market on the bishop of Winchester's manor of Farnham, 1263–1349', *Surrey Archaeological Collections*, 90 (2003), pp. 163–79 (hereafter 'Farnham'); idem, 'The peasant land market on the estate of the bishopric of Winchester before the Black Death', in Britnell (ed.), *Winchester pipe rolls*, pp. 61–80 (hereafter 'Estate'); J. Mullan, 'The transfer of customary land on the estates of the bishop of Winchester between the Black Death and the plague of 1361', in Britnell (ed.), *Winchester pipe rolls*, pp. 81–107; M. Page, 'The peasant land market in southern England: the estate of the bishops of Winchester, 1260–1350', in L. Feller and C. Whickham (eds), *Le marché de la terre au Moyen Âge* (Rome, 2005), pp. 315–40 (hereafter 'Southern England'); J. Mullan, 'The time and place of entry and marriage fines on the bishopric of Winchester estates: 1350–1400', in M. Bourin and P. Martínez Sopena (eds), *Pour une anthropologie du prélèvement seigneurial dans les campagnes médiévales (XIe–XIVe siècles): Les mots, les temps, les lieux* (Paris, 2007), pp. 399–414; J. Mullan, 'Accumulation and polarisation in two bailiwicks of Winchester bishopric estates, 1350–1410: regional similarities and contrasts', in B. Dodds and R.H. Britnell (eds), *Agriculture and rural society after the Black Death: common themes and regional variations* (Hertford, 2008), pp. 179–98.

30. G. Delille and G. Levi (eds), 'Il mercato della terra', *Quaderni storici*, new ser. 65 (1987), pp. 351–659.

31. L. Feller and C. Whickham (eds), *Le marché de la terre au Moyen Âge*.

debts.[32] Whether we would find the same structure in England we cannot tell, but certainly the pattern of debt recorded on the same manorial court rolls might well throw a new light on the peasant land market. In 2006 Chris Briggs published work on local litigation over debts, a topic that could well be carried further forward, not least through the Winchester pipe rolls.[33] The present work on the peasant land market can properly be seen simply as a sample of what these extraordinary records have to reveal.

The Winchester manors cannot be expected to offer a representative picture of the land market for the whole of England, since they were confined to southern counties. On the other hand, they were sufficiently scattered to comprise a wide range of different agrarian and commercial environments, and to that extent make it possible to analyse interregional differences. It is already apparent from existing studies that there is no simple explanation of differences in the intensity of transactions in land between one context and another. On the other hand, the volume and continuity of data to be obtained from the pipe rolls offer a unique opportunity to identify some of the principal sources of variation between manors and between regions, and to that extent they allow us to formulate more positive conclusions than those to be derived from single locations, however well documented.

---

32. A. Furió and A.J. Mirar Jódar, 'Le marché de la terre dans le pays de Valence au bas Moyen Âge', in Feller and Whickham (eds), *Le marché de la terre au Moyen Âge*, pp. 573–623.

33. C. Briggs, 'Manor court procedures, debt litigation levels, and rural credit provision in England, c.1290–c.1380', *Law and History Review*, 24 (2006), pp. 519–58.

Chapter 2

The bishop's estate

This study concerns the landholdings of thousands of small households located in hundreds of settlements scattered across seven counties of southern England. It examines the various ways in which they acquired and transferred parcels of land, discusses the extent to which a market in land existed, and explores the influences that affected transfers of property. The society of the late medieval English countryside was predominantly made up of such households, which made their living chiefly from agriculture. They produced most of the country's food supply, whether for consumption within their households or for sale in the market. By the thirteenth century they needed cash to pay rents and taxes, as well as to buy goods such as salt or metal goods that they could not themselves produce. Acquiring and retaining land, and successfully managing it, conditioned their formation and survival. The experiences of the individual households we shall be studying varied, but the common thread linking them was that ubiquitous feature of medieval life, lordship; they were all tenants of the bishop of Winchester. Recent research has highlighted how important lordship could be in determining the choices available to villeins in their holdings of land.[1] However, restriction of the evidence to the manors of a single lordship has a very positive value; it enables us to suggest how much variation between different peasant communities was owing to their local characteristics, and so unattributable to the preferences of different lords.

To be sure, it is now recognised that the Winchester episcopal estate cannot be considered a microcosm of medieval English society, despite its size, and despite the variations of customs, environments and soil types to be found across its numerous components. Most of the estate was located within the broad swathe of territory where open-field agriculture was practised, and most of the manors, for all their differences in size, were recognisably of southern and midland types, which differed from the characteristic institutional forms of northern England.[2] The variety to be found there nevertheless invites the use of the pipe roll evidence for comparative study. Titow has demonstrated the possibility of making local comparisons both between different manors of the estate and between groups of manors in different regional contexts.[3] The present study is devoted to examining intermanorial differences in the propensity for land to be transferred within and between families, and, where possible, explaining these differences by reference to the regional context.

---

1. J. Whittle, 'Individualism and the family-land bond: a reassessment of land transfer patterns among the English peasantry c.1270–1580', *Past and Present*, 160 (1998), pp. 25–63.

2. B.M.S. Campbell, 'A unique estate and a unique source: the Winchester pipe rolls in perspective', in Britnell (ed.), *Winchester pipe rolls*, pp. 21–43.

3. , Z. Titow, 'Some differences between manors and their effects on the conditions of the peasantry in the thirteenth century', *AHR*, 10 (1962), pp. 1–13, reprinted in W. Minchinton (ed.), *Essays in Agrarian History*, 2 vols (Newton Abbot, 1968), i, pp. 37–52.

Not all relevant considerations were regional, however, since other characteristics of manors, such as their size and complexity, had an important bearing on the volume and character of the land market.

The bishop of Winchester's estate

The estate of the bishop of Winchester was one of the largest and richest of medieval England, generating an income in the region of £4,000 a year.[4] In Hampshire, the heartland of the estate, the bishop at the end of the thirteenth century possessed a core of twenty-eight demesne manors and five boroughs. A further twenty-eight demesne manors and five boroughs were scattered across Berkshire, Buckinghamshire, Oxfordshire, Somerset, Surrey and Wiltshire. Some of these outlying properties, notably the Somerset manors, were sufficiently extensive to permit interregional comparison with those of the Hampshire core. Most of this vast property had been granted to the see before the Norman Conquest. However, the Winchester estate was not unchanging. In 1284 the bishop lost possession of his properties on the Isle of Wight, which were appropriated to the crown by Edward I, and received in return four manors on Hampshire's southern coast which had formerly belonged to Winchester Cathedral Priory.[5] More changes occurred under William Wykeham (1366–1404). Following his foundation and endowment of Winchester College and New College, Oxford, he recovered a number of manors that had been let to feudal tenants for nominal services.[6] From time to time other subinfeudated manors reverted temporarily to the bishop's own hands while their tenants were minors.[7] Finally, some large manors split into their constituent parts: Twyford and Marwell, for example, were administered together before 1347–8 but treated as separate manors afterwards.[8] For these reasons the number of manors that rendered financial accounts to the bishop varied from year to year.

Before the episcopate of William of Wykeham there were generally no more than sixty manors, but some were large enough to encompass a large number of separate settlements. Farnham, for example, was coextensive with the hundred of Farnham and measured about ten miles by six (16 x 9.5km) at its widest extent. It was divided into fifteen tithings, some of which later formed parishes in their own right.[9] The group of manors centred on Taunton occupied a still larger area and encompassed more than sixty tithings.[10] As late as 1822 Taunton was described as a complex of five hundreds – Holway, Hull, Poundisford, Staplegrove and Nailsbourne – containing thirty

4.   *PRBW 1301–2*, pp. xx–xxi; *PRBW 1409–10*, p. xxiv.

5.   *PRBW 1301–2*, p. ix.

6.   *PRBW 1409–10*, pp. xvi, xviii.

7.   *PRBW 1301–2*, pp. xii, 363–7; M. Page, 'A note on the manor of Limerstone, Isle of Wight', *Hampshire Field Club and Archaeological Society Newsletter*, 29 (1998), pp. 25–6.

8.   *PRBW 1301–2*, p. xii.

9.   Page, 'Farnham', pp. 164–5.

10. R.G.H. Whitty, *The court of Taunton in the sixteenth and seventeenth centuries* (Taunton, 1934).

tithings distributed across thirteen parishes.[11] The tithing, as well as the manor, is often a significant unit for describing and interpreting the character of tenants' landholdings. Even manors smaller than Farnham and Taunton comprised numerous settlements with different patterns of land transfer and social structures. There were demonstrably such differences between, for example, Ashton and Upham, two of eleven tithings within the manor of Bishops Waltham.[12]

At a higher level of administration, the bishopric manors were grouped into geographically separated bailiwicks (Table 2.1). Although these were not formalised until the later fourteenth century, bailiffs in charge of grouped manors occur in the earliest pipe rolls. Bailiffs oversaw the administration of the manors in their bailiwicks, held courts in between sessions of the steward's tourn, and accompanied reeves in presenting their accounts.[13] Some bailiwicks form a useful area for regional study because their manors shared common characteristics, such as inheritance customs, that influenced the pattern of land transfers in particular ways. For most purposes, however, we have adopted an alternative grouping of manors based more on characteristics of land type.

The pipe rolls

The evidence to be discussed derives largely from the 133 Winchester pipe rolls which survive between 1262–3 and 1414–15.[14] These are among the most celebrated of medieval manorial records. As long ago as 1929, Lord Beveridge considered them to be 'incomparably the longest and richest series of manorial accounts available for study by modern economic historians', an assessment that has not been overturned by all the scholarly effort that has since been expended in studying other estates.[15] The pipe rolls contain enrolled annual accounts, running from Michaelmas to Michaelmas, for each demesne manor on the bishopric estate, drawn up from individual manorial account rolls after these had been corrected at audit. As Chapter 1 has explained, the fact that they itemise the payment of court fines is of decisive importance for our purpose.

The heart of the material relating to the land market is the record of entry fines, most of which relate to the transfer of land held in villeinage or by families of villein status. Before recipients could receive property they had to pay the bishop an entry fine for the right to take up possession. These operations were formalised in each manor court: their only record was normally the note entered first in the bishop's court rolls and then enrolled in the pipe rolls. Similar fines were charged when property was involved in marriage settlements. The pipe rolls record payments for some other categories of tenure, including some freeholdings, and it is not always possible to

---

11. J. Toulmin, *The history of Taunton in the county of Somerset*, new edn enlarged by J. Savage (Taunton, 1822), pp. 46–7.

12. Page, 'Estate', pp. 70–2.

13. T.W. Mayberry, *Estate records of the bishops of Winchester in the Hampshire Record Office* (Hampshire County Council, 1988), pp. 17–18; *PRBW 1301–2*, pp. xvii–xviii.

14. HRO, 11M59/B1/29–161.

15. W.H. Beveridge, 'The Winchester rolls and their dating', *Economic History Review* 2 (1929), p. 93.

Table 2.1
Bailiwicks of the Winchester estate

Bailiwick	Manors
Taunton	Taunton borough, Nailsbourne and Kingstone St Mary, Staplegrove, Trull and Bishops Hull, Holway, Poundisford, Otterford, Rimpton
Downton	Downton and borough, East Knoyle, Upton, Bishops Fonthill, Bishopstone, Hindon borough
Witney	Witney and borough, Adderbury, Brightwell, Harwell, Morton
Wargrave	Wargrave, Ivinghoe, West Wycombe, Culham, Waltham St Lawrence, Warfield
Highclere	Overton and borough, North Waltham, Highclere, Burghclere, Ecchinswell, Woodhay, Ashmansworth
Twyford	Twyford, Marwell, Merdon, Crawley, Bishopstoke
Soke of Winchester	Soke of Winchester, Wolvesey
Bishops Sutton	Bishops Sutton, Cheriton, Beauworth, Alresford and borough, Wield
East Meon	Fareham and Gosport, Alverstoke, Brockhampton and Havant, East Meon, East Meon Church, Hambledon
Bishops Waltham	Bitterne, Bishops Waltham, Droxford
Farnham	Esher, Farnham, Bentley, Southwark

Source: T.W. Mayberry, *Estate records of the bishops of Winchester in the Hampshire Record Office* (Winchester, 1988), pp. 22–3

make a clear distinction between properties of different legal status. The present study, which takes into account all the transfers of property recorded in the pipe rolls in order to supply as complete an analysis of local variation as possible, will call attention to such ambiguities where necessary.

The entry fines recorded in the bishop's pipe rolls should constitute a complete record of transactions in customary property across his estate. The starting date for the study, 1262–3, the first year of the episcopate of John Gervais, was chosen partly because this was the first year in which the entry and marriage fines were recorded separately from the other sources of income generated by manorial courts. Previously all fines and amercements had been collected together under a single heading, *purchacia* or *purchasia* (usually translated 'perquisites').[16] Their separation under a distinct heading was influenced by an increasing enthusiasm for detail; over the course of the later Middle Ages receipts and expenses were subdivided into a growing number of specialised sub-sections.[17] This higher quality of information is another, and more compelling, reason for beginning this study no earlier than 1262–3. Even the four surviving rolls from the episcopate of John Gervais (1262–8) contain many unhelpfully laconic entries, recording only that a tenant paid a fine for an unspecified amount of land. Only in the episcopates of Nicholas of Ely (1268–80) and, especially, John of Pontoise (1282–1304) do entry fines come to be recorded in sufficient detail for a comprehensive study of the peasant land market. From that time

---

16. See Stocks, 'Payments', p. 49.

17. *PRBW 1301–2*, pp. xii, xx; Page, *Medieval bishops*, p. 14.

on the record normally names both new and former tenants, and describes the relationship (if any) between them. It then states the amount, type and location of the land being transferred, the amount paid as a fine, and any noteworthy circumstances relevant to the transfer.

Only twenty pipe rolls are missing from the period of study. Some of the most explicable gaps correspond to years of vacancy between bishops, and these cause special problems. On the death of a bishop the lands of the bishopric passed into the possession of the crown, to be administered by royal officials who accounted for the revenues at the Exchequer. Pipe rolls do not survive for the final year or years of the episcopates of Nicholas of Ely (1268–80), John of Pontoise (1282–1304), Rigaud of Assier (1319–23) and John Stratford (1323–33). Although the vacancy that followed the death of each of these bishops was mostly no more than a few weeks, this was time enough for the king to appropriate the revenues of their estate, and presumably also the records in which those revenues were set out. This can be demonstrated from the beginning of the episcopate of Rigaud of Assier, for which the pipe roll does survive. Rigaud was provided to the see of Winchester on 26 November 1319, following the death of his predecessor, John Sandale, on 2 November. The pipe roll for 1319–20 includes virtually no details of the transfers of land conducted during this year because the entry fines authorising them were paid directly to the king. A similar pattern followed the appointment of Rigaud's successor, John Stratford, in 1323. The end of one episcopate and the beginning of another was sometimes also accompanied by fluctuations in the number of entry fines recorded. The difference between 1344–5, the last year of Bishop Orleton, and 1345–6, the first year of Bishop Edington, is striking. The number of land transfers recorded in 1316–17, the first year of John Sandale's episcopate, was also far greater than normal, although this may only reflect the famine of that year. The most extensive single lacuna spans the final years of Nicholas of Ely's incumbency and the subsequent vacancy before the appointment of John of Pontoise (1278–82). The most serious interruption – not the result of a vacancy – is the loss of the accounts for the three years of famine between 1293 and 1296, when the land market might be expected to have had distinctive features.[18] It is unfortunate that without them it is impossible to make comparisons with other estates in this period. It is also a pity not to be able to compare this crisis with the more serious famine and agrarian crisis of 1315–22. A further unfortunate loss is the roll for 1380–1, the year of the Peasants' Revolt.

Although the series of pipe rolls lacks so few years, some survivors have suffered damage. The most severely impaired is that for 1269–70, from which only a single membrane is extant, accounting for the manors of Alresford and Wield. In 1302–3 the accounts for Alresford, Beauworth and Cheriton are missing, and several lines have been lost from the entry and marriage fines of Holway and Staplegrove. More severely, in 1271–2 the accounts of eight manors are missing or damaged, in 1285–6 six accounts are missing – including that for Witney, a manor on which the land market was usually very active – and in 1332–3 the accounts of seven manors are lost. Of the

---

18. P.R. Schofield, 'Dearth, debt and the local land market in a late thirteenth-century village community', *AHR*, 45 (1997), pp. 1–17. The pipe roll for 1295–6 may yet be found: Page, *Medieval bishops*, p. 13; Britnell, 'Winchester pipe rolls', p. 6.

fifty-nine surviving accounts between 1349–50 and 1414–15 we have complete data from thirty-one, and the only years for which more than three manors are missing are 1366–7 (five manors), 1374–5 (five manors), 1389–90 (four manors), 1399–1400 (six manors), 1402–3 (five manors and Taunton Borough), and 1405–6 (seven manors and Taunton Borough). It is often difficult to judge what correction needs to be made in overall figures to allow for these losses; in 1285–6 and 1332–3 it is possibly as much as 20 per cent of the total.

Some allowances have to be made, too, for administrative foibles. Not every transfer recorded in any given annual account actually took place that year, partly because clerks were sometimes unsure to which roll certain fines were to be assigned. In the account for East Meon in 1345–6 the last four entry fines recorded have been crossed through with the note that they are to be found instead in the pipe roll of the following year; all four duly appear in the account of 1346–7. The problems the clerks encountered can be illustrated by an example from a manorial account from Hambledon in 1345–6, one of the few surviving original accounts from which the pipe rolls were compiled. John Bramshott was recorded to have owed two payments for land he had inherited, but spaces were left for the sums due. The entries were then crossed through. Both payments were subsequently recorded in the pipe roll of the following year. Evidently the business of the courts continued to be conducted after the end of the financial year at Michaelmas, when accounts were being finalised, allowing scribes to include land transfers in one roll which should properly have belonged in the next. For this reason many of the figures used in this study are averaged over a decade.

The case of John Bramshott also shows how clerks could introduce mistakes into the pipe rolls through errors of transcription. According to the original account John Bramshott inherited his land from his father, William Chidden, but in the pipe roll William is described as John's brother.[19] Such mistakes were presumably exceptional; two other accounts, from Bishopstoke and Hambledon in 1347–8, were transcribed perfectly in the pipe roll of that year.

The number of recorded entry fines was at least partially affected by the varying assiduity of the episcopal administration. Estate officers had to decide whether it was worthwhile to exact entry fines for all sub-leases, even for those of very short duration, and of very small parcels of land. In this respect the administration under John of Pontoise appears to have been considerably more thorough than that of other bishops in the century before the Black Death: it is only between 1282 and 1303 that we find small-scale short-term sub-leases among the recorded entry fines. This may be the result of the exceptional detail with which fines were recorded under this bishop, but it is also possible that this type of entry fine was not normally collected, and that the figures gathered for these twenty years are inflated by heightened scrupulousness, in which case this development was perhaps related to other examples of administrative innovation aimed at maximising the bishop's revenues.[20]

---

19. HRO, 11M59/B2/20/1.

20. M. Page, 'Challenging custom: the auditors of the bishopric of Winchester, c.1300–c.1310', in M. Prestwich, R.H. Britnell and R. Frame (eds), *Thirteenth century England VI* (Woodbridge, 1997), pp. 39–48.

Although the Winchester pipe rolls have to be interpreted with care, and although their information relating to the peasant land market is more limited than that of the very best series of court rolls, they nevertheless remain a source of fundamental importance, well able to remedy the scarcity of quantitative studies relating to the transfer of customary land.[21] The many thousands of entry fines they record provide a larger base for the study of the peasant land market than has hitherto been available. For the present study, the numbers of entry fines paid in each year or on each manor have been categorised, tabulated and analysed, and the quantitative evidence is often complemented by qualitative evidence. Many recorded entry fines are accompanied by explanations detailing the circumstances behind the transfers of land, so allowing the considerations influencing peasants to be more fully understood. Some fines concern licences for marriage, usually paid by the father, but sometimes by the mother, the bride herself or more distant relatives. There are more than 7,000 of these, equating to almost 11 per cent of all fines. Although these have no immediate connection with the movement of property or the development of a land market they can contribute to an understanding of population and social trends that have a bearing on the transfers of land.

Other estate records

The bishopric of Winchester has few surviving estate surveys and custumals, but such as there are can usefully complement the information of the pipe rolls. A partially preserved custumal of the bishopric estate compiled originally in the thirteenth century survives in a sixteenth-century copy.[22] It includes surveys of over half of the bishopric manors, about thirty-five in all.[23] Few of the individual custumals are dated, but those that are range from 1244–5 (Wargrave) to 1278–9 (Ivinghoe). Although it is tempting to guess that the others were probably compiled between these years,[24] a comparison between the custumal for North Waltham and the entry fines recorded in the pipe rolls suggests that an original survey of about 1290 was updated at various times until about 1321.

Changes in the pattern of land tenure at Bishops Waltham can be followed with exceptional confidence. A solitary fourteenth-century rental for the manor, which can

---

21. R.M. Smith, 'Some issues concerning families and their property in England, 1250–1800', in *idem* (ed.), *Land, kinship and life-cycle*, p. 15.

22. BL, Egerton MS 2418. A microfilm of this manuscript is kept at Hampshire Record Office (M405). See also J.Z. Titow, *English rural society, 1200–1350* (London, 1969), p. 86.

23. The pipe rolls refer to custumals of other manors as well, such as Ashmansworth and Highclere: *PRBW 1409–10*, pp. xv, 225, 253, 255. The number of manors depends on how the sub-manors of Taunton and Wargrave are counted. The manors included are Alresford, Beauworth, Bishops Sutton, Bishopstoke, Bishopstone, Bishops Waltham, Bitterne, Brightwell, Cheriton, Crawley, Culham, Downton, Droxford, East Knoyle, East Meon, East Meon Church, Ecchinswell, Hambledon, Harwell, Ivinghoe, Merdon, Morton, North Waltham, Rimpton, Taunton, Twyford, Upton, Waltham St Lawrence, Warfield, Wargrave, West Wycombe, Wield, Witney.

24. J.Z. Titow, 'Land and population on the bishop of Winchester's estates 1209–1350' (unpublished PhD thesis, University of Cambridge, 1962), p. 3.

be dated to about 1332, lists tenants tithing by tithing, the lands they held and the rents they owed.[25] It can be compared both with a custumal of 1259–60 and with the entry fines recorded in the pipe rolls. These comparisons illustrate the range of experience between tenants who accumulated land and those who dispersed their holdings. It shows that although peasant tenements were liable to fragment, each portion being occupied by an independent household, this was not the norm in this period. Most holdings remained intact, stayed within the family and were passed down the generations. These documents tell of stability as much as they do of change.

A final document to be considered is the customary of the bishop's estate, compiled by Sir Charles Montagu, the bishopric steward, in 1617.[26] The chief areas of his concern were inheritance, alienation, entry fines, heriots and forfeitures, although he also considered various other issues. Predictably, most of the rules he recorded were based on seventeenth-century practice, but many reflect older tradition. The rules governing inheritance, for example, are compatible with the evidence of the thirteenth-century pipe rolls; they usefully distinguish between manors that practised primogeniture and those where ultimogeniture prevailed. Montagu frequently accompanied statements of custom with precedents extracted from pipe rolls of the fourteenth, fifteenth and sixteenth centuries. Annotations in the margins of the pipe rolls bear witness to the scale of his research, which clearly exposes the heterogeneity of the Winchester estate. The rules for widows, in particular, varied from manor to manor: on some a widow was obliged to pay an entry fine in order to retain her husband's land while on others she was not; on some she was entitled to retain her land and remarry, but on others remarriage meant the confiscation of her estate. These variations in custom explain why certain types of entry fine and land transfer are recorded on some manors and not on others. A comparison of the customary and the pipe rolls can also indicate whether customs were respected or ignored. Custom, in particular as it affected tenure, was a powerful force, a weapon that could be wielded by either lord or tenant in resisting changes that threatened their interests. If it can be demonstrated that custom was manipulated either for or against the interests of the tenants, this is valuable evidence of the strength or weakness of their position in an era of changing economic and social circumstances.

Principal sources of supply

The local operation of the land market on the bishopric estate was inevitably affected by differences in the supply of land. Thirteenth-century land hunger, the outcome of several centuries of population growth, gave way in the fourteenth century to a relative abundance of property as a result of demographic contraction. The increased availability of land resulting from the mid-fourteenth-century epidemics of 1348–9 and 1361–2 had a major impact on the development of the market.[27] But although this

---

25. HRO, 11M59/E2/159512/1. The observations here rely heavily upon J.Z. Titow's transcription of this document, now HRO, 97M97/B12.

26. HRO, 11M59/E2/415808.

27. J.Z. Titow, 'Lost rents, vacant holdings and the contraction of peasant cultivation after the Black Death', *AHR*, 42 (1994), pp. 97–114.

contrast between a period of scarcity and a period of abundance makes a useful starting point for examining fluctuations in the supply of land, it is necessary to explore further the interregional variation that was characteristic of the Winchester estate and, *a fortiori*, of the southern English shires. The supply of available land, both in quality, quantity and terms of tenure, was unevenly distributed. The ancient distinction between customary and free tenures had been reshaped and hardened by legal developments of the twelfth and thirteenth centuries, and further distinctions need to be made between ancient tenures and those newly created from forests and waste in response to the high land values of the late twelfth and thirteenth centuries. Long-standing circumstances affecting the legitimacy of either dividing or accumulating formerly independent properties could affect what was available at a local level. Differences in location and soil quality made land more attractive in some locations than others. In addition, decisions on whether to expand or contract demesne farming were governed to some extent by distance from Winchester, and so were to that extent independent of local circumstances. It will help to clarify later discussions of the land market if at this stage some of these differences in manorial endowment and context are examined more closely.

Customary holdings

The customary holdings central to our enquiry were characteristically hereditary, and so, particularly when land was in short supply, frequently descended within families without entering the land market. Yet as the supply of available land improved during the fourteenth century, and as the land market developed accordingly, they too became more liable to be bought and sold. It will help to have an overview of their relative importance between manors. No evidence of the spatial distribution of customary tenements manors is good enough for exact measurement, but since we are chiefly interested in establishing ranking, and observing difference, some rough and ready indications will do. Table 2.2 shows, to the nearest pound, the gross levels of *gabulum* – otherwise known as rent of assize – that were due on the Winchester bishopric manors at the time of the first surviving pipe roll in 1208–9. These sums antedate the assarting movement of the thirteenth century, and so indicate levels of money rent at a time when customary holdings formed a larger proportion of the total than they did between 1260 and 1415. The composition of this sum cannot be precisely analysed, and on some manors it included rents from cleared land that was unlikely to be held by customary tenure. On numerous manors there are recorded small increments to the *gabulum* whose status cannot be determined. Customary tenants characteristically owed labour services as well as money rents, and the figures in Table 2.2 do not allow for intermanorial differences in the relative importance of cash payments. It is also perhaps misleading to compare the level of *gabulum* from Taunton with that from other manors, since it was later managed as a group of manors rather than a single unit. However, the great contrasts suggested by these figures are sufficiently significant to introduce this aspect of the estate's endowment of peasant customary land. The *gabulum* from Farnham was twenty times the amount of that from the smallest manors. The table does not include figures from all the manors that occur in the later pipe rolls, but it serves as a useful introduction to some of the largest; these will inevitably figure prominently in any account of the land market simply because there was more land there in peasant hands.

Table 2.2
Receipts from gabulum *on different bishopric manors in 1208–9 (median value: £20)*

Gabulum	Manors (gabulum *in 1208–9, to the nearest pound*)
>£50	Taunton (£132), Farnham (£80), East Meon (£75)
£40–50	Bishops Waltham (£47), West Wycombe (£44), Twyford (£41), Witney (£40)
£30–40	Bishops Sutton (£41), Downton (£35)
£20–30	Alresford (£27), Wargrave (£26), Adderbury (£24), Cheriton (£24), Hambledon (£23), Fareham (£23), Merdon (£21)
£10–20	Overton (£19), Highclere (£18), Harwell (£15), Bishopstoke (£14), Knoyle (£14), Brightwell (£13), Crawley (£10)
<£10	Ecchinswell (£8), Bitterne and Fawley (£7), Wield (£6), Meon Church (£5), Rimpton (£4), Woodhay (£4), Beauworth (£4), Ashmansworth (£4)

Source: H. Hall (ed.), *The pipe roll of the bishopric of Winchester, 1208–9* (London, 1903)

Demesne

Most of the bishop of Winchester's manors had demesne lands. In the earlier part of the period these were normally cultivated directly to the bishop's advantage under the supervision of local men and estate officials, and a large proportion of their output was sold. They varied considerably in size. Average sown acres on each manor before our study period, shown in Table 2.3, do not correspond to the total available acreage, since much of the land, often a third or more, was fallowed each year. However, these figures indicate the relative importance of the demesne on different manors. A comparison between Table 2.2 and Table 2.3 shows that the manors with large demesnes were characteristically those with large numbers of customary tenements as well. The relationship was not finely predictable; the ratio of demesne to *gabulum* was much higher on the Taunton manors than at Farnham, for example. But Taunton, Farnham, East Meon, Bishops Waltham, West Wycombe, Twyford, Witney, Bishops Sutton, Downton, Wargrave, Cheriton, Fareham and Merdon were all above the median values on both counts.

Because of the correspondence between numerous tenures and extensive demesnes, these large manors were also the ones where peasant agriculture could be more than usually extended by the abandonment of direct demesne management. The larger demesnes, of 300 sown acres or more, were distributed erratically about the estate. Of the Hampshire manors, Twyford, Bishops Waltham, Merdon and Cheriton were south of Winchester, East Meon, Burghclere, Crawley and Overton to the north. But some of the largest demesnes were scattered at a considerable distance from Winchester: Taunton in Somerset, Downton and Knoyle in Wiltshire, Witney in Oxfordshire, Wargrave in Berkshire, West Wycombe and Ivinghoe in Buckinghamshire. These manors were likely to be particularly affected by rising transport costs, which adversely affected the profits of estate management during the fourteenth century.

An indication of the amount of land converted to alternative uses on different manors of the estate can be gauged by comparing acreages sown under direct demesne management in the period 1209–70 with those in 1408–11 (Table 2.4). These figures do not correspond to the amounts of demesne actually released to

Table 2.3
The average sown acreages of the bishop's demesnes, 1209–70 (median value: 255)

Acres	Manors (acreage in brackets)
>800	Taunton (1829)
700–799	Downton (758)
600–699	Twyford (633), East Meon (619)
500–599	Bishops Waltham (532)
400–499	Witney (436), Wargrave (405)
300–399	Knoyle (397), Merdon (396), Cheriton (381), Burghclere (376), West Wycombe (364), Crawley (358), Ivinghoe (346), Overton (307)
200–299	Fareham (286), Bishopstone (269), Bishops Sutton (262), Farnham with Seal (256), Hambledon (254), Alresford (247), Woodhay (238), Rimpton (237), Adderbury (236), Brightwell (223), North Waltham (221), Wield (206), Fonthill (201)
100–199	Bentley (187), Ashmansworth (185), Ecchinswell (166), Highclere (157), Morton (153), Stoke (148), Beauworth (140), Harwell (137)
<100	Bitterne (94), East Meon Church (92)

Source: J.Z. Titow, *Winchester yields: a study in medieval agricultural productivity* (Cambridge, 1972), pp. 136–9

tenants; the sown area was not the total area of the demesne, and land abandoned from cropping might be kept under the bishop's direct management for other agrarian purposes. Nor do the figures indicate anything of the social consequences of declining demesne leasing, since demesnes might be leased in larger or smaller blocks, and not always to tenants of peasant status. However, Table 2.4 has the merit of demonstrating how the impact of declining demesne agriculture was likely to vary between manors. On many of the Hampshire manors the area released cannot have exceeded a few hundred acres, but on the larger manors, especially those remote from Winchester whose administrative costs were higher, the potential for transforming the peasant land market with large inputs of demesne land was much greater. On some of the bishop's larger manors demesne cultivation was cut particularly severely: the acreage sown by the bishop's own servants declined between 1292–70 and 1408–11 by 100 per cent at Downton, Witney, Wargrave, Knoyle, Burghclere and West Wycombe, and by 75 per cent at Taunton, as against a contraction of 71 per cent for the estate as a whole.

Evidence from the Winchester demesnes also allows us to suggest a rough ranking in terms of output per acre. This is not a measure of natural fertility, since the productivity of demesne lands depended upon inputs of labour, manure and seed which varied according to the administrators' perception of profitability. That would depend upon more considerations than soil type alone.[28] However, this is the nearest indication we can get of which demesne lands were the most desirable. In Table 2.5

---

28. C.C. Thornton, 'The level of arable productivity on the bishopric of Winchester's manor of Taunton, 1283–1348', in Britnell (ed.), *Winchester pipe rolls*, pp. 109–37.

Table 2.4
The reduction in the sown area of the bishop's demesnes between 1209–70 and 1408–11

Reduction in sown area (acres)	Manors (acres withdrawn from cultivation in brackets)
>600 acres	Taunton (1379)
500–599	Downton (591)
400–499	Witney (436), Wargrave (405), Bishops Waltham (403)
300–399	Knoyle (397), Burghclere (376), Twyford (376), West Wycombe (364)
200–299	East Meon (293), Farnham (256), Woodhay (238), Rimpton (237), Adderbury (236), Wield (206), Fonthill (201)
100–199	Cheriton (186), Ashmansworth (185), Crawley (177), Fareham (166), Overton (163), Highclere (157), Morton (153), Bishopstoke (148), Mardon (147), Bishopstone (139), Bishops Sutton (133), North Waltham (127), Brightwell (110), Alresford (102), Hambledon (101)
<100	Bitterne (94), Ivinghoe (79), Beauworth (73), Ecchinswell (72), Harwell (58), Bentley (53), East Meon Church (39)

Source: as Table 2.3

manors are classified in terms of the average output of wheat and barley per acre in the period 1325–49, weighted by prices of the years 1331–47. This evidence implies that there was little relationship between the size of demesnes and their quality. Of the fifteen largest in 1209–70, six were above the median quality and nine below it. Some, at least, of the demesne land entering the peasant market from demesnes at Witney, Wargrave and Downton, for example, was probably of good quality, although it is impossible from our data to say how it would compare with land already in tenancies on those manors.

Assart and purpresture

Beside customary land and demesne land, the property market on different manors was heavily affected by the existence of newly cleared land in neither category. The word 'assart' (from the Latin *assartum*), commonly used by historians to describe a cultivated area cleared from woodland, in fact occurs on very few of the bishop's manors, being found predominately at Witney in Oxfordshire and at Ivinghoe in Buckinghamshire. It is used only occasionally elsewhere, for example at Bitterne and Highclere, in the south and north of Hampshire respectively. Much more common across the estate, especially on the colonising manors of Farnham and Wargrave, is the word 'purpresture' (*purprestura*), which was less specific than 'assart' and could cover any sort of encroachment.[29] The fines tell of such encroachments, for instance, 'in the heath' at Merdon in 1266, 'in the marsh' at Bishops Waltham in 1275, but also beside the houses and tenements of village streets.[30]

Both the form and tenure of these newer lands were distinctive from older tenements in that they were more erratic in size and usually held for money rents.

---

29. *PRBW 1409–10,* p. 458.

30. As at Cheriton in 1285, East Meon in 1286, Farnham in 1287, Woodhay in 1288.

Table 2.5
Average yields per acre of wheat and barley on bishopric demesnes, weighted by price, 1325–49
(median yield: 11.06)

Average yield per acre	Manors (yield per acre in brackets)
Top quartile (17.12–20.28)	Harwell (20.28), Brightwell (19.08),
Third quartile (13.96–17.12)	Ivinghoe (16.22), Wargrave (14.76), Bishopstone (14.66), Hambledon (14.25), Adderbury (14.04)
Second quartile (10.80–13.96)	Highclere (13.43), Bentley (13.24), East Meon (13.21), Fareham (13.03), Morton (12.55), Farnham (12.01), Ecchinswell (11.77), Downton (11.58), Woodhay (11.50), Taunton (11.27), Witney (11.19), Rimpton (11.15), Fonthill (11.06), Bitterne (10.99)
Bottom quartile	East Meon Church (10.79), Burghclere (10.74), Crawley (10.49), Knoyle (10.41),
(7.65–10.80)	Bishops Waltham (10.35), Alresford (10.22), Bishopstoke (10.19), West Wycombe (10.17), Merdon (9.74), North Waltham (9.53), Wield (9.49), Cheriton (9.47), Ashmansworth (9.40), Overton (8.79), Beauworth (8.67), Twyford (8.56), Bishops Sutton (7.78), Esher (7.65)

Sources: J.Z. Titow, *Winchester yields: a study in medieval agricultural productivity* (Cambridge, 1972), pp. 121–35; D.L. Farmer, 'Prices and wages [1042–1350]', in H.E. Hallam (ed.), *The agrarian history of England and Wales, II: 1042–1350* (Cambridge, 1988), p. 787

Intermanorial differences in their availability created some of the most marked contrasts between the bishop's manors. Titow, working from thirteenth-century custumals, contrasted the Taunton group, having 'no colonizable resources worth speaking of left to it by the middle of the thirteenth century', with Witney and Wargrave, 'the two most colonizing manors of the bishopric'. The latter were already large manors, whether judged by the amount of assized rent in 1208–9 or by the sown area of the bishop's demesne (Tables 2.2 and 2.3). Between 1256 and 1306 both had cleared almost identical extents of new land, 660 acres at Witney and 680 at Wargrave, but Witney's assarting came principally in three great chunks, in 1285, 1293 and 1303, whereas at Wargrave it was piecemeal and continuous. In either case these additions to the local supply of land allowed an increase in population and output.[31] The evidence of entry fines complements this picture by indicating more broadly the distribution and availability of such land. Table 2.6 includes properties described as new assart and purpresture as well as purprestures transferred amongst tenants in the period between 1263 and 1349. It shows that the impact on the land market of such new lands, variously described as assarts or purprestures,[32] could be transformative. Fines for assart at Witney and Warfield, amounting respectively to 62 per cent and 51 per cent of all transfers, put these two manors at the head of the league for more recently expanded resources. High levels of colonisation had also been experienced by most manors of the Wargrave group (straddling Berkshire and Buckinghamshire), those around Burghclere in North Hampshire, and also Farnham and Bentley on either side of the border between Surrey and Hampshire.

31. Titow, 'Some differences', pp. 2, 8–9.
32. See Chapter 3 for more detailed discussion of these terms.

Table 2.6
Fines for assart and purpresture as a proportion of the total number of fines within each manor, 1263–1349

Entry fines concerning cleared assarts and purprestures (%)	Number of manors	Manors
>50	2	Witney, Warfield
30–49.9	8	Wargrave, Waltham St Lawrence, Culham, Highclere, Ashmansworth, Burghclere, Woodhay, Marwell
20–29.9	3	Farnham, Bentley, Merdon
10–19.9	11	Ivinghoe, West Wycombe, Bishops Waltham, Overton, Bishops Sutton, Alresford, Beauworth, Cheriton, Wield, Twyford, Bishopstoke
0.1–9.9	22	Holway, Poundisford, Bishops Hull, Staplegrove, Nailsbourne, Adderbury, Morton, Downton, East Knoyle, Bishops Fonthill, Otterford, Rimpton, Esher, Bitterne, Droxford, Ecchinswell, East Meon, East Meon Church, Fareham, Hambledon, Havant/ Brockhampton, Crawley
0	7	Brightwell, Harwell, Bishopstone, Upton, Billingbear, North Waltham, Alverstoke

Note: Whilst the majority of these transactions are for 'free standing' assart and purpresture, these lands are sometimes engrossed with customary holdings, and on some manors more than others.

Titow has argued that, with respect to the welfare of the peasantry, the extent to which assarting was possible constituted the most important source of differences between manors.[33] 'The two most colonizing manors' have to be placed in a class of their own. On other manors, the effects of forest clearance, although nowhere so conspicuous, varied greatly. In North Hampshire, Highclere, Burghclere, Ashmansworth and Woodhay had assarts – indeed, Titow identified Woodhay as largely a mid-thirteenth-century creation 'built around a small nucleus of original customary holdings' – but Overton and Ecchinswell had markedly fewer and North Waltham none. In the manors of Buckinghamshire, Berkshire and Oxfordshire there were similar contrasts. Although woodland clearance had transformed the land market at Witney, there were few assarts at either Morton or Adderbury, and none at all at Brightwell and Harwell. Meanwhile, in South Hampshire, only Merdon, with 20 per cent of transfers involving purpresture, had expanded its landed resources significantly in recent times. In the more westerly manors of the estate, too, colonisation had been slight or absent. The Taunton and Wiltshire groups had very little assart or purpresture, and although there were numerous transactions at Taunton involving 'overland', a class of property whose origin is uncertain, this was certainly not land reclaimed within the period under discussion.

Throughout southern England much of the land available for clearance had been taken up before our period of study, and already by the 1260s such property was being

---

33. Titow, 'Some differences', p. 2.

inherited and otherwise transferred.[34] In the late 1280s the pipe rolls twice record 'old assart' at Ivinghoe in the 1280s, 'old purpresture' at West Wycombe, Hambledon and Fareham in the 1290s, and 'old assart' and 'old purpresture' at Ivinghoe in the first two decades of the fourteenth century. Yet some entry fines imply ongoing creation of new holdings in the later thirteenth century. The phrases 'new purpresture' and 'new assart' usually occur without any reference to any previous tenant. There are eighty-three such fines over the estate, of which seventy-three occur before 1300, the majority being at Witney, Ivinghoe, Highclere, Burghclere and Woodhay. Either because of original dissimilarities, or because old clearances varied in their performance over the long term, assarted land differed greatly from manor to manor in quality by the later fourteenth century. There is no reference to 'new purpresture' after 1350, when fines for assarts and purprestures became exclusively a matter of transfers between peasants rather than of new creations.

Population

The bishop's manors differed in the size of their population as well as in other respects, and the number of potential buyers and sellers could in turn have an independent impact upon both synchronic and diachronic differences between manors. Evidence from the Taunton manors implies a peak of population at the beginning of the fourteenth century. In 1311 there were 1,453 males over the age of twelve in the manors of Otterford, Bishops Hull, Nailsbourne, Staplegrove, Holway and Poundisford.[35] This suggests a total population of at least 4,000 at that time on those manors. Their ranking on the Winchester estate can be roughly assessed from the intermanorial distribution of fines for marriage transfers (Table 2.7), which suggests that between 1263 and 1349 Holway, Poundisford and Staplegrove were among the ten most populous bishopric manors. The variability between manors of the portion of families that owed marriage fines restricts the range of inferences to be drawn from Table 2.7, which nevertheless suggests the probability that the Taunton manors were exceptionally populous. Predictably, there is a rough relationship between the ranking of manors in this table and the indicators of size in Tables 2.2 and 2.3.

In England as a whole it is likely that population declined by at least 50 per cent between the early fourteenth century and its final quarter from a high point of perhaps six million.[36] This was the result of famine in 1315–18, the Black Death of 1348–9, and

---

34. M.M. Postan, 'Medieval agrarian society in its prime: England', in *idem* (ed.), *The Cambridge economic history of Europe, I: The agrarian life of the Middle Ages* (Cambridge, 1966), pp. 548–52; E. Miller and J. Hatcher, *Medieval England: rural society and economic change, 1086–1348* (London, 1978), pp. 53–63.

35. We owe these figure to Dr. C.C. Thornton.

36. R.M. Smith, 'Plagues and peoples: the long demographic cycle, 1250–1670', in P. Slack and R. Ward (eds), *The peopling of Britain: the shaping of a human landscape* (Oxford, 2002), p. 181. For a lower estimate, see B.M.S. Campbell, *English seigniorial agriculture, 1250–1450* (Cambridge, 2000), p. 402. The assumptions behind Campbell's argument are questioned by D. Stone, *Decision-making in medieval agriculture* (Oxford, 2005), pp. 262–72, and *idem*, 'The consumption of field crops in late medieval England', in C.M. Woolgar, D. Serjeantson and T. Waldron (eds), *Food in medieval England: diet and nutrition* (Oxford, 2006), pp. 19–20.

Table 2.7
The intermanorial distribution of marriage fines, 1263–1349

Number	Manor and total
300–399	Farnham (351), Bishops Waltham (323)
200–299	Downton (276), East Meon (271), Merdon (265), Holway (263), Ivinghoe (240), Marwell and Twyford (229), Poundisford (217)
150–199	Staplegrove (196), Bishopstoke (190), Fareham (176), Witney (162), Bishops Sutton (161)
100–149	Burghclere (131), Trull and Bishops Hull (127), Harwell (115), Adderbury (110), Ecchinswell (108), Woodhay (105), Overton (101), Brightwell (100)
50–99	Crawley (92), Bitterne (91), Kingstone St Mary and Nailsbourne (82), Wargrave (80), Droxford (79), West Wycombe (79), Bishopstone (77), Hambledon (65), Bentley (58), Alverstoke (56), Cheriton (55), Highclere (50)
<50	Havant/Brockhampton (49), Ashmansworth (47), Calbourne (36), Bishops Fonthill (34), North Waltham (27), Waltham St Lawrence (26), East Meon Church (22), Beauworth (19), East Knoyle (18), Ringwood (16), Otterford (14), Wield (13), Morton (12), Brighstone (8), Esher (8), Culham (7), Fulford (4), Mill Lane (4), Upton (4), Corfe (3), Cove (1), Gosport (0), Rimpton (0)

recurrent epidemics in later years.[37] A comparison between hundred-penny totals of 1311 and the poll tax evidence of 1377 suggests that numbers on the Taunton manors had fallen by 54 per cent.[38] Some of the bishop's manors have left visible evidence of shrinkage in the later Middle Ages, although it is impossible to judge from such evidence how far they had declined by 1415.[39] It is not possible to chart with precision how high mortality, migration and economic change affected the ranking by population of bishopric manors during the Black Death and the sixty-five years following, but a comparison between Tables 2.7 and 2.8 suggests some continuity. Of the fourteen most populous manors in the period 1263–1349, as measured by the number of marriage fines (those with 150 or more), twelve were still among the top fourteen in 1350–1415. These included Holway and Staplegrove, whose combined adult male population had fallen by about 48 per cent between 1311 and 1377. This suggests that the experience of the Taunton manors was not exceptional. The number of marriage fines is not itself a measure of the extent of declining population, since liability to pay this fine was affected by widespread changes in the relationship between the bishop and his tenants; the number of those liable to pay the fine fell considerably more steeply than the number of those marrying.

---

37. For crisis mortality on the bishopric estates up to 1349, see M.M. Postan and J.Z. Titow, 'Heriots and prices on Winchester manors', *Economic History Review*, 2nd series, 11 (1966), pp. 383–411, reprinted in M.M. Postan, *Essays on medieval agriculture and general problems of the medieval economy* (Cambridge, 1973), pp. 150–85.

38. We are grateful to Dr. C.C. Thornton for this calculation.

39. M. Aston, 'Deserted settlements in the west of England', in M. Aston, D. Austin and C. Dyer (eds), *The rural settlements of medieval England: studies dedicated to Maurice Beresford and John Hurst* (Oxford, 1989), pp. 120–1; J. Hare, 'Agriculture and rural settlement in the chalklands of Wilthire and Hampshire from c. 1200–c. 1500', in M. Aston and C. Lewis (eds), *The medieval landscape of Wessex* (Oxford, 1994), pp. 162, 165–6 (Bishopstone), 167 (Burghclere, Highclere).

Table 2.8
The intermanorial distribution of marriage fines 1350–1415

Number	Manor and total
50–99	Downton (90), Bishops Sutton (81), Merdon (76), Ivinghoe (74), Bishops Waltham (69), Ecchinswell (60), East Meon (60), Holway (60), Fareham (58), Marwell and Twyford (57), Farnham (51), Staplegrove (50)
<50	Bishops Hull (49), Bishopstoke (44), Burghclere (44), Brightwell (42), Overton (42), Woodhay (40), Nailsbourne (39), Poundisford (39), Crawley (38), Harwell (36), Bitterne (31), East Knoyle (31), Droxford (30), Adderbury (27), Cheriton (27), West Wycombe (27), Wield (27), Rimpton (24), Alverstoke (22), Bentley (21), Bishopstone (21), Ashmansworth (20), Hambledon (19), North Waltham (16), Bishops Fonthill (15), Morton (13), Wargrave (11), Highclere (10), Otterford (10), Waltham St Lawrence (10), Witney (8), East Meon Church (7), Brockhampton (6), Beauworth (6), Brighstone (8), Esher (8), Culham (4), Upton (4), Gosport (0)

Location and commerce

By the later thirteenth century the development of local trade in southern England had progressed so far that none of the bishop's manors was beyond the influence of commercial considerations in the management of land. The bishop himself was one of the most commercially minded of English landlords, and in the thirteenth century used the demesnes of all his manors as a source of cash. Not all manors were equally well positioned, and some had exceptional opportunities for trade. One distinctive group of manors in South Hampshire, to be examined shortly, was close to Southampton and the south coast. Bishopstone and Downton were both about six miles (9.6km) from Salisbury; the latter, at least, benefited from the development of Salisbury's textile industry in the later fourteenth century, and particularly from the city's growing demand for barley.[40] Taunton offered a good outlet for produce, at least in some periods of the later fourteenth century. Esher was the nearest rural property to London, and although it was fifteen miles (24km) away from the capital it had easy access to river traffic along the Thames. These considerations benefited property values at various times. But any new opportunities arising from proximity to a town depended on the fortunes of the town in question and cannot be taken for granted. The fact that Twyford, Crawley and Cheriton were within about six miles (9.6km) of Winchester allowed them no great scope for development within our period of study.

One particular difference between manors worth highlighting in this context is the presence, in some, of their own marketing centres in the form of boroughs established by the bishops of Winchester.[41] Families in such communities were more heavily dependent upon manufacturing and trade than those of most rural settlements. Chapter 3 will suggest that there were comparable concentrations of quasi-urban population even on some manors of the bishopric that had no borough,

---

40. A.R. Bridbury, *Medieval English clothmaking: an economic survey* (London, 1982), pp. 66–82; J. Hare, 'Lord, tenant and the market: some tithe evidence from the Wessex region', in Dodds and Britnell (eds), *Rural society and agriculture*, pp. 140–3.

41. M.W. Beresford, 'The six new towns of the bishops of Winchester, 1200–55', *Medieval Archaeology*, 3 (1959), pp. 187–215.

Table 2.9
The bishop of Winchester's net income from his boroughs, 1301–2

Borough	Net income
Taunton	£34 8s 8d
Alresford	£19 17s 9d
Witney	£12 19s ½d
Overton	£12 8s 4½d
Farnham	£12 0s 0d
Downton	£8 1s 2d
Newtown in Burghclere	£7 17s 5½d
Hindon	£7 7s 4½d

Source: PRBW 1301–2, pp. 39–40, 50–1, 67, 99–100, 111–12, 144–6, 207, 328
Note: The figure for Farnham is not directly comparable with the others because the borough was leased as a whole.

such as Bishops Waltham and Hambledon, although in these instances no distinction was made in the manorial accounting between 'urban' rents and others. A resident population of tradesmen constituted a ready market for some forms of property as a source of supplementary income or as a long-term investment. It is not always easy to distinguish between the smallholdings of burgesses and those of the more rurally based populations around them, but the activity of burgesses could significantly increase transactions in assarts and purprestures, as at Witney.[42] They could also affect, if only indirectly, the management of customary land. The fragmentation of customary holdings was particularly advanced on the Taunton manors, and at Witney and Farnham, and part of this may be attributed to an exceptional local demand for smallholdings. Not all the bishop's boroughs were of equal significance in this respect. Table 2.9 ranks them according to the rent of assize they owed in 1302; the higher the ranking the larger the independent impact of the burgesses on the demand for land is likely to have been. Yet even boroughs of comparable size, such as Witney and Farnham, did not determine the character of the local land market; as we shall see, the extrafamilial transfer of assarts operated very differently in the two manors. The presence of burgesses was only one of the many independent circumstances that affected the way the land market developed on the Winchester estates.

The regional distribution of fines

The differences between manors that we have discussed will explain a good deal of intermanorial variation in the number of fines. Witney, Bishops Waltham, Farnham, East Meon and Taunton (especially Holway) always had a significantly large number. Most of these have been identified as particularly large manors. Smaller manors, such as Upton, Culham and Beauworth, had consistently few, in some years recording no fines at all. It is hardly surprising that the size of manors was a principal determinant of the number of transactions recorded by entry fines, not only because large manors had more land of all types to be transferred, but also because they commonly acquired

42. Page, 'Estate', p. 74.

other characteristics favourable to the development of the land market. They were more likely to have forest or moor that could be assarted, creating small properties held by money rents. They were also more likely to have attached markets or boroughs. However, not all large manors had the same characteristics, or the same customs, and we shall have occasion to observe numerous variations in detail that affected their development.

In addition to demonstrating local contrasts between manors, the evidence of the pipe rolls permits discussion of regional variation in the turnover of properties. It would be helpful to be able to measure the proportion of tenant land that changed hands between families, but the absence of reliable information about the total area in tenant hands rules out this approach. It is nevertheless possible to assess the number of transfers on each manor in relation to the amount of assized rent due to the bishop. This does not measure commercial transactions in land directly because it neither takes account of differences in the size of properties transferred nor distinguishes between intrafamilial and extrafamilial transactions. A region with smaller units of property will register a higher turnover of property simply because of the larger number of families per unit of land. Nevertheless, the measure can serve to establish an initial contrast between different parts of the estate, which can then be refined in the light of other data.

For this purpose the manors of the bishopric estate have been divided into eight groups to bring out regional differences that would otherwise be obscured. These groups differ from those of the bailiwicks adopted by the bishopric for administrative purposes. The index of activity shown in Table 2.10 is calculated for the period 1263–1349 by dividing the number of entry fines recorded for each period by the total assized rent – in pounds sterling – recorded in the pipe roll of 1300–1. The formula adopted is:

$$\frac{\text{total fines for each period}}{10 \times \text{assized rent in 1300–1 (£)}}$$

Boroughs are excluded from the calculation, on the grounds that little of the property there was customary, the number of recorded fines is consequently very small in relation to the rent they generated, and their evidence would merely muddy any conclusions to be derived from the manorial evidence. For the Winchester estates as a whole between 1263 and 1349 the average ratio is 2.9, but the range between individual manors is between 0.8 (Alverstoke) and 7.8 (Bitterne). Table 2.10 lists the different regions in descending order of activity so recorded, and demonstrates what differences there were between them. This figure for each group is rounded to a single digit to emphasise that the results of the exercise cannot be considered exact. Viewed in this way there was only slight variation in activity across the estate, but three groups of manors were outstanding for their number of transfers. These deserve some comment in the light of our understanding of their local economies, imperfect though that inevitably is. None of them had a particularly high concentration of lay wealth; in fact, in 1330 they were poorer than Wiltshire, which does not show up so strongly as a region of high activity.[43]

---

43. B.M.S. Campbell and K. Bartley, *England on the eve of the Black Death: an atlas of lay lordship, land and wealth, 1300–1349* (Manchester, 2006), p. 194.

The Woodland group that heads the table, even though it did not include the individually highest-scoring manors, is a distinctive subset of the widely scattered Northern group of manors rather than an independently defined region. It comprises the two manors of Witney in Oxfordshire and Wargrave in Berkshire. These both lay above the Thames Valley. Wargrave had a small seigniorial borough first recorded in 1225, but also had ready access to the Henley market from which London was supplied.[44] Witney, the largest of the bishop's manors whether measured by the amount of assized rent or by the number of transfer fines, had an attached seigniorial borough, and one of some significance; it ranks ninety-first in Alan Dyer's list of towns in 1334, ahead of Guildford and Bath.[45] The manor was also within the supply region of Oxford, about ten miles (16km) away. To judge from the crop yields of the demesne, the arable was of good quality at Wargrave, but little better than the mean for the bishop's estate at Witney. But the local characteristic that most decisively affected the level of land transactions in these two manors was extensive late assarting, a topic first explored by Titow. On both manors there were many unvirgated smallholdings created from assarted land that were more readily exchanged than properties held by customary tenure. The remaining manors in the northern part of the estate, grouped in Table 2.10 as Northern, were closer to the norm for the whole estate, although the level of activity was above average, with an index of 4, in Ivinghoe, Waltham St Lawrence and Culham.[46] On the latter two manors, as at Witney and Wargrave, assarts constituted a high proportion of total transfers (Table 2.6). The high turnover of land on these manors is a valid indicator of the vigour of the land market, since the proportion of extrafamilial transfers was above average (see Tables 6.3, 6.4, 6.5) and the proportion of transfers by inheritance particularly low.[47]

The Somerset manors comprise the Taunton group, together with Rimpton. Apart from Otterford, all these manors had higher than average ratios of transfer fines to assized rents, the highest being at Trull and Bishops Hull, Staplegrove and Poundisford. Titow has demonstrated that land was exceptionally valuable on the Taunton manors. He related this phenomenon, in contrast to the situation at Witney and Wargrave, to the exhaustion of available reserves of reclaimable land and the consequent absence of assarts.[48] There are other considerations. The rich loams of these manors were exceptionally good; John Billingsley reported to the Board of Agriculture in the late eighteenth century that 'the climate, particularly of that part

---

44. B.M.S. Campbell, J.A. Galloway, D. Keene and M. Murphy, *A medieval capital and its grain supply: agrarian production and distribution in the London region c. 1300* (London, 1993), pp. 47, 49, 51, 169; D. Farmer, 'Marketing the produce of the countryside, 1200–1500', in *AHEW* III, pp. 370–2; P.D.A. Harvey, *A medieval Oxfordshire village: Cuxham, 1240–1400* (London, 1965), pp. 103, 110; S. Letters, *Gazetteer of markets and fairs in England and Wales to 1516*, 2 vols (London, 2003), I, p. 58.

45. A. Dyer, 'Appendix: ranking lists of English medieval towns', in D.M. Palliser (ed.), *The Cambridge urban history of Britain, I: 600–1540* (Cambridge, 2000), p. 757. See, however, Page, 'Esate', p. 74, and the judgement that 'Witney borough failed to prosper'.

46. The only other manors with a ratio of 4 elsewhere on the estate were the small manor of East Meon Church in the East Meon group and Mardon in the Twyford group.

47. Page, 'Estate', p. 65.

48. Titow, 'Some differences', pp. 4–6.

Table 2.10
Regional indices of the turnover of property (excluding towns), 1263–1349

Region	Assised rent (£)	No. of entry fines	Index	Range
Woodland	92.31	5814	6	6
Somerset	190.30	7180	4	1–5
South Hampshire	215.96	7800	4	1–8
North Hampshire	102.98	2660	3	2–3
Northern	171.10	4069	2	2–4
Wiltshire	94.79	2055	2	1–2
Hampshire Chalk Plateau	439.55	9250	2	1–4
Eastern	158.18	3168	2	2–3

Note: The regional groups above are constituted as follows: Woodland): Witney and Wargrave. Somerset: Taunton manors and Rimpton. South Hampshire: Bitterne, Alverstoke, Havant and Brockhampton, Fareham, Bishops Waltham, Bishopstoke. North Hampshire: Highclere, Burghclere, Ecchinswell, Woodhay, Ashmansworth. Northern: Adderbury, Brightwell, Harwell, Morton, Ivinghoe, Culham, Waltham St Lawrence, Warfield, West Wycombe. Wiltshire: East Knoyle, Upton, Bishops Fonthill, Downton, Bishopstone. Hampshire Chalk Plateau: Overton, North Waltham, East Meon, East Meon Church, Hambledon, Droxford, Bishops Sutton, Cheriton, Beauworth, Alresford, Wield, Merdon, Crawley, Twyford and Marwell. Eastern: Farnham, Bentley, Esher.

which is called *Vale of Taunton Dean* is particularly mild and serene; and the soil highly fertile and productive'.[49] Ultimogeniture was the normal mode of descent between generations, which probably increased the pressure of demand for land.[50] A high level of commercial activity also stimulated employment and market demand; the Taunton manors all benefited from proximity to the ancient borough of Taunton.[51] On these manors, as we have seen, customary units were exceptionally subdivided, as in South Hampshire; the quarter virgate was a standard unit of property (see Table 3.4). A high proportion of transfers involved cottages, purprestures and detached fragments of older tenements.[52] The high transfer of land is again, as on the Woodland manors, a valid indicator of an active land market, since the proportion of extrafamilial transfers on the Taunton manors was above average. The level of commercial activity was more muted at Rimpton, whose trade was dependent chiefly on local rural markets.[53]

The South Hampshire group comprised the six manors of Bitterne, Alverstoke with Gosport, Fareham, Havant with Brockhampton, Bishops Waltham and Bishopstoke. Of these, Bitterne was the highest scoring of the bishop's manors by the criteria adopted for Table 2.10, with a score of 8; the others had scores of 4 or 5 except for Alverstoke,

49. J. Billingsley, *General view of the agriculture of the county of Somerset* (Bath, 1798), p. 263–4.
50. This point is discussed in greater detail in Chapter 8.
51. M. Beresford and H.P.R. Finberg, *English medieval boroughs: a handlist* (Newton Abbot, 1973), pp. 158–9.
52. Chapter 3, pp. 48–52.
53. Tables 6.3, 6.4, 6.5; C. Thornton, 'The determinants of land productivity on the bishop of Winchester's demesne of Rimpton, 1208 to 1403', in B.M.S. Campbell and M. Overton (eds), *Land, labour and livestock: historical studies in European agricultural productivity* (Manchester, 1991), pp. 187–8.

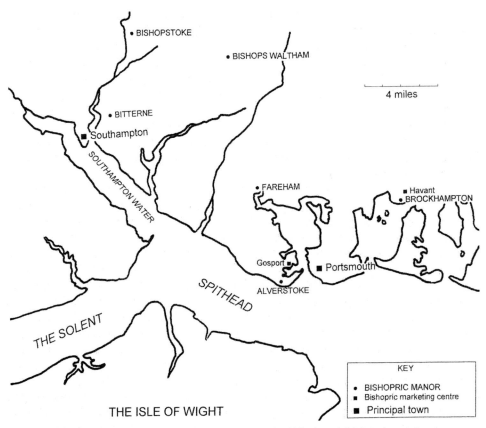

Figure 2.1 The South Hampshire group of manors on the Winchester bishopric estate.

whose ratio was below 1. The land market on these manors was less developed than this implies, since the proportion of extrafamilial transfers was generally below average. Both at Alverstoke and at Bishopstoke the proportion of extrafamilial transfers between 1320 and 1349 was exceptionally low, implying that the land market there was in fact little developed at that time; by this criterion it was most advanced at Bitterne and Brockhampton (see Table 6.3). It has not been possible to test whether average assised rents were lower in this region than elsewhere, which would mean that the index of land transfers in Table 2.10 is correspondingly inflated.[54] The quality of the land for arable husbandry was a mixed assortment of loams and clays, better drained around the coast at Bitterne and Brockhampton than further inland at Fareham and Bishops Waltham. There were some fertile soils along the coast, but they were acid elsewhere, and no better than in other parts of Hampshire.[55]

---

54. In 1810 rents in this region were often *higher* than elsewhere in the county: C. Vancouver, *General view of the agriculture of Hampshire and the Isle of Wight* (London, 1810), pp. 77, 80, 82, 84, 86.

55. Table 2.4; Campbell and Bartley, *England on the eve of the Black Death*, map 11.4, p. 194c; D.L. Farmer, 'Prices and wages [1042–1350]', in H.E. Hallam (ed.), *The agrarian history of England and Wales, II: 1042–1350* (Cambridge, 1988), p. 740; Hampshire County Council, *Audit of Hampshire soils* (Winchester, 2004), pp. 7–9.

An analysis of 1810 distinguished between lighter loams in the western and central part of this region (including Alverstoke, Bitterne, Bishops Waltham, Bishopstoke), and heavier, flinty loams further east (including Havant and Brockhampton).[56] If the high turnover of properties implies that they were in high demand, presumably among the members of tenant families, this cannot be explained by superior crop yields. Nor is it related to a high rate of abandonment; the extent to which properties passed by inheritance was higher than on most manors of the estate – over 40 per cent of all land transfers – at Bitterne, Fareham, Bishopstoke, Alverstoke and Gosport between 1269 and the Black Death.[57] There were features of local custom and of the regional economy that would allow an exceptional capacity to accommodate family members on smaller units of property. Ultimogeniture was practised at Bishops Waltham, Bitterne, Bishopstoke and Fareham.[58] Customary units of tenure were exceptionally subdivided on some of these manors, as at Bitterne and Bishops Waltham, where quarter virgates accounted for over 60 per cent of all transfers.[59] A higher than average demand for small properties may relate to the variety of economic opportunities made possible by the proximity of Southampton Water, Portsmouth Harbour and the Solent. Bitterne, above the east bank of the River Itchen near its estuary, is now a suburb of Southampton. Fareham, with a borough large enough to send members to the parliament of 1306, was a small port at the head of Portsmouth Harbour, near the mouth of the River Wallington.[60] The large manor of Alverstoke, acquired from the monks of St Swithun, Winchester, in 1284, stretched along the western shore of Portsmouth Harbour, and contained the harbour of Gosport.[61] Havant, with a market chartered in 1200, was another small port, situated close to the north shore of Langstone Harbour, to the north of Hayling Island.[62] Situations so close to the coast not only facilitated the disposal of agrarian products but also created opportunities for non-agricultural employment. Fishing for salmon and mackerel were local specialities; the former is well attested at Bitterne,[63] which also had salt pans.[64] Bishops Waltham and Bishopstoke were also within this region – further from the

---

56. Vancouver, *General view*, fold-out map and p. 9.

57. Page, 'Estate', p. 65.

58. Chapter 7, pp. 108–9.

59. See also Chapter 3, pp. 44–8.

60. H.A. Doubleday *et al.* (eds), *The Victoria history of Hampshire and the Isle of Wight*, 5 vols and index (London, 1900–14), III, p. 211, Beresford and Finberg, *English medieval boroughs*, p. 118; C. Fenwick (ed.), *The poll taxes of 1377, 1379 and 1381*, 3 vols, Records of the Social and Economic History of England and Wales, new ser. 27, 29, 37 (Oxford, 1998–2005), I, pp. 348–9.

61. Doubleday *et al.* (eds), *Victoria history of Hampshire*, III, pp. 123, 203, 205, 484.

62. Letters, *Gazetteer*, I, p. 154.

63. Campbell, 'Unique estate', p. 38; E.M. Hewitt, 'Fisheries', in Doubleday *et al.* (eds), *Victoria history of Hampshire*, V, p. 466; M. Kowaleski, 'Fish production, trade and consumption, c1300–1530, 2: the western fisheries', in D.J. Starkey, C. Reid and N. Ashcroft (eds), *England's sea fisheries: the commercial sea fisheries of England and Wales since 1300* (London, 2000), p. 25; PRBW 1301–2, pp. 243, 245.

64. Farmer, 'Prices and wages [1042–1350]', p. 730; E.M. Hewitt, 'Salt', in Doubleday *et al.* (eds), *Victoria history of Hampshire*, V, p. 469.

Table 2.11

The reduction in the number of entry fines by region (excluding towns), 1350–1415

Region	No. of entry fines		% reduction
	1263–1349	*1350–1415*	
Woodland	5814	2001	66
Somerset	7180	5962	17
South Hampshire	7800	3773	52
North Hampshire	2660	1280	52
Northern	4069	2474	39
Wiltshire	2055	1210	41
Hampshire Chalk Plateau	9250	5023	46
Eastern	3168	1731	45
Total	41996	23454	44

coast, but well within the marketing radius of the port of Southampton. Bishops Waltham, ten miles (16km) away, was a substantial settlement with its own market.[65]

The reasons for high levels of activity in the three regions described above are accordingly very different, and because of the regions' different characters, they experienced very varied fortunes after the Black Death. Table 2.11 shows the number of fines registered in the period 1350–1415, and compares for each region the percentage by which this had fallen since 1263–1349. From this table it seems that activity on manors of the South Hampshire manors declined to much the same extent as across the estate as a whole. However, the Somerset group, including Rimpton, fared very considerably better than average, and the Woodland group fared distinctly worse. The performance of the Somerset manors can be linked, if only imperfectly, to a variety of circumstances that continued to benefit the commerce of south-western England in the later Middle Ages. The poorer performance of the Woodland manors seems to be directly implied by its greater dependence upon agriculture and the unattractiveness of much of the land there. The different circumstances that had stimulated the land market in the period before 1349 had direct implications for the extent to which that activity was sustainable as population declined.

The other groupings of manors in Tables 2.10 and 2.11 show less variation between manors and less contrast between regions. Some of them – the Northern and Eastern groupings in particular – are poorly defined regionally. The three manors of the Eastern group deserve some comment because the measure of activity there is dominated by the evidence of the large manor of Farnham; the smaller manors of Bentley and Esher register a level of activity slightly above the estate average. The range of differences within the other groups hardly justifies making strong distinctions at this level of analysis. Hampshire, where the bishop had his greatest concentration of manors, may be divided into three principal soil regions, of which the mixed soils of the south, which we have already discussed, is one.[66] The Chalk Plateau region accounts for a large number of manors in a broad belt running diagonally across the

65. Letters, *Gazetteer*, I, p. 151.

66. Hampshire County Council, *Audit of Hampshire soils*, pp. 4–9.

county from the north-western border toward the south-east. The soils vary from loams rich in lime in the valleys to shallow soils directly overlying chalk on the downlands.[67] In the early nineteenth century tillage in this region was described as 'difficult and expensive',[68] and bishops of Winchester were generally contented with relatively low crop yields (Table 2.5). Yet the downs offered the alternative possibility of extensive natural pasture for sheep, and ensured that the larger properties, at least, would practise mixed farming.[69] Although Winchester was a prominent marketing centre, the region's trade was predominantly very local. The level of activity in the land market was relatively low (Table 2.10), exceeding the mean calculated for the whole estate only at Merdon and on the tiny manor of East Meon Church. Activity in the land market was somewhat greater in the third soil region, a strip of territory to the north of the Chalk Plateau region, where the soils were generally wetter and contained more clay.[70] At Burghclere, Ecchinswell and Ashmansworth the measure of activity adopted for Table 2.10 tipped slightly above the estate average. The difference from the rest of Hampshire is not great enough to justify any very strong hypothesis, but it is noteworthy that the manors of this region were at least within striking distance of trade with the Kennet Valley. However, the land market was poorly sustained between 1350 and 1415, a period preceding Newbury's emergence as a focal point for industrial growth.[71]

Conclusion

The Winchester pipe rolls supply an unequalled wealth of data about transfers of different kinds of land in different parts of southern England and on manors of different quality. A number of identifiable circumstances influenced the level and character of transfers of land on different manors. Intermanorial comparisons were inevitably affected strongly by the size of the manors in question, which not only affected the amount of tenant land available for transfer but also had an impact upon other relevant environmental characteristics, such as the level of local market demand for agricultural produce. The size of the bishops' demesnes, the presence of assarted land outside customary tenures, the size of manorial populations and the association of some manors with markets and towns were all local circumstances affecting supply and demand that were commonly related to the size of manors. Yet even large manors varied greatly in their particular mix of attributes, so that they do not constitute a uniform category.

67. They were broadly classified in 1810 as 'strong flinty loams and hazel-coloured mould on chalk, occasionally veined with gravel: more or less peat in most of the vallies': Vancouver, *General view*, fold-out map and p. 8.
68. Vancouver, *General view*, p. 134.
69. J. Hare, 'The bishop and the prior: demesne agriculture in medieval Hampshire', *AHR*, 54 (2006), pp. 194–7; *idem*, 'Agriculture and rural settlement', pp. 160–1.
70. The region was described in 1810 as comprising 'woodlands and the wastes of Bagshot, clay, sand, gravel and peat; the last found upon the wastes and in some of the enclosed low grounds': Vancouver, *General view*, fold-out map and p. 8.
71. M. Yates, *Town and countryside in western Berkshire, c.1327–c.1600: social and economic change* (Woodbridge, 2007), pp. 73, 83.

Regional differences, crudely assessed in Tables 2.10 and 2.11, suggest that the availability of assarted land and the commercial opportunities offered by the local economy were the two most important determinants of regional variation on the Winchester estate. The three groups of manors where the turnover of tenant property was most rapid – Witney and Wargrave, South Hampshire, Somerset – illustrate the separate effects of these different circumstances. The impact of commercial opportunities is of particular interest. Much of the discussion of the demand for land in the period between 1263 and 1415 has explored the consequence of a changing relationship between population and resources, using a model that excludes any significant independent role for money and commerce. However, the importance we can attach to commercial environments in affecting the turnover of peasant property implies that this limited analysis is not enough to account for the principal differences between manors or economic regions. Nor, given the importance of commercial environments, can it be expected to account for all the changes during the period, important though the fourteenth-century decline in population undoubtedly was. Local commercial opportunities were not constant, and the period under consideration was one of recurrent instability. Across the estate there were accordingly large and complex changes in the volume and composition of transfers between 1269 and 1415 that are not easily predictable from the population–resources model, and one of the objects of the following chapters will be to assess their timing and character.

Chapter 3

Units of property

As the differences examined in Chapter 2 imply, entries in the pipe rolls record the transfer of properties of widely differing character and scale. Besides standard customary units of tenure – virgates and their fractions – a large number of fines also involve the transfer of discarded demesne land, assarts and purprestures that had entered more recently into the peasant land market. A significant proportion of fines are also concerned with a varied array of homesteads, smallholdings, individual acres and plots, woods, groves, rents, fish-weirs and mills. The analysis of peasant transfers on the Winchester bishopric estate involves categorising and describing this range of properties, as well as analysing changes affecting their character and size.

The sources are inconsistent in the descriptions they give to some types of holding and in the measurement of certain others. Such inconsistencies not only occur from manor to manor but across time as well. Especially before 1300, it was common for transferred property to be described laconically as 'land', sometimes as 'a house and land', 'a messuage and land', or 'lands and tenements'. Amongst the Taunton group of manors, mere 'land' occurs some 684 times, 608 of them before 1300. This bare description was employed increasingly less frequently at Taunton over succeeding years; it was rare after about 1320, and does not appear at all after 1341. The picture is very similar over the estate as a whole; more than a third of transferred properties are described as 'land', but almost 90 per cent of these instances (4,030 out of 4,522) occur before 1300. Before 1300 neif land (*terra nativa*) is so designated only eight times, and customary land (*terra custumaria*) only seven times.

It seems likely that 'land' refers in most instances to older peasant tenures, including virgated land, since from the earliest years included in this study the pipe rolls make special note of the conveyance of assarts, pieces of demesne and other distinctive properties such as woodland and mills. Some of the more particular types of holding have their own problems of definition that cannot be finely resolved since it cannot be determined to what extent different terms were synonymous. 'Overland' is found chiefly on the downland of Somerset attached to the Taunton manors. 'Bordland' or 'bordage land' was especially characteristic of the Wiltshire manors of Downton and Bishopstone, although it occurs elsewhere. It seems likely that these terms shared roughly the same meaning: an enclosure from the waste which was then used for cultivation. 'Purpresture', an important and widespread category of property, seems technically to have described encroachments on common land, or roads, or on demesne land, but in practice overlapped in meaning with overland and bordland. 'Assart' was probably reserved to denote encroachments on woodland. All four descriptions – overland, bordland, purpresture and assart – were employed at Downton, and on many of the estate's manors two, or even three, can be found side by side.[1]

---

1. *PRBW 1409–10*, pp. 449–50, 457–8; A.E. Levett, 'The Black Death on the estates of the see of Winchester', in P. Vinogradoff (ed.), *Oxford studies in social and legal history, V* (Oxford, 1916), p. 70.

Clearances from woodland, downland and heath were often at the edges of manors: Highclere, Woodhay and Burghclere all record assarts at a location called the 'Wash', which was presumably adjacent to all three. The nomenclature and other locational details of the fines also frequently imply that the land use was formerly marsh, moor or heath. There were purprestures at 'Bradmore' belonging to both Highclere and Burghclere, at 'Damemor' in Highclere and at 'Wodemour' in Overton. The place-name element 'end' suggests a remote location: there were purprestures at 'Hethhende' and 'Fouleweyeshend' in Woodhay, and at the 'Brokehende' in West Wycombe. Such lands, therefore, not only constituted new categories of property, but also formed distinct territorial blocks and zones.

In time, fuller descriptions take the place of the earlier vague terminology relating to standard holdings. Our first half virgate, a standard unit of customary land, appears in 1283. References to associated buildings also become more exact. Messuages are more commonly recorded from the 1290s, and cottages appear from 1306. By 1340 the term 'neif land' (*terra nativa*) was used, albeit inconsistently, both on the manors which had experienced extensive recent colonisation and on those which had no colonisable resources at all. By the time of the Black Death in 1348–9, full descriptions of property were the norm.

For much of our period we lack details of legal status, and unfortunately we cannot assume that undifferentiated 'land' was necessarily held by customary tenure. Free land, too, often owed the lord a fine from an incoming tenant. There are forty-two mentions of free land in the fines prior to 1349, sixteen of them at Alverstoke. 'Reliefs', which were equivalent to entry fines for some kinds of free tenure, occur on 839 occasions before 1349, of which 272 were at Alverstoke, 186 at Witney and 71 at Fareham. The high concentration of explicitly free lands in Alverstoke, and the fact that 63 per cent of a relatively small number of recorded reliefs were from only three manors, encourages us to suppose that most of the early fines for 'land' probably related to tenures of villein status, although we are here inevitably on uncertain ground. It is improbable that indications of free tenure would concentrate so strongly in only a few manors purely by chance. Once we have more detailed descriptions of properties, it is reasonable to suppose that holdings described as a messuage and virgate, or ferling, or ten acres, were customary tenures. Most bishopric manors had a nucleus of standard customary tenements based on the virgate from which rents and services were extracted. The custumals can be helpful in this respect, indicating the range of customary holdings which existed at the time that these records were compiled.

Virgated tenements

The size of the virgate varied from region to region, from manor to manor, and even within some manors.[2] In the earlier part of the period there is little evidence anywhere what this size was, but in 1368–9, the second year of Bishop Wykeham's episcopate, the accountants began regularly to record the acreage of customary holdings, often 'by estimation'. This new concern may have arisen from the need to calculate

---

2.   Levett, 'Black Death', p. 50.

Table 3.1
Variations in the size of virgates by region and manor

Region	Manor and acreages
Somerset	Bishops Hull (**40**), Holway (**40**), Nailsbourne (**40**), Otterford (**40**), Poundisford (**40**), Staplegrove (**40**), Rimpton (**32**, **40**)
North Hampshire	Ashmansworth (**40**), Burghclere (**40**), Ecchinswell (**40**), Highclere (**40**, **32**), Woodhay (**40**)
Hampshire Chalk Plateau and South Hampshire	Bishopstoke (**40**), Bishops Waltham (**40**, **30**, **20**), Fareham (**32**), Bitterne (**32**, 30, 16), Brockhampton (**16**, 40, 20), Bishops Sutton (**40**), Droxford (**40**), Merdon (**40**), Overton Borough (**40**), East Meon (60, 50, 40, 38, 34, 32, 26, 22, 20, 14, 10), East Meon Church (**40**, 32, 28, 20), Hambledon (**40**, 32, 30), Crawley (**32**, 45, 44, 30), North Waltham (**32**, 40, 44), Overton (**32**, 40), Cheriton (32, 40), Beauworth (32, 40), Wield (**32**), Alresford (**32**, 30, 22, 20, 12), Twyford (**20**, 40), Marwell (**20**)
Eastern	Bentley (**32**), Esher (**32**), Farnham (**32**, 30)
Woodland and Northern	Witney (**30**, 24), Wargrave (**24**, 20), Billingbear (**26**), Ivinghoe (**24**, 30, 20, 18,16), Waltham St Lawrence (**24**, 34, 20, 16), Adderbury (**24**, 32, 28), Warfield (**20**, 40), West Wycombe (36, 32, 30, 24, 20), Brightwell (20, 24, 34), Harwell (**20**), Morton (**20**, 40,16)
Wiltshire	Bishops Fonthill (**24**, 34, 20), Downton (34, 32, 30, 28, 24, 18, 16), East Knoyle (**20**, 30), Bishopstone (**16**)

Note: The sole or predominant acreage is printed in bold.

services, rents and entry fines more precisely during a time of difficulties with vacant tenements. Table 3.1 lists the estate's manors by the stated acreage of their virgate holdings.

There is some systematic regional variation in these acreages. Virgates on the Taunton group of manors were consistently of forty acres, and this was also the regular figure for the North Hampshire group. A thirty-two-acre virgate characterises the Eastern group, Farnham, Esher and Bentley, and occurs randomly as the commonest size elsewhere, notably at Rimpton, Fareham and Bitterne. Virgates in the Wiltshire and Northern groups – to which the Woodland manors of Witney and Wargrave have been united for this purpose – were smaller, ranging between sixteen and thirty acres, but with no predominant size. The rest of Hampshire, both South Hampshire and the Chalk Plateau region, is characterised by remarkable inconsistency; both forty-acre and thirty-two-acre virgates were widespread, but there were many other sizes as well, both larger and smaller. Table 3.1 demonstrates how common it was for single manors to have virgates of more than one size, although East Meon is quite exceptional for its plethora of different virgates, ranging from ten to sixty acres. Either there were different virgates for different purposes, or they had been created at different times according to different principles, or there had never been even an estimated acreage in mind.

Direct evidence of measured acres is sparse, and relates to non-customary holdings particularly of small individual plots and former demesne lands. In 1306–7, at Staplegrove, John Palmer fined for half an acre adjacent to his land 'which he held before unmeasured and without a fine'. The measure used in these cases was perhaps the 'king's perch' of 16½ feet, as in the case of a plot acquired by William Plummer at West Wycombe in 1342–3.[3]

In addition to the recorded size of virgate holdings there was also considerable manorial and regional variation in the relative proportions of virgates, half virgates and ferlings (quarter virgates). These distinctions do not correspond directly to differences in the level of activity in the land market, as indicated by the evidence of Chapter 2, and relate to other local circumstances. At Witney and Wargrave, where the land market was chiefly in assarted land, transactions in virgated land mostly involved whole virgates, as also on most of the manors in the Northern group; ferlings account for less than 1 per cent of all transfers before 1349 and do not occur at all between 1350 and 1415. On the Taunton manors, by contrast, the land market had developed through subdivisions of the virgate. The ferling was there the commonest recorded unit of virgated land, accounting for over half of all transfers on all the manors except Trull and Bishops Hull before 1349, and all manors without exception between 1350 and 1415.[4] Less than 10 per cent of all transfers involved whole virgates. The Taunton manors had only in recent times undergone a process of decentralisation from a single unit, a process observable from the layout of the pipe rolls of the later thirteenth and early fourteenth centuries, and this may account for the strong similarities between them.[5] At Rimpton, also in the Somerset group, whole virgates and half virgates were more commonly transferred than around Taunton, but the share of ferlings in the market – 33 per cent between 1263 and 1349, 30 per cent between 1350 and 1415 – was again relatively high. The South Hampshire manors, different again, show no common pattern. Whole virgates were the chief unit of transfer at Alverstoke and Brockhampton with Havant, but ferlings predominated at Bitterne and Bishops Waltham. Half virgates were the most common unit of transfer among the North Hampshire group of manors (except at Highclere, where the whole virgate predominated) and again in the Wiltshire group. In both regions the ferling was apparently rare. Whole virgates and half virgates were the most usual units of transfer on the manors of the Hampshire Chalk Plateau region, although there was a good deal of variation, and ferlings were exceptionally numerous at Merdon, Crawley, Droxford and Hambledon (Table 3.2).

Virgated tenements had several distinctive characteristics that affected their role in the land market throughout our period. They were more likely than other sorts of land to attract family loyalty, and to pass within families rather than by sale to outsiders. This is demonstrated by Table 3.3, which shows that the transfer of virgated tenements by extrafamilial transactions *inter vivos* was always significantly more unusual than for other types of property. However, the strength of family bonds was

---

3. D. Oschinsky (ed.), *Walter of Henley and other treatises on estate management and accounting* (Oxford, 1971), p. 314: Walter of Henley, 'Hosbandrye', c.28; but cf. in *ibid.* the anonymous 'Husbandry', c.63, p. 444.

4. See also Levett, 'Black Death', p. 70.

5. Thornton, 'Arable productivity', pp. 109–37.

Table 3.2
Numbers of virgates, half virgates and ferlings transferred as percentages of total transfers of virgated land within each manor of the Hampshire Chalk Plateau region, 1263–1349 and 1350–1415

Manor	Virgate		Half virgate		Ferling	
	1263–1349 (%)	1350–1415 (%)	1263–1349 (%)	1350–1415 (%)	1263–1349 (%)	1350–1415 (%)
North Waltham*	86	93	13	7	2	0
Beauworth*	86	92	11	8	3	0
East Meon	69	79	26	16	5	6
Cheriton	66	87	32	14	3	0
Alresford	64	88	35	12	1	0
East Meon Church	56	63	41	31	3	6
Overton	54	86	44	14	2	0
Twyford and Marwell	54	32	30	47	16	21
Wield*	42	74	58	27	0	0
Crawley	42	36	48	16	10	48
Bishops Sutton	33	56	50	44	18	0
Hambledon	27	51	38	23	35	26
Droxford	15	17	41	36	44	47
Merdon	6	6	58	37	36	57

Note: Manors marked with an asterisk have fewer than 100 fines from the years 1350–1415 (Appendix).

Table 3.3
Property types transferred by inheritance and by extrafamilial transactions inter vivos 1320–1415

Property type	Period	Total	Inheritance (%)	Extrafamilial inter vivos (%)	Other (%)
Virgated holdings	1320–49	4340	60.0	10.7	29.3
	1350–79	4179	37.4	21.9	40.7
	1380–1415	3177	37.7	22.4	39.9
Cottages, messuages and cotlands	1320–49	4087	42.7	29.1	28.2
	1350–79	3279	29.3	40.2	30.5
	1380–1415	1913	27.6	41.1	31.3
Fragments: acres and plots	1320–49	3547	16.6	47.2	36.2
	1350–79	2801	19.5	53.0	27.5
	1380–1415	1739	11.2	51.3	37.5
Assart and purpresture	1320–49	2522	30.7	45.9	23.4
	1350–79	2686	27.9	42.0	30.1
	1380–1415	1897	25.0	46.3	28.7

Note: Virgated tenements include, full virgates, ½ virgates, ferlings, fractions and accumulations of customary virgate tenements. Fragments and acres are those pieces of land without dwellings and reckoned to be customary land, for which see the discussion in chapter 3. The column others are all other types of transfer: by marriage, by extrafamilal transfers post mortem, by intrafamilial transfers *inter-vivos*, and by uptake from the lord without any preceding surrender.

weakened by the high mortality of the mid-fourteenth century, which resulted in numerous failures of succession. After 1349 the disposal of virgated units by extrafamilial transfer became more frequent relative to transfer by inheritance (Table 3.3). This was barely significant on the Taunton manors, or on the eastern manors of Farnham and Esher, but elsewhere it was widespread. Even so, the extrafamilial transfer of virgates *inter vivos* remained less usual than that of other categories of holding.

Two other observations concerning virgated holdings require comment at greater length because of their direct relevance to the development of a market in peasant land. One is the widespread resistance to their engrossment, and the other a similar resistance to their fragmentation.

The amalgamation of virgated units

Although no consistent policy was applied on every manor, either before or after the Black Death, the manor courts of the bishopric of Winchester, with or without the direct instructions of the bishop's officers, sometimes interfered in the land transactions of tenants to restrict the accumulation of customary holdings.[6] This conservatism had some advantages from the lord's point of view, since separate holdings were easier for estate officers to identify and administer than those which were combined, and the buildings on them were less likely to be run down. Labour services, especially week-work, and other customary dues were attached to each individual holding, and it was upon the fulfilment of these obligations that the demesne economy relied. It was less likely that tenants of accumulated tenements could supply the services due. However, the fact that custom varied across the estate, and that the accumulation of customary tenures was allowable on some manors, like Bishops Waltham,[7] but not on others, suggests that custom, rather than episcopal preference, was the principal safeguard of the status quo. The preferences of the bishop's officers for maintaining traditional structures of tenure could coincide with the interests of village communities in a period when property was hard to come by.

To judge from the small number of recorded interventions by courts to prohibit accumulation of customary holdings, the informal pressure of local opinion must have been the most usual sanction of customary rules in this respect. No more than fifteen have been found out of all the thousands of recorded fines,[8] but these few nevertheless constitute a good indicator of what some manorial courts regarded as desirable. In almost all cases the proposed accumulation was the accidental result of customary patterns of inheritance. At West Wycombe in 1301–2, Jordan atte Vyninge was prevented from inheriting his mother's half-virgate 'because he held other land and the lord bishop does not allow one man to hold two villein lands'. He had to choose which land he would hold, and opted to keep what he had already; the

6. This topic is also discussed by Page, *Medieval bishops*, pp. 333–5.
7. For Bishops Waltham, see Page, *Medieval bishops*, p. 20.
8. Page, 'Southern England', p. 333.
9. *PRBW 1301–2*, p. 162; Page, 'Southern England', p. 334.

available half virgate was then given to one of his female kin.[9] The case is interesting in demonstrating the court's regard for family continuity; a member of the family, although a woman and merely 'consanguineous' with Jordan, was found to fine for the tenement. A similar regard for the right of kin is found in other cases. At Droxford in 1312–13, Henry, son of Geoffrey Mitchell, obtained a messuage and ferling only after his brother, who had succeeded to a virgate holding the same year, had been prevented from so doing; he 'was not allowed because he held another tenement of the same status'. Similarly, at Farnham in 1313–14, John Godwin was refused permission to inherit the messuage and virgate of his father, which he 'ought to have held but was not allowed because he holds another tenement of the same status and they were always accustomed to be separate'. There are only two known cases, at North Waltham in 1316–17 and North Wield in 1301–2, where the prohibition of accumulation by inheritance caused a break in the bond between family and tenement.[10]

On particular issues the bishop's officers often had some independent role, but they operated within the context of existing custom, either to interpret it or to relax it in particular cases. In some instances, rules prohibiting accumulation were formally waived by the bishop, presumably with the consent of the suitors at the manor court. At Droxford in 1335–6, William, son of William Attwood, paid two fines for inherited property, first for a messuage and half virgate and secondly for a toft and a half ferling, 'though the custom of the manor is that no one is able to hold two tenements except by the lord's grace, only for his time and not for his heirs'. At Fareham in 1324–5, the bishop allowed sixteen tenants to hold more than one customary tenement; each tenant paid a fine to retain his additional land, for which he had already paid an entry fine, 'on condition that he performs all the due and accustomed services of the said tenements, and that he will give a heriot after his death for each tenement that he holds, that is, one beast for each tenement'. In this case the court was accepting a *fait accompli*. Henry Stile, who was allowed to retain two messuages, 1½ virgates and eight acres, had begun to accumulate property in 1310–11, when he inherited a messuage and half virgate from his mother. In the same year he had acquired a messuage and ferling, and in 1315–16 a messuage and virgate, both surrendered by unrelated tenants. Because he had accumulated these properties he was able to provide for his children during his lifetime. In 1335–6 he began their redistribution by granting his daughter, Isabella, the messuage and ferling. His son, Thomas, received the messuage and half-virgate in 1337–8. Finally, in 1338–9, his youngest son, John, inherited the remaining messuage and virgate.[11] The tenants of Fareham evidently had a relaxed attitude to modest accumulation such as Henry Stile's even before the Black Death, since the court must have known about it long before 1324–5, and the bishop's officers were less interested in enforcing the rules than in an opportunity to collect some additional court revenue.

The latest example of a tenant being prohibited from possessing more than one customary tenement, from Witney in 1347–8, implies that the decision was founded

---

10. Page, 'Southern England', p. 334.
11. At Fareham the custom of ultimogeniture was practised: HRO, 11M59/E2/415808, fo. 27.

on manorial custom rather than episcopal fiat. Walter, son of Richard Dodd, fined £2 2s for a virgate in Hailey 'which Isolda, widow of William Dodd, held in her widowhood, and for which Richard Dodd, who is next of kin to William, refused to fine because he holds another messuage and virgate of villein land and according to the manor it is not possible to hold two villein tenements'. There are no instances of such prohibition after 1348.

The fragmentation of virgated units

Historians of the medieval peasant land market in England have found great contrasts in the degree to which customary holdings were allowed to disintegrate, and in the chronology of their disintegration. The process started earliest and proceeded most rapidly in the eastern counties. It is associated with the early development of a peasant land market in that region, although not all subdivisions of customary units can be assumed to be market-related.[12] On the estates of the bishopric of Ely, villein tenements were subdivided and alienated as a way of coping with population growth during the twelfth and thirteenth centuries, creating fractional virgates but also allowing the accumulation of property by a 'village aristocracy' of villeins.[13] The market was exceptionally active in years of high grain prices, indicating that sales were motivated chiefly by the need to raise cash in times of hardship.[14] By 1292 most of the standard holdings at the manor of Martham in Norfolk 'had become fragmented beyond all but administrative recognition'.[15] In Suffolk, too, although the fragmentation of villein tenures proceeded more slowly than that of free tenures, it was well advanced by 1300 on all types of estate, including even that of the powerful abbey of Bury St Edmunds.[16] In some instances, as at Martham, fragmentation is attributable to the practice of partible inheritance as well as to population pressure. But whilst fragmented standard holdings are clearly discernible in these regions, they were not universal even there before the Black Death, and elsewhere their appearance was long delayed.[17] At Halesowen, in Worcestershire, although many tenants sold properties piecemeal to meet debts and to endow family members, this was from lands other than the customary holding, so that between 1270 and the Black Death the integrity of such holdings was preserved.[18] At Kibworth Harcourt, in

---

12. G.C. Homans, *English villagers of the thirteenth century* (New York, 1960), p. 204; Hyams, 'Peasant land market', pp. 19, 27–8.

13. E. Miller, *The abbey and bishopric of Ely: the social history of an ecclesiastical estate from the tenth century to the early fourteenth century* (Cambridge, 1951), pp. 142–51.

14. B.M.S. Campbell, 'Population pressure, inheritance and the land market in a fourteenth-century peasant community', in Smith (ed.), *Land, kinship and life-cycle*, pp. 107–20.

15. P.D.A. Harvey, 'Introduction', in Harvey (ed.), *Peasant land market*, p. 8; J. Williamson, 'Norfolk: thirteenth century', in Harvey (ed.), *Peasant land market*, pp. 69–71.

16. M. Bailey, *Medieval Suffolk: an economic and social history, 1200–1500* (Woodbridge, 2007), pp. 43, 54–5.

17. R.J. Faith, 'Peasant families and inheritance customs in medieval England', *AHR*, 14 (1966), p. 86.

18. Razi, *Life, marriage and death*, pp. 5–9.

Leicestershire, although there were numerous holdings of half a virgate, and although villeins sometimes created temporary leases, before the Black Death the permanent alienation of customary land, except by inheritance, was restricted to exchanges of minute parcels.[19] There was little fragmentation of customary virgates and half virgates on Westminster Abbey manors even after the Black Death, except in the case of some that had to be leased.[20] At Leighton Buzzard, in Bedfordshire, such fragmentation, coming in the form of the disappearance of virgates and half virgates, was a fifteenth-century phenomenon, to some extent licensed by the lord.[21] On the Winchester bishopric estates, meanwhile, the timing varied, and there is little evidence for any general episcopal policy that could explain the variety of what the pipe rolls reveal.

The fragmentation of customary tenements, like their accumulation, could indeed be opposed by manorial courts on the grounds that the tenants of these lands were bound to provide both cash rents and labour services to their lord; the manorial economy would be threatened if they were unable to do so because tenements were no longer large enough to sustain a family in its obligations.[22] One of the clearest expressions of this policy is from Esher in 1314–15, when William Wexford recovered an acre from Henry Firth 'which was his land of old, and which he surrendered into the lord's hands for the use of Henry, which surrender was not allowed because it was by dismemberment (*demembratio*)'. Similarly, at Poundisford in 1325–6, Walter Coffin recovered half an acre from Adam Archer 'as parcel of a ferling, because according to the custom of the manor it is not able to be dismembered'. This policy explains other, similar, instances. At Droxford in 1325–6, Richard Illes recovered from Walter Millward a plot with a house built on it, which was 'a parcel of a ferling'. At Cheriton in 1348–9, John Creech acquired a messuage and 3½ acres from Richard Amfrith, 'which was a parcel of a virgate which John now holds'.

Many such recoveries of land were effected in the name of manorial custom through the manorial court, 'by inquest', 'by jurors', or 'by the free men and others of the hundred'. At Bishops Waltham in 1347–8, Adam Scott secured the surrender of a messuage and ferling from John Caker by verdict of twelve customary jurors of Bishops Waltham after it was found that John's ferling was part of Adam's tenement 'because the messuage and ferling which Adam holds and the said ferling now surrendered were one whole tenement in the time of Adam's grandfather, Richard'. At Alresford in 1289–90, an inquest of the manor court allowed William Woodford to recover from Hugh Woodford three acres 'which pertained to the land which he now holds'. In 1276–7 Hosanna Hook recovered a messuage and two acres 'which sometime pertained to her land, as testified by the free men and others of the hundred of Hambledon'. In a later fine the same land was said to have been recovered 'in full hundred before the steward as her right because it was unjustly alienated from

19. Howell, *Land, family and inheritance*, pp. 242, 249–53.

20. Harvey, *Westminster Abbey*, pp. 264–5.

21. A. Jones, 'Bedfordshire: fifteenth century', in Harvey (ed.), *Peasant land market*, p. 198.

22. Harvey, *Westminster Abbey*, pp. 212–13; Kosminsky, *Studies in the agrarian history of England*, p. 207.

her holding for a long time'. We cannot be sure to what extent resistance to fragmentation was driven by episcopal policy, rather than simply supported by the bishop's officers when courts drew it to their attention as an issue. Many recoveries of land no doubt served the best interests of the larger customary tenants who might be expected to have dominated the manorial court. Lord and tenants apparently worked well together to restore fragmented tenements to their former size.[23] That episcopal policy was not the dominant force is suggested by the fact that the courts made different decisions, and allowed different outcomes, on different manors.

Opposition to the dismemberment of units was far from universal, and in fact there were already many fractional and dismembered virgates on the Winchester estate by the mid-fourteenth century. A useful indicator is the varying proportion of fragments of virgated holdings apparently not attached to dwellings. The absence of dwellings indicates that such pieces had either not yet formed separate households or were in the process of detaching from one holding to become part of another. On almost all manors such fragments occur already in the 1260s and 1270s. The first appearances of detached lands at North Waltham in 1290–1 and at Waltham St Lawrence in 1297–8 are exceptionally late. Already between 1263 and 1349 fragments of customary holdings were accounting for over a quarter of all transfers in south Hampshire on the manors of Brockhampton, Alverstoke and Bitterne, and on most manors they made up at least 10 per cent of transfers. Table 3.4 tabulates the evidence for the years 1263–1349. A high degree of disintegration is characteristic of the Woodland manors of Witney and Wargrave, the Somerset manors (except Rimpton), the South Hampshire manors, and the Eastern group of Esher and Farnham. Manors with the least fragmented tenements include many smaller ones, such as Bishopstone and at Bishops Fonthill; with small populations and fewer land transactions, pressures to subdivide holdings were perhaps lower there than in more crowded settlements. However, the size of a rural community was only a very imperfect indicator of the likelihood of fragmentation. Esher was another small manor, but its tenurial structure was dominated by cottage tenements, and there was a large proportion of acre and sub-acre pieces of land with and without dwellings. Fragments of customary tenures had accounted for over a quarter of all transfers between 1263 and 1349. Esher's proximity to London perhaps encouraged settlement by families not primarily engaged in agriculture; to judge from the evidence of demesne productivity there the land was poor, and in proportion to the amount of assized rent the land market was not particularly lively.[24] One wonders whether fragmentation in these circumstances depended more on local interest, on episcopal indifference, or on a combination of the two.

Besides fractions of customary tenements, on some manors the fines also record a number of fractions of cottages, messuages and houses. At Staplegrove in 1325–6, for instance, Margery, daughter of Nicholas Kynele, fined for 'a third part of a cottage

---

23. M.M. Postan, 'The charters of the villeins', in Brooke and Postan (eds), *Carte nativorum*, pp. xxxvi–xxxvii, reprinted in Postan, *Essays on medieval agriculture*, p. 117.

24. Assized rent in 1301–2 was £5 19s 11d, and the number of fines between 1263 and 1349 was 178, which means that the ratio used in Table 2.9 as an index of activity was 3.

Table 3.4
Fragments of customary holdings transferred as a percentage of all transfers, 1263–1349

Total transfers (%)	Manors (actual percentages in brackets)
>20	Havant and Brockhampton (37.8), Alverstoke (32.1), Esher (29.8), Bitterne (26.9), Trull and Bishops Hull (24.3), Witney (24), Warfield (22.6), East Meon Church (22.4), Holway (22.2), Adderbury (21), Wargrave (20)
15–19.9	Farnham (19.4), East Meon (19.2), Woodhay (17.9), Bentley (17.4), Bishops Waltham (17.1), Poundisford (16.9), Staplegrove (16.8), Hambledon (16.4), Culham (15.1)
10–14.9	East Knoyle (14.5), Downton (13.6), Ivinghoe (12.7), Morton (12.2), Waltham St Lawrence (12), Marwell and Twyford (11.8), Highclere (10.9), Kingstone St Mary and Nailsbourne (10.9), Fareham (10.6), Wield (10.5), Overton (10.4), Bishopstoke (10.3), Merdon (10.3)
5–9.9	Droxford (8.6), Alresford (8.3), Brighstone (7.8), Ecchinswell (7.4), Bishops Sutton (7.3), Crawley (7), Cheriton (6.8), West Wycombe (5.9), Upton (5.6)
<5	Ashmansworth (4.9), Gosport (4.8), Bishopstone (4.6), North Waltham (3.4), Bishops Fonthill (3), Brightwell (2.8), Otterford (2.7), Harwell (1.9), Rimpton (1.2), Burghclere (0.9), Beauworth (0),

with a curtilage containing one daywork'. These fines imply pressure on accommodation, which is likely to have been particularly acute when Taunton's population was at its peak in the early fourteenth century. It is difficult to see how what appears to be a divided dwelling would work in practice, but such expressions may refer to the conversion of outbuildings to dwellings on a divided holding. The distribution of these over the estate is largely in keeping with the picture of fragmentation so far; the most divided customary dwellings are found on the Taunton manors, notably at Poundisford, Staplegrove and Holway. They are numerous elsewhere where the fines also reveal a high proportion of smallholdings, especially at Brockhampton (8.7 per cent of all transfers), Bitterne (8.0 per cent) and Droxford (5.3 per cent) in south Hampshire, and at Adderbury in Oxfordshire (7.3 per cent).[25]

An interesting and further indicator of the exceptional circumstances of the Taunton manors appears in the form of fines for the creation of easements and other rights of way. More than half such fines (nineteen out of thirty-five between 1262–3 and 1415–15) are from the Taunton group. At Poundisford in 1305–6, when pressure on land resources was about at its height, William Gore fined for a ten-foot road to his land, between the lord's wood and tenements of the prior of Taunton, because he was unable to have access to his land elsewhere; he was bound to enclose the wood with a good ditch six feet wide and five feet deep and to plant two rows of quickset along the road.

The varying degree of splintering of holdings and dwellings, in the most general terms, suggests uneven pressure on the land available to the peasantry in the earlier part of the period. To some extent this is likely to be related to different rates of population growth, although cause and effect are not clearly distinguishable since the fragmentation of holdings and dwellings encouraged numbers to increase by

---

25. Such divided dwellings do not constitute more than 5 per cent of transfers on any manor apart from those named, and in most the proportion is below 1 per cent.

facilitating earlier marriages or permitting immigration. More than three-quarters of fragmented dwellings occur before 1350. They imply an impressive capacity on the part of some manors, such as Taunton, to absorb increasing numbers. But such fragmentation was not a final state. Later chapters will demonstrate the recombination of holdings once divided and the amalgamation of previously independent properties, particularly in the later fourteenth century.

These observations illustrate well the complex issues involved in a discussion of the effect of manorial custom. On the one hand, the strength of family ties, and prejudice in favour of maintaining holdings intact, often retarded the development of a land market, in some cases for centuries. At Bishopstoke, where there were no tenures other than customary ones, there was no commercial land market until after the end of our period.[26] On the other hand, there is a strong relationship across England between commercial development, population growth, high demand for land and the fragmentation of customary tenures. This is best seen in the precocious development of the East Anglian land market, but is also suggested by the fragmentation of holdings on the Taunton manors.[27] The implication of these contrasting tendencies is that institutional conservatism and radicalism were at least in part environmentally conditioned, the switch from one to the other depending upon features of economic development that advanced unevenly across the country. Landlords and villagers stood more to gain than to lose by allowing virgates to be broken up as social relations became more monetised and as the advantages of flexible choice that landlords and some peasant families were allowed by market relations came to outweigh the greater security of fixed and indivisible obligations.

Unvirgated lands

Virgated holdings and fractions of virgates, including those that formed part of larger accumulated holdings, account for only about a quarter of all property transfers on the Winchester estate between 1263 and 1349 and about a third between 1350 and 1415. A large number of other entry fines concern transfers of former demesne, forest, downland and heath – including the overlands, bordlands, purprestures and assarts which we have already discussed – which made an important contribution to the possibility of buying and selling property. This evidence, which is in accord with Titow's observations from the custumals, adds to what we have discovered concerning patterns of intermanorial and interregional variation across the estate.

Assarts and purprestures accounted for 22 per cent of all land exchanged on the estate, although the size of individual transactions was often very small. Particularly where there was little scope for clearance from wasteland or woodland, many purprestures were no more than small plots amongst existing tenements. At Bishops Sutton in 1274–5, Roger Clerk fined 10s for 'one and half acres of new purpresture at a certain Rammescumbe between the enclosures of John Beadle on the one side and

---

26. Page, *Medieval bishops*, pp. 18–19.

27. For population pressure on the Taunton manors in the thirteenth century, see Titow, 'Some differences', pp. 1–13; Postan and Titow, 'Heriots and prices'.

John Torshaghe on the other'. They were often measured in feet or perches. At Adderbury, in Oxfordshire, where only 1.5 per cent of land transfers were of purpresture, Richard Wilkins in 1334–5 paid a fine of 6d for a plot of purpresture measuring one perch long and four feet wide 'to enlarge his tenement'. At East Meon in 1301–2, John Miles paid a fine of 1s to 'retain a certain purpresture 12 feet long and four feet wide at one end and 1½ feet at the other end, which before he had encroached upon without licence'. Even where there was scope for more extensive reclamation, a lot of the work was piecemeal and resulted in very small units. There were, nevertheless, larger assarts and purprestures in regions where there had been extensive scope for clearing new land. At Witney in 1284–5 James Crawley and Roger Herring fined for 140 acres of new purpresture, and in 1292–3 James Crawley leased a further twenty acres of new assart. In 1302–3 a further 87½ acres and half a ferling of new assart were said to have been 'assarted this year from the lord's demesne, this being the first year, at 2s per acre'; it is not stated who paid the large fine of £18 15s 3d, and it may be that the village community paid it jointly.

As the demand for land relaxed in the fourteenth century, many assarts and purprestures were abandoned. In the Highclere group, twenty-six of the forty-two properties abandoned after 1350 were purprestures. At Burghclere and at Woodhay small acreages of purpresture were in the lord's hands 'because they lie in la Wasshe and no one wished to lease them'. On these manors, at least, the evidence seems to point to a proportionately higher retreat from the newer lands than from standard holdings.[28] But assart and purpresture did not disappear from the land market. At both Witney and Wargrave a vigorous market in those assart holdings that remained occupied, many of them now well over a century old, continued through the fourteenth century, often as part of larger accumulations of property.

Nearly 1,300 fines concern the movement of detached parcels of waste and demesne from lord to tenant and, to a lesser degree, between tenants themselves. This represents only about 3 per cent of all transfers. The share rose to 9 per cent at Downton, and was also uniformly higher than usual on the Somerset manors, but rarely exceeded 3 per cent elsewhere.[29] Parcels of waste chiefly comprised small plots measured in feet or perches, often adjacent to holdings. Many of them seem to have been previously unoccupied scraps. For example, at East Meon in 1353–4 John Trondenham fined 1s for 'a plot of the lord's waste adjoining his tenement in Meon between the royal highway and the river bank on the western side beyond the river'. Although only 4 releases of waste are recorded before 1310, the number then increased to 155 during the 1330s and 215 in the 1340s before dropping after the Black Death to an average of only 30 a decade between 1350 and 1415. The demesne properties transferred through the manor courts and recorded among the entry fines were more significant in number and size, although most were less than ten acres,

---

28. Postan, 'Medieval agrarian society in its prime', pp. 551–2, 566; *idem, The medieval economy and society* (London, 1972), p. 35.

29. 6.8 per cent at Rimpton, 5.1 per cent at Kingstone St Mary and Nailsbourne, 4.7 per cent at Trull and Bishops Hull, 4.6 per cent at Staplegrove, 3.7 per cent at Poundisford.

most frequently being between two and five acres. As former demesne lands entered into the peasant economy, their exchange between peasant households increased in importance relative to transfers from the bishop to his tenants. Whereas about 88 per cent of demesne and waste in the period 1263–1349 was secured directly from the lord, only 59 per cent was acquired this way between 1350 and 1415. This parallels the similar transformation in the recorded exchange of purprestures.

The entry fines in this sample nevertheless give only a very partial account of demesne leasing on the bishop's estate, especially in the later fourteenth and early fifteenth centuries, as we learn from other sections of the pipe rolls, especially from those specifically recording leases (*firme*). At Holway in 1409–10, for example, there were thirteen leases of demesne land, only three of which are recorded in the fines.[30] The leasing of the bishop's demesnes will need more extended discussion (see Chapter 4).

Besides land designated as assart, purpresture, demesne or waste, parcels of moor, heath and woodland occur in 338 transactions and once again their distribution provides an interesting insight into the tenurial and topographic make-up of a number of manors. Entry fines concerning moor and heathland between 1263 and 1415 were most numerous at Farnham (72) and on the Taunton manors (29). Transfers of woodland were numerous at East Meon (56). There were eighteen such transfers at Bishops Sutton and fifteen at Hambledon, but the Taunton manors had only a dozen between them, and no other manor registered more than seven. Even within manors the location of woodland property tends to be concentrated: at East Meon, for example, all the pieces of grove and wood are in 'Hyden' and at Farnham all heath is said to be at 'Elstede'.

The newer and non-customary status of assarts and purprestures affected their significance in the land market. They were less likely than customary holdings to be integrated into common fields, and more likely to be enclosed.[31] They were also less identified with particular families, moved between families more easily than customary holdings, and so were more likely to be used to meet ephemeral requirements. Like freehold, they facilitated a more rapid development of a peasant land market. Where they were numerous, as at Witney, their presence protected the integrity of customary holdings, since through them the needs of resident families could be accommodated without the need to subdivide virgates.

The contrast between the subdivided virgates of the Somerset group of manors and the unvirgated assarts of the Woodland manors confirms that the land market operated in very different contexts in these two regions of the Winchester bishopric estate. The evidence suggests that they were both regions in which exchanges of property were exceptionally numerous in relation to the rental value of tenant land. The Taunton manors at least probably experienced exceptional population growth and density of settlement, and the same is likely to have been true of Witney and Wargrave. Yet the way in which population growth was accommodated in the two

---

30. *PRBW 1409–10*, pp. 16–17. Three of these are for the farm of pasturage, and so would not be expected to appear in the fines.

31. D. Roden, 'Field systems of the Chiltern Hills and their environs', in A.R.H. Baker and R.A. Butlin (eds), *Studies of field systems in the British Isles* (Cambridge, 1973), pp. 351–3.

regions, as Titow observed, was fundamentally different – subdivision of virgated holdings at Taunton, reclamation from woodland at Witney and Wargrave. In neither case can the exceptional responsiveness of the land market be associated with above-average standards of peasant welfare. The assarts of the Woodland manors, although they allowed an expansion of agricultural resources, characteristically did so in such small units that their occupants were poorly endowed: in spite of the far greater subdivision of virgates on the Taunton manors, tenants there had larger holdings than at Witney. The thirteenth-century custumals show that those holding over thirty acres from the bishop constituted 7.6 per cent of the tenant population of the Taunton manors, but only 5.3 per cent of that at Witney; by contrast, tenants with fewer than fifteen acres were 56 per cent of the total at Taunton but 73.6 per cent at Witney, and tenants with fewer than five acres were 13 per cent of the Taunton total but 51.5 per cent at Witney.[32]

Cottages, cotlands, messuages and houses

Many other entry fines concern dwellings with small customary smallholdings; these form about a quarter of land transfers across the estate, nearly equivalent in number to the larger standard holdings. However, the nomenclature and size of these holdings among the fines is extremely varied. Cottages are the most numerous, but the typology of smallholdings also includes the cotland (*cotlanda*), the messuage (*mesuagium*), the messuage with attached cotland, as well as the individual house attached to various numbers of acres or with crofts and other plots of land. Not all such diminutive tenements were customary, however; some were developments on purprestures or assarts. Smallholdings were characteristically derived from forest and waste land on manors where there had been recent clearance, as at Witney, Wargrave, Warfield, West Wycombe, Merdon, Bishops Waltham and Farnham. At Farnham, 62 per cent of messuage holdings and 85 per cent of cottage holdings are described as purpresture.[33] In the Taunton group cottage holdings were chiefly, although by no means exclusively, overland tenements, with a minority of customary smallholdings; 688 cottage holdings were transferred before 1349 and 1,176 after, and of these 1,079 were associated with overland.

Even without the large number of purprestures and assarts, on some manors the volume of smallholdings was impressive. On the Taunton group of manors, beside the cottage holdings already mentioned, over a thousand messuages with smallholdings were transferred over the whole period of study, 513 before 1349 and 519 after. The majority were of villein status.[34] Of those whose acreages are stated, almost 75 per

32. Titow, 'Some differences', pp. 3–4. He warns that, because we do not know the number of landless peasants, these differences do not necessarily imply that average standards of welfare were lower in Witney. See, too, M.M. Postan, 'Subtenants on some manors of the bishops of Winchester', in Brooke and Postan (eds), *Carte nativorum*, p. lxiii.

33. For the market in purprestures at Farnham, see Page, 'Farnham', pp. 174–6.

34. Before 1349, 156 messuages are called 'villein' and 116 'overland'. After 1349, 429 were 'villein' and 65 'overland'.

cent were half ferlings and 14 per cent were three-quarters of a ferling. Elsewhere, holdings tended to be even smaller. At Bishops Waltham, for example, throughout the period cottages are associated with a range of appendages from a quarter acre to as many as eight acres, and messuage holdings with between one acre and six, whilst houses were usually associated with just a couple of acres, roods or even dayworks. The daywork (*dayna*) was a unit of uncertain size, found chiefly on the Somerset manors, equivalent to the amount of land that could be worked in one day. In Kent and south Essex, and at Wellingborough in Northamptonshire, it was equivalent to four perches or one-tenth of a rood, and that seems to be the reckoning on the Taunton manors; when dayworks are mentioned in conjunction with roods they are never more than nine, suggesting that ten dayworks were equal to the rood, one-fortieth of an acre.[35]

Often these smallholdings were measured as fractions of a virgate, and may in some cases have originated from the fragmentation of virgates, although it is likely that many were originally created as service tenements for slaves or *famuli* who would be expected to spend most of their time working on demesne land.[36] The cotland, usually attached to a messuage, was nearly always of villein or customary status. Cotlands are chiefly confined to the North Hampshire group of manors and adjacent parts of the Hampshire chalklands: between 1263–4 and 1414–15, 104 were transferred at Woodhay, 69 at Ecchinswell, 44 at Highclere, 54 at Burghclere, 31 at Ashmansworth, 23 at Overton, and 13 at North Waltham. In the later fourteenth century, when acreages are commonly given, we learn that they were mostly equivalent in acreage to the ferling. At Bishops Waltham, Highclere, Ecchinswell and at Woodhay, where virgates were of forty acres, cotlands were usually of ten. At Farnham, where we find the thirty-two-acre virgate, the small number of cotlands were of eight acres. But this was not standard across the estate. At Fareham in 1354, Thomas Crocker fined to take Christine Hugh in marriage with her messuage and four acres 'called Cotlond in the tithing of Cammoysbishop', which was equivalent to a half ferling on this manor. At Ivinghoe in 1373, where most recorded virgates were of twenty-four acres, two transactions of a cottage and four acres 'called Cotlond' suggest a holding of one-sixth of a virgate. Whether cotlands were regarded as synonymous with ferlings in origins and status is nevertheless unclear, since both are found on some manors. In some rare instances cotlands bear no relation to the virgate system. At Downton the single mention of a cotland is of '32½ acres of cotland with four crofts and a meadow', but the wording may signify an accumulation of several cotlands. At Bishopstoke the fines record the transfer of a nine-acre cotland where the forty-acre virgate was the norm. A handful of similar anomalies can be found at Overton, Twyford and Crawley.

Smallholdings not described as cotlands, but attached to cottages and messuages, were also sometimes fractions of a virgate. On the Taunton group smallholdings were

---

35. *PRBW 1409–10*, p. 452; P.D.A. Harvey, 'A manuscript estate map by Christopher Saxton', *The British Museum Quarterly*, 23 (3) (1960–1), p. 66; H.L. Gray, *English field systems* (Cambridge, Mass., 1915), pp. 300–1.

36. H.C. Darby, *Domesday England* (Cambridge, 1977), pp. 69–71; C. Dyer, *Lords and peasants in a changing society: the estates of the bishopric of Worcester, 680–1540* (Cambridge, 1980), pp. 97–8.

commonly of 5 or even 2½ acres, equivalent to a half ferling and a quarter ferling. Similar units are found in several other manors, especially Bishopstone and East Knoyle, some of the north Hampshire group, Bitterne, Hambledon, Bentley, Farnham and Fareham. At Bishopstone both cottage and messuage holdings were nearly all of eight acres, equivalent to a half virgate; half virgates are rarely described as such on this manor, and this peculiarity of alternative nomenclature may explain why. At Bitterne in South Hampshire, where the virgate was of thirty-two acres, messuage holdings are most frequently of four, eight and sixteen acres. In many instances, then, cottage or messuage holdings were not the smallest tenements on any manor. When these cottage holdings are taken into account, many manors had more holdings at least equivalent to the ferling, or even the half virgate, than the nomenclature of the pipe rolls would imply. At Bishops Sutton in the period 1263–1349, for example, one may add to the recorded ferling holdings a further ninety messuages, cottages and cotlands of ten acres, and eight other holdings of twenty acres were equivalent in size to half virgates.

In most manors, nevertheless, both cottage and messuage holdings other than cotlands seem to bear no relationship to the virgate. Some may have been purprestures of irregular size, and others were perhaps fragments of larger customary holding that had acquired an independent dwelling. In the tithing of Headley on the manor of Bishops Sutton, although about a third of messuage holdings are described as villein land, more than half the remainder are defined by their rent. One fine, for example, transfers 'one messuage and 6s and 9 pennyworths of land', and another 'one messuage and 3s 2d of rent'. This suggests the creation at Bishops Sutton, at least, of many messuages with small holdings outside the regular standard holdings, and probably in more recent times.

Holdings of these kinds broadened the lower part of a pyramidal cross-section of property holding among manorial tenants. At Bishops Waltham in about 1332, smallholders of less than ten acres comprised slightly over half of the total tenements, and tenants of between a ferling and virgate a little over 40 per cent. Meanwhile, those holding a virgate or more comprised only 8.5 per cent. Between 1263 and 1349, over three-quarters of holdings transferred were either cottages and messuage holdings (48.6 per cent) or ferlings (31.0 per cent); only 3.7 per cent were of virgates or larger units.[37] This finding tallies with the evidence of those historians of medieval rural society who have been impressed by the high proportion of tenants with land inadequate or barely adequate to sustain a family.[38]

In addition to these smaller customary holdings the entry fines also record large numbers of independent acres and many hundreds of smaller sub-acre pieces of land of roods, dayworks, butts, crofts and a whole range of plots of various descriptions, all without dwellings. While many of these were assarts, purprestures and parcels of demesne, a notable proportion were categorised by the fines as villein land, and the assumption of villein status is a reasonable one to make in cases where no alternative

---

37. See also Titow, *English rural society*, p. 86.

38. Kosminsky, *Studies in the agrarian history of England*, pp. 206–27; Postan, 'Medieval agrarian society in its prime', pp. 618–22; Titow, *English rural society*, pp. 78–96.

origin is stated. Throughout the estate the bulk of these fall between half an acre and a ferling and they form about 17 per cent of all land transferred. Not only do these 'loose' acres and sub-acre pieces of customary land form a significant proportion of transfers across the estate, they can add to our perception of the process of the disintegration of customary holdings over the period.

In the absence of large reserves of uncultivated farm land, the cottages, messuages and smallholdings required to maintain a growing number of families were more easily created than the larger holdings required for subsistence farming. Their number increased during the twelfth and thirteenth centuries, partly through deliberate provision by the many landlords who developed villages and towns to increase their income from rents. Such holdings were less likely to attract family loyalty than peasant farms, and there were few social obstacles to their being transferred between families. The declining population that was such a marked feature of the fourteenth century had an immediate effect on the demand for housing, so that cottages and messuages were in excess supply through much of the century, and many were abandoned.[39] Some were integrated into larger tenures, either for use or for the site value, but many disappeared from the property market altogether and any lands attached to them were amalgamated with other properties. The declining demand for cottages and smallholdings is important in accounting for a number of statistical trends we shall have cause to observe from the period after the Black Death, including the tendency for average entry fines to increase despite a fall in average land values.

Property outside agriculture

Some recorded transfers are a reminder that the rural economy of the Middle Ages was not wholly concerned with producing food from the land. The 357 transfers of mills are a case in point. Most are described simply as mills or water mills, but transfers of fulling mills occurred at various times at Taunton and Bishops Hull in Somerset, Downton in Wiltshire, Wargrave in Berkshire, Farnham in Surrey, and at Alresford, Bishops Sutton, Bishops Waltham, Bitterne and East Meon in Hampshire.[40] There were transactions involving windmills at East Knoyle in Wiltshire and at Bitterne and Gosport on the southern coast of Hampshire. Horse mills occur at Fareham, Woodhay and East Meon, all after 1380. Water mills were often associated with weirs, fisheries and fish-traps, which were sometimes transferred with the mills but on other occasions acquired separately or independently. A fine at Culham in 1322–3 was for a messuage, a half share of two water-mills and half a fishery attached to the mills. Forty-nine fines are concerned with the transfer of forges, illustrating the

---

39. M.M. Postan, 'Some agrarian evidence of a declining population in the later Middle Ages', *Economic History Review*, 2nd series, 2 (1950), p. 243–4, reprinted in *idem, Essays on medieval agriculture*, pp. 210–11.

40. For the multiplication of rural fulling mills, see E.M. Carus-Wilson, 'An industrial revolution of the thirteenth century', *Economic History Review*, 1st series, 11 (1941), pp. 39–60, reprinted in *eadem, Medieval merchant venturers*, 2nd edn (London, 1967), pp. 183–210; J. Langdon, *Mills in the medieval economy: England, 1300–1540* (Oxford, 2004), pp. 40–7.

importance of smith work for the maintenance of ploughs, carts and other equipment. Many forges were associated with a dwelling, a small piece of land, or both. They occur on twenty-one manors across the estate, as one might expect given the universal need for smithies.[41]

The entry fines also concern the transfer of property within the boroughs of the estate, although they account for only a small proportion of the total. On the manors of Fareham, Farnham and Gosport there was no separate account for the boroughs they contained; entry fines for burghal properties are mixed with others. In these cases estimates may be attempted by calculating the number of properties where the transfer is said to be within the borough and by adding to this the number of properties that are specifically urban in nature, such as shops or burgage plots. Fareham, with about 300 such property transfers recorded between 1263 and 1415, had by far the busiest market in urban property; there were only 154 at Taunton, and about 67 at Farnham. Downton, Witney, Hindon, Overton, Gosport and Alresford had no more than 80 recorded transfers between them. However, it is likely that these figures underestimate the number of borough transfers since locational detail relating to messuages and cottages is often not supplied. Most of Fareham's urban properties, and about half those of Farnham, are described as burgage tenements, but these are rarely found on other manors. At Downton there are only three instances. Elsewhere we see an indiscriminate mixture of plots, parcels, messuages, houses, stalls, selds and shops.

Urban and sub-urban property was by no means confined to the boroughs. Some other manors had shops, stalls, selds and pentices as well as a 'high street'. The largest number of such installations was apparently in Havant (recorded in the Brockhampton accounts), where eighty-five shops were transferred between 1263 and 1415. In the same period twenty-one shops were transferred at Bishops Waltham, nineteen at Hambledon and seventeen at Ivinghoe; there are fewer than half a dozen from anywhere else on the estate. The rental of c.1332 for Bishops Waltham implies that nearly 46 per cent of the manor's smallholders were inhabitants of the town, including sixty-six of the eighty-two tenants holding a cottage only, or a cottage and a few acres.[42] This suggests that many small holdings recorded on Winchester manors may in fact have been quite urban in character.

Conclusion

Although there was a core of virgated tenements on the Winchester estates, there were regional, intermanorial and intramanorial differences in the size of virgates and – long before the Black Death – many local differences in the extent to which they were split up. Inhibitions against accumulating customary tenures were generally stronger before the Black Death than inhibitions against fragmenting them: despite pipe roll

---

41. Alresford (1), Bishopstoke (4), Brightwell (2), Bishops Waltham (2), Cheriton (2), Droxford (1), East Knoyle (1), Fareham (1), Highclere (3), Holway (3), Harwell (1), Ivinghoe (5), Kingstone St Mary and Nailsbourne (1), Merdon (1), Mill lane (1), Morton (1), North Waltham (2), Overton (1), Poundisford (1), Trull and Bishops Hull (2), Twyford (2), Wield (2), Waltham St Lawrence (3).

42. HRO, 11M59/E2/159512/1; Titow, *English rural society*, p. 86.

evidence that in some contexts manorial custom made it difficult to subdivide virgated units, the desirability of accommodating more inhabitants had often encouraged the halving and quartering of virgates long before the mid-fourteenth century. It is impossible to ascribe to the bishops of Winchester any fixed policy in this respect. In exceptional circumstances – notably on the Taunton manors and at Bishops Waltham in South Hampshire – environmental pressures had led estate officials and village communities to tolerate considerable subdivision of customary units, although the outcome was less radical than in parts of eastern England, where even halves and quarters of virgates were commonly being broken down into irregular numbers of acres.

The subdivision of customary tenures was less necessary, even to facilitate population growth and commercial expansion, where there were unused reserves of forest, downland or heath. The existence of new properties outside the system of virgated tenures, especially on large manors, created a pool of properties whose transfer was less likely to be inhibited by respect for their integrity or their associations with a particular family. They could more readily be alienated for the endowment of non-inheriting family members, or simply sold to a new family to raise cash in times of hardship. Numerous purprestures and assarts, in particular, by creating a division between more and less negotiable types of land, permitted a distinctly different formation of the land market from that depending predominantly upon customary tenures.

Independent cottages and cottages with smallholdings sometimes originated from the fragmentation of customary units, but many are likely to have had a separate origin even where their dimensions are stated as fractions of a virgate. They were less likely than more substantial holdings to attract strong family loyalties, and in some circumstances – in boroughs and industrial villages – they account for a large proportion of the total number of fines, even though the total extent and value of property they represent must have been less significant than their share of the documentation. Industrial properties such as mills and forges, and urban properties, also occur in the entry fines of many manors, since many rural property owners had interests outside agriculture. In the course of the period smallholdings of all kinds were readily amalgamated, with kaleidoscopic variation, in the creation of larger holdings, particularly as a result of a declining demand for cottages and messuages during the fourteenth century.

Chapter 4

Tenures

The tenurial structure was an important source of variation between manors insofar as it affected the facility with which land could be transferred. In the course of time, however, widespread changes in the terms on which many tenants held their properties accompanied the development of a market in peasant lands. Leasehold from the bishop, not only of customary holdings but also of demesne and other lands, increased greatly in importance. In addition, there were mutations of custom affecting villeinage, the form and impact of which varied between manors and regions. The context of most such developments implies tension between the interests of the bishop and his tenants, as each sought to take advantage of local and wider changes. The estate administrators needed to maintain the bishop's income when it was under threat, which required complex decisions. Should they maintain the direct cultivation of demesne lands and the keeping of livestock, or should they release land to tenants? Should they insist on traditional rents and services from tenants despite the risk that these terms of tenure might seem unattractively burdensome? Meanwhile, peasant families, within the context of a freer market after the Black Death, increasingly found themselves in a position to better their tenurial conditions and personal status. Labour services were associated with unfree status all through our period of study and could deter tenants from taking up vacant holdings. At Twyford in 1308–9, a messuage and two virgates in Owslebury tithing escheated to the bishop 'because no one wished to hold it on account of the labour services', and they were, therefore, commuted for 6s 4d. At Cheriton at the later date of 1341–2 the record is blunter still; a toft and ten acres was granted to a new tenant in return for 2s for the labour services 'because there was no one who wanted to hold the land by doing the labour services'. After 1349 it was easier for tenants to negotiate freedom from such services, either by challenging the bishop's officers or by leaving the episcopal estate in search of freer conditions elsewhere. In challenging the bishop, however, they risked failure and penal amercements, and in abandoning family holdings they forfeited the hereditary rights that had protected them in harder times. The ways in which these various tendencies worked out in different situations is an important matter for investigation.

The long-term trend in the relationship between lords and tenants in England is well known. Villeinage declined in favour of a greater freedom of tenure; rents and other incidents of villeinage fell in value; labour services – a principal indicator of servile status – were heavily reduced in favour of money rents. But some of these changes, especially the multiplication of short-term leases, occasioned greater insecurity of tenure. So did negotiated changes in custom, although uncertainties were to some extent counteracted by increased dependence on written evidence.[1] In

---

1.   For general discussion of this point, see R.H. Britnell, *The commercialisation of English society, 1000–1500*, 2nd edn (Manchester, 1996), pp. 217–23; C. Dyer, *Making a living in the Middle Ages: the people of Britain, 850–1520* (New Haven, 2002), pp. 335–7, 349–54; R.H. Hilton, *The decline of serfdom in medieval England* (London, 1969), pp. 32–51.

a number of ways the entry fines of the Winchester estate, in their long sequence and geographical diversity, can contribute to an understanding of these phenomena.

Changes affecting customary tenure

Modifications of customary tenure were in part an adaptation to the changing requirements of demesne cultivation. When demesnes were expanding and profits were to be made by direct management the bishop's needs for labour had increased, but this expansion was subsequently reversed.[2] On some manors the demesne began to be reduced as early as the mid-thirteenth century, and contraction became more widespread and more pronounced in the course of the fourteenth and fifteenth centuries. More than 10,500 acres of demesne across the estate were under seed in 1301–2, but this had fallen to a little more than 7,000 by 1349–50 and to just 4,500 by 1409–10.[3] By the mid-fifteenth century the arable worked directly under the estate's management was less than a tenth of what it had been a century earlier, although some manors were much more affected than others.[4]

In the late thirteenth and early fourteenth centuries it suited the bishop to sell some of his labour services as a means of realising cash.[5] Titow calculated that *ad hoc* sales brought in just over £12 in 1225, a figure that rose to almost £98 in 1300, more than £140 in 1321 and £250 in 1348.[6] Sales of labour services were then expedients year by year, with no commitment by the lord to any permanent change in the terms of tenure; there are only thirteen recorded examples of permanent commutation across the whole estate between 1267–8 and the Black Death. The pattern of intermanorial variation provides confirming evidence that in this period the sale of works was at the bishop's discretion; sales of labour services were generally higher where there was a falling demand for labour on the demesne. At Bishops Waltham, Twyford, Bishopstoke, Hambledon, Farnham and Downton, where the sown acreage shrank between the third quarter of the thirteenth century and the 1340s, the level of sales was exceptionally high. On manors where the sown acreage declined very little, as at Adderbury and Ivinghoe, the level of sales was correspondingly lower.[7] Because

---

2. M.M. Postan, 'The chronology of labour services', *Transactions of the Royal Historical Society*, 4th series, 20 (1937), pp. 169–93, reprinted in *idem, Essays on medieval agriculture*, pp. 89–106.

3. Titow, 'Land and population', p. 21a; *idem, English rural society*, p. 52. The acreage for 1409–10 was calculated by Mark Page and includes the sown acres for leased manors: *PRBW 1409–10*, p. xx.

4. E. Miller, 'The occupation of the land: the southern counties', in *AHEW* III, pp. 142–3. See also Table 2.4.

5. Levett, 'Black Death', pp. 86–7; Titow, *English rural society*, p. 52.

6. J.Z. Titow, 'Labour problems and policies on the Winchester estates, 1208–1275' (unpublished paper presented to the British Agricultural History Society in 1995).

7. Titow has calculated that at Bishops Waltham the sown acreage in the 1340s was 30.2 per cent of what it had been in the 1270s, at Taunton 47.7 per cent, at Bishopstoke 46.7 per cent, at Farnham 52.2 per cent, at Twyford 55.6 per cent, and at Hambledon 68.6 per cent. In contrast, for example, the sown acreage at Adderbury over the same period was 90.9 per cent of its earlier level, and at Ivinghoe 99.8 per cent: Titow, 'Labour problems', table 1.

sales of labour services were the result of *ad hoc* managerial decisions, the accounts at first normally recorded the cash receipts amongst the miscellaneous 'issues of the manor'. By the mid-fourteenth century, because such sales were greatly increased, it had become usual to record this income under its own heading.

Although the plague of 1348–9 placed a significant brake on estate administrators' willingness to sell labour services – since rising wage rates made it more advantageous to use customary labour – the bishop's interests became increasingly subject to challenges from his more substantial tenants. The need to retain tenants suggests that their preferences had to be taken into consideration more than in the past. Although in the years immediately after the Black Death fewer works were sold on some manors in response to the interests of management, this was an untenable defiance of the logic of the situation; in effect, tenants were being expected to contribute more to the lord's economy at a time when their bargaining power was greater. Villeins who would have formerly inherited heavily burdened holdings were now better able to pick and choose amongst various options and were consequently in a position to influence the conditions of their tenure. Traditional labour services could be sufficiently unattractive to undermine the strength of family attachments to particular lands and particular manors, and the resentment of labour services may lie behind some of the numerous fines in which an out-going tenant was said to 'refuse to hold any longer', or others where none of a deceased tenant's kin was willing to fine for his land. The terms of commutation vary from fine to fine, allowing us to view the process as it happened. Most such modifications of tenure were made in the course of negotiating extrafamilial transfers of customary virgates and half virgates *post mortem*. Many quittances of services in the 1350s and 1360s were temporary, particularly in the Downton group, where there were many vacant tenements: at East Knoyle in 1356–7 the labour services of an incoming tenant to a half virgate were released only until Lammas Day (1 August). Through the third quarter of the fourteenth century, works were usually commuted for a few years, but no more. Sometimes, however, the terms of commutation were left indeterminate. At Witney and Downton problems of vacant tenements were especially acute, and the bishop's hand was forced earlier than was typical elsewhere.[8] Thus at Witney in 1359–60 some entry fines released labour services with no specified term, and the following year similar grants were made there 'at the lord's pleasure'.

Even as commutations became more permanent the bishop let go only what was necessary to secure tenants in difficult times, so that many fines offered only partial relief from servile services. At Twyford in 1362–3, when William Hersey took up a toft and half virgate of villein land with an acre of purpresture that had escheated into lord's hands, he paid a fine of 2s together with 4s for the relaxation of all works 'except the washing and shearing of the lord's sheep with his neighbours'. This latter exception – especially common at Witney and Twyford, but found also at Marwell, Overton and Alresford – reflects a concern for the management of the increasing demesne flocks.[9] William Godwin, who fined for a toft and virgate of villein land at

---

8. A. Ballard, 'The manors of Witney, Brightwell and Downton', in P. Vinogradoff (ed.), *Oxford studies in social and legal history*, V (Oxford, 1916), pp. 198–9, 213–14.

9. Miller, 'Occupation of the land', p. 144.

Alresford in 1405–6, was to perform no labour services other than finding two men to wash and shear the lord's sheep. At Overton in 1366–7, Stephen Baston fined for a messuage and cotland, and paid an additional 3s to be released from works, but he was still obliged to participate in haymaking, sheep-washing and shearing, and in the performance of autumn boon-works, alongside other cotters. Commutation was sometimes accompanied by seigniorial pressure on tenants to enter a vacant property, implying that compulsion was thought reasonable or feasible only with the added inducement of modified terms of tenure.

The progress of commutation did not proceed everywhere at the same speed. The willingness of estate officers to commute services was affected by the difficulty they had in finding tenants. Tenants from the manors in the Downton bailiwick and at Witney, Twyford and Wargrave fined most frequently for the abandonment of labour services, and it is precisely in these manors that Titow noticed the largest and most persistent number of vacant holdings in the 1360s and beyond.[10] Often several commutations occurred together: at Witney fourteen were agreed in 1359–60, and a further three the following year, all for lands in the townships of Curbridge and Hailey; and there were nine commutations at Twyford in 1362–3. On Wargrave manor, by contrast, commutation came late in the period under review, chiefly in 1402–3.

Sales of services increased more rapidly following the collapse of grain prices in the 1380s, when the episcopal administration hesitantly began to farm out its manors and to abandon demesne cultivation. The episcopal administration came to accept that the effects of a reduced demand for land were there to stay, and it is not obvious that at any stage they sacrificed income for the sake of conservative principles. It became more common for labour services to be formally commuted rather than simply sold *ad hoc*, although this tendency still had some way to go in 1415.[11] The contrast with the beginning of the fourteenth century can be easily demonstrated by comparing the published pipe rolls for 1301–2 and 1409–10. At North Waltham, where no labour services were sold in 1301–2, the bishop received £3 9s 3½d in 1409–10 for the labour services of fifteen virgates and three half virgates; he retained only 'the washing and shearing of sheep and enclosing the park'. At other manors in North Hampshire sales of labour dues were extensive in 1409–10, even though they had been absent in 1301–2. At Ashmansworth, six virgaters, seven half virgaters and six cotlanders bought their annual services for £4 15s 10d. Services were also abandoned from twenty-four half virgaters, three cotlanders and three half cotlanders at Burghclere, and from eighteen tenants, mostly virgaters, at Highclere.[12] In the Taunton group of manors there are no sales of works at all in 1301–2 but a great many in 1409–10, when income from sales of works at Holway, Staplegrove, Bishops Hull, Nailsbourne and Poundisford totalled £83 18s 10¼d.[13] Commutations for life begin to be recorded from the end of our period, one from Downton in 1410–11 being the

10. Titow, 'Lost rents', pp. 109–10; *idem*, 'Labour problems'.

11. For an extended analysis of this matter, see Levett, 'Black Death', pp. 86–121, and Ballard, 'Manors of Witney, Brightwell and Downton', pp. 197–200, 208–9, 214–16.

12. Highclere, Burghclere, Cole Henley, Ashmansworth and Woodhay manors were leased out by this time: *PRBW 1409–10*, pp. 207–58.

13. *PRBW 1409–10*, pp. 19, 30, 36, 42, 47.

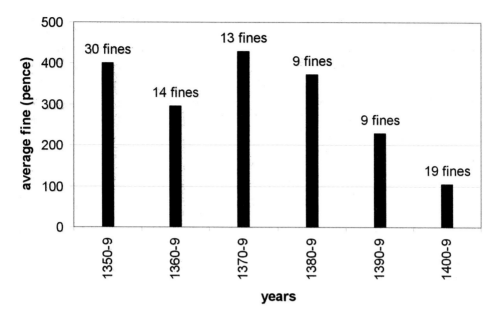

Figure 4.1 Average fines (pence) at Downton for all virgate holdings, 1350–1410.

earliest. Untenanted holdings are sometimes recorded as still owing labour services in the early fifteenth century, as at Beauworth and North Waltham, which might imply that this was the reason for their being unoccupied. However, the flexibility of the bishop's administrators elsewhere, when necessity dictated it, implies that this may be false reasoning, and that there were probably other reasons for the undesirability of these lands.

Besides the negotiated sale or commutation of labour services, other concessions had to be made by the bishop in order to secure tenants. On some manors, especially where vacant holdings were a particular problem, the administration lowered entry fines, as at Downton (Figure 4.1). This development will be discussed more extensively in Chapter 5.[14] We shall also find, in Chapter 6, that fines for those taking up vacant properties that had escheated to the bishop were normally appreciably lower than those on properties that passed by inheritance between family members. Sometimes, too, the contractual nature of the commutation of services was even more explicitly recognised by the simultaneous conversion of a tenure to leasehold. There is only a single example of a standard tenement leased without such commutation, whether for a term of years or for life: at Bishops Sutton in 1367–8, Roger Haywood fined for a toft and a virgate of villein land that he had 'by concession of Bishop William Edington, to hold for the term of his life'.

Many of those who took up standard holdings with commuted services in the aftermath of the Black Death had not previously been associated with the manors in question. Migrants could improve their lot by obtaining title to abandoned and semi-

---

14.   Mullan, 'Transfer of customary land', p. 87.

derelict customary holdings for which the estate officers were willing to change the terms of tenure. Some of these tenants came from manors other than the bishop's, but others may have arrived from neighbouring manors of the estate, with the assent of the bishop's officers, or even at their invitation. Richard Boys, for example, who appears in 1366–7 at Marwell, south-west of Winchester, fined 3s 4d for a toft and virgate holding on which most services had been commuted for 4s. Richard had not fined for land on the manor before, but some years previously a villein of the same name had inherited an acre of meadow at Bishopstoke, a few miles to the south. The family name crops up also at Bitterne, not much further away, as well as at other manors in South Hampshire. Likewise, John Mere, who secured a customary holding with a two-year relaxation of works at East Knoyle in 1359–60, may be identified with John Mere, a smallholder, of Downton.

Once a widespread process of permanent commutation was under way it was self-perpetuating. The continued performance of those services that remained was increasingly resented as a symbol of social inferiority. Any conservatism of the bishop's officers on this point was then likely to breed resentment over tenurial conditions. The only identified example in the pipe rolls of tenants causing serious trouble comes some years beyond our period: in 1461 at East Meon no manorial courts were held because 'the tenants rebelled against the lord'. In the same year at Merdon tenants refused to perform autumn services and the cost of the harvest consequently rose from the usual £3 to over £21.[15] But at an earlier date we find lesser forms of collective resistance. At Staplegrove in the Taunton group, for instance, a number of tenants were fined in 1409–10 'because they refused to perform the lord's labour services at the mill of Taunton and in hundreds other than the hundred of Staplegrove',[16] the latter phrase implying an organised and collectively reasoned argument for defiance. Troubling as it must have been for the steward to hear this collective voice in the manorial court, it serves to remind us where authority continued to lie, for the fine was imposed and no concessions were allowed.

The commutation of services significantly eased the problems of tenants wanting to accumulate property, a development to be examined in greater detail in Chapter 8. In 1395–6 William Godwin of Wargrave inherited a large composite holding consisting of two messuages, two virgates, some purpresture and a croft with pasture. Ten years later he secured a toft and virgate that had escheated to the lord, for which he paid an annual rent of 2s and 13s 4d for commuted services, except that he still had to wash and shear the lord's sheep. He was also required to build a house of 'two long bays'. Similarly, Nicholas Kirkby of Twyford, who came from an established family of that manor, was able in 1366–7 to acquire for 4s a year an abandoned and escheated customary holding, from which all services, other than those for care of the demesne flocks, were commuted. Nicholas remained active in the local land market through the following decade. In 1402–3 he secured an escheated toft and half virgate to hold for an annual rent of 6s and a further 7s a year for all services, with the additional benefit 'that he should not henceforth be elected to any office in court'. Tenants would have

_____

15. Titow, 'Labour problems'. Unfortunately the pipe roll for 1380–1, the year of revolt, does not survive.

16. *PRBW 1409–10*, pp. 30–1.

been inhibited from engrossing such units had they become liable for all the labour services previously owed, especially considering the rising expense of acquitting them by means of hired labour.

The sale of works in this period was not invariably in the interests of lesser tenants, however, especially in times when regular employment was hard to come by, since it depended on the increase in freedom being worth the money price that had to be paid.[17] Not all villeins could afford to make an annual payment in exchange for labour services, and conservatism in this respect was not uniquely the characteristic of the bishop's men. Commutation of services was a phenomenon that separated larger tenants from smaller; those tenants who were eager to commute their works were those exceptionally able to raise the necessary cash, and among long-standing tenants the commutation of services was accordingly commonest among the wealthier families. Of the nine consecutive commutations of services at Twyford in 1362–3, seven were to the advantage of principal families long resident on the manor's customary virgates; all seven were for escheated properties, mostly virgates, and their tenants typically paid around 5s a year for the release from the services due. For an individual to secure a commutation on anything much smaller than a half virgate was unusual.

The increasing commutation of services did not imply, in the period before 1415, any abandonment of the legal distinction between free and villein tenure. On the estates of Westminster Abbey the terminology of villeinage 'was dropping out of the conveyancing vocabulary used in the respect of customary land by 1400',[18] but this development was not universal at such an early date. Although the number of villeins on the estates of the bishopric of Worcester was declining as families died out or migrated, the bishop's officers continued to insist upon the servile status of those who remained.[19] Such persistence could lead, perhaps after confrontation with tenants, to major concessions concerning terms of tenure, or to a necessary acceptance on the part of the estate of mounting arrears of rent and increasing numbers of vacant properties.[20] The spasmodic absence of reference to the villein status of customary lands in the Winchester pipe rolls was merely a matter of clerical omission. Between 1349–50 and 1414–15 some 250 virgate and half-virgate holdings are not described as held in villein or customary tenure. However, half of these were enrolled before 1370, and they are disproportionately numerous in 1349–50, so they have no significance for the long-term development of terminology. The large number of entry fines in the

---

17. J. Hatcher, 'English serfdom and villeinage: towards a reassessment', *Past and Present*, 90 (1981), p. 12.

18. In most places words of servile meaning finally fell out of use only in the period c.1430 to c.1470: Harvey, *Westminster Abbey*, p. 275.

19. Dyer, *Lords and peasants*, pp. 270–5.

20. E.B. Burstall, 'A monastic agreement of the fourteenth century', *Norfolk Archaeology*, 31 (1957), pp. 211–18; C. Dyer, 'A redistribution of incomes in fifteenth-century England?' *Past and Present*, 39 (1968), pp. 11–33, reprinted in R.H. Hilton (ed.), *Peasants, knights and heretics: studies in medieval English social history* (Cambridge, 1976), pp. 203–7; R.H. Hilton, *The English peasantry in the later Middle Ages* (Oxford, 1975), pp. 54–73; E. Searle, *Lordship and community: Battle Abbey and its banlieu, 1066–1538* (Toronto, 1974), pp. 382–3.

aftermath of the Black Death merely encouraged clerks to save both time and space by omitting what at times must have seemed like superfluous words.

Changes affecting non-customary tenure

A widespread feature of the period after 1349 was that a larger proportion of tenants held property that had never been customary. Assarts, waste and demesne, as we have seen, were more available on some manors than others, and more in some years than others. Nevertheless, where available they created exceptional new opportunities for an increasingly creative and adaptable land market. Many of the bishop's wealthier tenants were able to accumulate several holdings and these were often held under a variety of terms and conditions; customary holdings were held in conjunction with assarts, purpresture and former demesne, all of which might be held either by hereditary titles or on lease.

The episcopal administration was more flexible in managing assarts than customary lands. This is most evident at Witney, partly because of the large number of assart holdings on this manor but also because of the high proportion of vacant lands there. Assart lands were subject chiefly to money rent, which was significantly reduced on ten of these holdings at Witney between 1388 and 1400. In 1390–1, for example, John Smith, for a fine of 6d, was admitted to three acres of assart which had previously rendered 6d per acre; they were now to be held for 4d per acre. But just as there were often limitations on the length of time for which services were commuted on customary holdings, so there were restrictions here too. Most reductions of rent on assart were accompanied by a clause that the new tenant would hold the property under new conditions only until another should come forward to accept it on the customary terms.

Unlike assarts, the impact of which on the land market was already important by the end of the thirteenth century, the impact of demesne lettings came mostly during the following centuries, and was slight until the final three or four decades of our period, despite a retreat from demesne arable farming from as early as 1269.[21] Entry fines in the bishopric manor courts (Figure 4.2) can give only an imperfect impression of the overall course of this process, since demesnes might be leased as a whole by a contract independent of manor-court procedure. However, the more piecemeal alienation of demesne to tenants needs to be considered to the extent that it affected the peasant land market on some manors. Localised increases in the number of such transfers from the mid-1320s to the 1340s were probably induced by a new phase of disappointing prices and profits.[22] This upsurge was ended by the Black Death, presumably because of the sudden availability of vacant tenant land.

Choices made by the bishops and their staff might have little to do with specifically local conditions, since decisions relating to individual manors had to take account of operating costs, which depended in part on distance from Winchester and associated administrative and transport expenses. By far the largest number of transfers of demesne through the manor court was on the Taunton group of manors, the most

---

21. J.Z. Titow, *Winchester yields: a study in medieval agricultural productivity* (Cambridge, 1972), p. 10.
22. Miller and Hatcher, *Medieval England*, pp. 60–1.

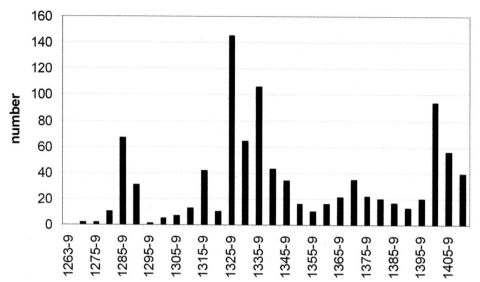

Figure 4.2 The number of transfers of demesne through manorial courts over the whole estate of the bishop of Winchester, 1263–1415.

remote from Winchester, which collectively experienced a greater reduction of demesne acreages than other manors (Table 2.4). Good land here had been hard to come by, so when manorial demesne was made available tenants were prepared to pay a high rent.[23] Leasing began early here; there were large numbers of leases in 1318–19, and again in the 1330s.

There were 139 recorded transfers of demesne land before 1349 in the Downton cluster of manors, which were also remote from Winchester. These were mostly in Downton itself, which experienced an exceptionally severe reduction of demesne cultivation (Table 2.4). Transfers occurred chiefly between the mid 1320s and about 1340, a period during which the demesne contracted to about half the size it had been during the 1290s.[24] Downton suffered particularly badly during the Black Death and the large proportion of vacant customary holdings with reduced entry fines must have detracted from any interest in additional demesne property.[25] In spite of this, in 1357–8 eighty-eight acres of arable from the demesne at Downton were leased to several tenants, and an enclosed croft was leased separately.[26] Labour was in short supply, profits were threatened, and the farming-out of this large area demonstrates the lord's exceptional determination to be rid of unprofitable land.

There were comparatively few such early releases of demesne except at Taunton and Downton, despite a general reduction of demesne acreages, and most of those

23. Titow, 'Lost rents', pp. 109–10; Thornton, 'Arable productivity', pp. 109–37.

24. Titow, 'Labour problems'.

25. Ballard, 'Manors of Witney, Brightwell and Downton', pp. 213–15.

26. These eighty-eight acres were still leased in 1409–10: *PRBW 1409–10*, p. 56.

that occurred came after 1325.[27] At Farnham and Bentley there were six transfers of demesne to tenants and in Wargrave bailiwick only four. Most demesne transfers transacted through manor courts were of small size; before the mid-fourteenth century they were usually of three acres or less, and although larger thereafter they rarely exceeded ten acres.

Although the terms of tenure of these holdings are rarely recorded there are sufficient numbers of examples to form some picture. Until the famine years of around 1315 parcels of demesne were commonly leased for a year. From then on they were leased for somewhat longer periods, as we can tell from rents recorded in the pipe rolls, which note how far the lease had run. Most commonly in the Taunton manors, the demesne lettings are recorded as 'let to him this the first year', 'let to him this the second year', and so on. Their rents varied between 3d and 1s an acre. The majority of demesne transfers, for which no terms of tenure are recorded, were perhaps held at will, signifying that the bishop would resume direct control at any time that suited him.

In the course of time, fragments of demesne permanently alienated by the bishop, and described as 'former' demesne, entered the inter-peasant land market, adding to a growing variety of terms of tenure. Our earliest example is from 1292–3, when John Mitchell secured by marriage half an acre formerly of the lord's demesne at Trull or Bishops Hull. An extrafamilial surrender of demesne occurs at North Waltham in 1307–8, and the following year at Alresford twenty-seven acres were surrendered by Roger Clerk to his son. But the exchange of demesne land between peasants at this time was unusual: there were only four instances before 1320. In the 1320s, following the larger increase of seigniorial releases of demesne, they became more frequent, but the total area involved was never large. Some parcels occur as appendages to customary holdings, but increasingly from the 1320s, former demesne properties had dwellings upon them.

Demesne leasing became both more extensive and more widespread in the 1380s.[28] The substitution of leases for direct management was observable across many estates at this time, especially ecclesiastical ones.[29] It was intimately connected with the declining profitability of large-scale arable husbandry in the later fourteenth century as labour costs rose and prices fell, although the precise timing depended much upon guesswork about what the uncertain future held.[30] In this context demesnes were more likely than previously to be leased as a whole, but there was nevertheless still some piecemeal release of demesne land into peasant agriculture. The amount of demesne leasing on the Taunton manors was particularly active in the

---

27. Before 1350 there were 58 in Bishops Waltham bailiwick, 49 in Witney bailiwick, 37 in Highclere bailiwick, 35 in Twyford bailiwick, 27 in East Meon bailiwick and 23 in Bishops Sutton bailiwick.

28. For the large acreages involved, see *PRBW 1409–19*, p. xx

29. W. Bean, 'Landlords', in *AHEW III*, pp. 573–5; Britnell, *Commercialisation*, pp. 187–9; Harvey, *Westminster Abbey*, pp. 148–51; F.R.H. Du Boulay, *The lordship of Canterbury: an essay on medieval society* (London, 1966), pp. 218–37; Dyer, *Lords and peasants*, pp. 146–9, 209–17; J.N. Hare, 'The demesne leases of fifteenth-century Wiltshire', *AHR*, 29 (1981), pp. 1–15.

30. Bean, 'Landlords', pp. 573–6; R.H. Britnell, 'English agricultural output and prices, 1350–1450: national trends and regional divergences', in Dodds and Britnell (eds), *Rural society and agriculture*, pp. 26–8; Campbell, 'Unique estate', p. 32; Dyer, *Lords and peasants*, pp. 146–9; Harvey, *Westminster Abbey*, pp. 148–51.

early 1400s: some measure of the demand here can be seen at Poundisford in 1395–6, when Nicholas Grey paid 3s 4d for 'two acres of newly broken land called Sydefurlong from the lord's demesne in the tithing of Southtrendle, rendering thence an annual increment of rent of 2s'. For the first time in this period the bishop was occasionally willing to allow demesne leases for life; seven occur between 1384–5 and 1415.

The opportunity to acquire small parcels of demesne was overshadowed, however, by an increasing tendency for the episcopal administration to farm out demesnes as a whole. There had been some farming-out of manors well before this time; the irregular sub-manors of Seal in Farnham, Billingbear in Wargrave and Otterford in Taunton, and the two small manors of Morton and Esher, had all been let out at various times even before 1350.[31] A more concerted effort at retreat from direct management came with the 1380s, even though 'the bishops were reluctant leasers'.[32] A new scale of indirect management began with the leasing out of the demesne of Ashmansworth in 1383. A few other manors of the estate were leased in the last few years of the century; in 1396–7, for example, the small manors of Morton, Wield, Otterford, Culham, Cole Henley and Easton were at farm and over the next few years a few more were added, notably the much larger manor of Witney. From 1406–7 a great many more manors were suddenly added to the list, including larger manors such as Woodhay and Waltham St Lawrence, although even in 1409–10 many demesnes were directly managed.[33] By the mid-fifteenth century only Merdon and Ecchinswell remained in hand; they were finally leased only in 1473.[34]

The terms of leasehold varied from manor to manor not only in the length of tenure and the rent payable but also in the composition of the leased property. In most cases only the demesne was leased, together with the livestock and other facilities needed to work it. In other cases whole manors were farmed out, tenancies as well as the demesne. In 1409–10, twenty-eight manors were leased, the demesne alone on seventeen, the rents also on the remainder. When the bishop leased the tenancies with the manor he retained his rights of lordship and jurisdiction, and so retained various profits arising from court business; this was expressed in formula excepting from leases 'pleas of the court, wards, marriages, reliefs, entry fines, heriots, wood and all profits accruing from the steward's tourn'. Even by the end of our period, these wholesale leases might be temporary arrangements. In 1414–15, for example, manors such as Bishopstoke, Burghclere, Highclere, Farnham and Wargrave were back in hand, although, in subsequent years, they were let once more.[35]

Examination of the entry fines allows us some insight to those who took up these farms. A handful were apparently only smallholders on the bishop's estate, although they may have had other property. John Wynerd, lessee of Bishopstoke in 1409–10,

---

31. Seal and Otterford, for example, were leased in 1301–2: *PRBW 1301–2*, pp. 38–9, 206.

32. Campbell, 'Unique estate', p. 32.

33. *PRBW, 1409–10*. The demesnes leased at this time are listed in *ibid.*, pp. xxii–xxiii. See also D.L. Farmer, 'Grain yields on the Winchester manors in the later Middle Ages', *Economic History Review*, 2nd series, 30 (1977), pp. 561–2.

34. See also Hare, 'Bishop and the prior', pp. 209–11.

35. For a list of the manors leased in 1409–10, see *PRBW 1409–10*, pp. xxii–xxiii. See, too, pp. 71, 75, 84, 121, 125, 140, 145, 148.

held just a ferling, and Walter Douglas, who leased Culham from 1405–6 for nine years, accumulated a small holding of a cottage, curtilage, toft and croft, with a purpresture and further plot of demesne. More characteristically, they were tenants of larger customary holdings within the manor they leased. John Brite, for instance, who held a twelve-year lease on the farm of East Knoyle manor from the early fifteenth century, was a virgater of the manor and this was typical of a number of others. John Aillward, farmer of Wield in 1405–6, was a virgater, and John Wexy, farmer of Woodhay in 1409–10, was a half virgater of the manor. Others were from the more successful tenant families, who had managed to accumulate holdings of a significant size. John Lylye, farmer of Wargrave, left on his death in 1413–14 a substantial estate consisting of a toft and croft, three cottages with a curtilage and two crofts, two messuages with two half virgates, an additional acre and also a purpresture. William Lythewey, who leased the manor of West Wycombe, held a composite holding comprising messuages and three half virgates, a ferling and an indeterminate plot of land. He added to this by the continued acquisition of cottages and acres of villein land and assart during his time as lessee. Many farmers had been reeves, and so had managerial experience under the old order of things. Initially it seems likely that differences in management style were not greatly changed, although it must be supposed that, with lower overhead administrative costs, the new lessees were better placed to make a profit than the bishop's estate officials had been able to do. In these circumstances demesne leasing contributed greatly to the accumulation of wealth and power in the hands of a minority of peasant farmers, a topic to be examined in greater detail in Chapters 9 and 10.

Tenures and the written word

In matters concerning terms of tenure, increasing faith was placed in the written word of the pipe rolls during the fourteenth century. From about 1300 the record of entry fines became increasingly full, supplying a fuller description of properties, their location and their status, the names of all parties involved in the transaction, and the terms of the fine.[36] The detail became even richer through the later fourteenth century. The acreages of virgated tenements are frequently given, terms of leases are more fully recorded, and there is more detail about the reason why a holding was transferred. The initiative for this elaboration doubtless came from the episcopal administration, not only in order to record more fully the determinants of its income from entry fines, but also to facilitate judgements concerning the descent of property. However, it was a development that villeins were willing to encourage for their own purposes.

Increasingly manor courts referred to the pipe rolls as an authoritative record. In particular, entry fines following actions for the recovery of land frequently show that judgement had depended on reference to the written record. There are only two examples before 1330; one from East Meon in 1271–2, when a judgement was given 'as attested by the pipe rolls of Wolvesey', and the other from Trull and Bishops Hull in 1325–6. But such cases occur with some frequency from the 1330s. At Ecchinswell in 1336–7, Henry Alfred established his claim against a rival and fined 'to hold a messuage and cotland containing ten acres as of his right, as was found by the record

---

36. Chapter 2, p. 14 above.

of the pipe rolls of Wolvesey, the time of the surrender being well remembered as was found by an inquest'. This singular fine allows an insight into a moment in time when local, unwritten knowledge was still in balance with the gathering authority of a court roll. But already the rolls were sometimes given precedence over oral testimony. In the previous year at Brightwell, custom interpreted by a local jury had been overturned by written evidence. Thomas Atwell and his son John paid a fine of 12d to retain a cottage at the lord's will and to be quit from all action of Robert son of Juliana Trip. An inquest had found in favour of Robert's right 'according to the custom of the manor' although 'contrary to the pipe rolls of Wolvesey', but the authority of the latter, in the event, turned the judgement in the Atwells' favour. From this time judgements by local juries in more complex matters of inheritance often looked to the rolls as a matter of course. Although perhaps incapable of affecting straightforward inheritance, their evidence was authoritative for more complex and ambiguous matters, especially when they depended upon transactions in the distant past. At Hambledon in 1344–5, for example, evidence establishing John Plaistow's title to a messuage he had probably acquired by marriage was found 'in the pipe rolls of Wolvesey from the time of the vacancy after the death of Henry Wodelok, bishop of Winchester': that is, from 1316. The recurring expression 'the pipe rolls of Wolvesey' is explained by the fact that the pipe rolls were stored in the bishop's palace at Wolvesey, near Winchester.[37]

Tenants often lost claims over tenements because they were unable to show evidence of right in the rolls. In an early example from 1325–6 at Trull and Bishops Hull, Juliana Keen fined 3s to recover from Thomas Upcot a plot of pasture called 'Kenesplot' because Thomas was unable to produce 'the record of the pipe rolls of Wolvesey which was called as evidence before'. Most examples are more laconic and note simply that the previous tenant lost the tenement 'for default of record'. In 1357–8 at Bishops Waltham, John Martin fined 2s for a messuage and a half ferling recovered against John Bond, whose claim had failed 'for default of record'. Indeed, no reference to an earlier entry by John Bond can be found. Meanwhile, the use of local inquests to establish title to land, common in the later thirteenth and early fourteenth centuries, is rarely mentioned after the 1340s.

The reasons for this focus of attention upon the importance of the written word by both administrators and tenants are not be difficult to see. In an earlier period the homage had the local knowledge to gainsay any unjust claims to title. However, reliance on oral custom became increasingly inadequate as family ties to land were broken and the force of custom weakened. The formation of an extrafamilial land market undermined the capacity of local knowledge to verify titles to land and increased the need for families to establish evidence for their claim. This process accelerated after the mid-fourteenth century when, temporarily at least, it became more common for more distant relatives to inherit. High mortality, migration, more atypical and complex inheritances, an increasing number of extrafamilial transfers of property and recurrent changes in the terms of tenure all added to the burden of memory alone as a foundation for local knowledge. A similar set of considerations was, on other estates, giving rise to the practice of giving tenants a copy of the court roll entry by which their title was recorded.[38]

---

37. Page, 'Estate', p. 315.

38. Britnell, *Commercialisation*, p. 222; Harvey, *Westminster Abbey*, pp. 284–5.

There remain unanswered questions. The Winchester pipe rolls seem to have served the purpose of the court rolls on other estates, yet they do not contain the non-financial information that would have enabled them to replace court rolls altogether.[39] The reason for the peculiarity of the episcopal administration in this respect remains an unresolved puzzle.

Conclusion

Despite a generally conservative attitude, shared with most English landlords, towards the preservation of customary tenures, the bishops of Winchester and their officials were obliged to make many concessions to tenants in the course of the fourteenth century. The distinction between free land and villein land was not abandoned before 1415, but money payments were substituted for labour services, especially on properties taken up by new families, and some customary tenements were leased. Labour services were often sold rather than permanently commuted, even in the early fifteenth century, and the bishop sometimes retained a few services, particularly those relating to the care of sheep. But the rising cost of labour, which made labour services all the more valuable for use on the bishop's demesne, meant that they were all the more resented by tenants. The smaller number of potential tenants after the Black Death often obliged estate administrators to satisfy the interests of tenants, particularly on manors where customary land was in excess supply. Relaxation of labour services facilitated the accumulation of property by wealthier peasants, although it did not necessarily serve the interests of lesser tenants with fewer means of raising cash. The terms on which assarted land was held also became easier, as at Witney, where its rentable value began to decline in the late fourteenth century.

During the fourteenth century, because of rising costs and falling profits, demesne arable farming contracted and the bishop released a large amount of former demesne into peasant hands. Before 1380 this was chiefly observable on the Taunton manors and at Downton, and there were few grants of demesne elsewhere. But after about 1380 the practice of alienating demesne became less piecemeal and more widespread, and expanded the amount of land that could be bought and sold by tenants. These changes were responsible for differences between manors, depending upon the acreage of demesne land released. Leases and alienations of demesne land, like the modification of customary terms of tenure, were generally more favourable to large tenants than to smaller ones and facilitated their accumulation of property.

The weakening of continuity of tenure during the fourteenth century, coupled with changes in terms of tenure, meant that the memory of old men ceased to be as reliable as it had been in the past as evidence for the rights of lord and tenant. In these circumstances greater emphasis came to be placed on the written evidence of manor court records, and on the Winchester estate this meant the evidence of the pipe rolls, which were commonly appealed to as evidence of title. This finding constitutes valuable additional testimony to the social impact of changes in the land market during this period of upheaval.

---

39. Harvey, *Manorial records*, p. 41.

Chapter 5

Entry fines

The 133 surviving pipe rolls between 1263 and 1415 record 65,891 separate transactions in 6,073 enrolled manorial accounts covering as many as eighty-three manors and boroughs. They concern the transfer of 58,657 properties and supply the names of 65,786 tenants and other involved parties. Fewer than 11 per cent are marriage fines. A tiny fraction are an undifferentiated group of fines for matters other than the transfer of land – for freedom from manorial office, for transgressions, and for licences to take marl, to build or to dwell outside the manor. From our assessment of the magnitude of the losses of the documents themselves, we may estimate that the true number of fines over the period was around 80,000. But the surviving fines over a period of 152 years allow an exceptional opportunity to look to the broader trends and causes of change in the land market.

The changing number of transfers

We might expect the number of fines in the earlier decades of our period to increase, indicating a period of rising population and economic growth. But for the period from 1263 to 1349, across the estate as a whole, the figure was stable, normally ranging between about 550 and 650 a year. Figure 5.1 shows the raw data, making no estimates for missing manors and missing years, but its testimony is adequate for present purposes.[1] It implies more institutional stability from the 1270s than is compatible with a continuous process of agrarian development. Little new land was coming into peasant hands, since the main phase of assarting was over, and manorial courts were commonly hostile to the amalgamation or subdivision of virgated tenements. However, the land market was quickened by occasional flurries of exceptional activity associated with years of high mortality. Particularly high rates on several Winchester manors have been noted in 1258, 1272, 1289 and 1308. The number of fines rose sharply because of increased rates of mortality at the height of the great famine of 1315–18, and again in 1349 because of the Black Death; heritable transfers of land rose from 204 in 1315–16 to 377 in 1316–17, and from 170 in 1347–8 to 1,830 in 1348–9.[2] But for the rest of the late thirteenth and early fourteenth centuries, fluctuations in the number of land transfers recorded were not especially marked.

Attention to individual manors shows that these aggregate fluctuations did not always imply common experience. Even the comparative stability of Figure 5.1 was not characteristic of all the individual manors; at Farnham, for example, the long-term trend was downward between the 1260s and the 1340s, and the variation from year

---

1. For another representation of this data, see Page, 'Estate', p. 320, and *idem*, 'Farnham', p. 167.
2. Page, 'Estate', pp. 318–19. See also Postan and Titow, 'Heriots and prices', pp. 404–7, and graphs I and II.

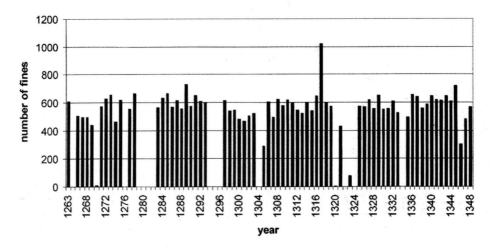

Figure 5.1 The number of entry fines in the pipe rolls, 1263–1348. The 2711 fines recorded for 1349 are too numerous to be shown conveniently on the same graph.

to year was significantly greater than across the estate as a whole.[3] The manors clustered around Wargrave reveal a decline in volume in the late 1320s and early 1330s at a time when the overall trend was stable. The impact of crises was also different on different manors. On some manors there were major peaks of activity in the 1280s: at Wargrave, for instance, there were over 100 fines in 1284–5 and over 80 in 1286–7, as compared with only 17 in 1316–17 and 59 in 1348–9. At Downton, too, the number of fines in 1284–5 was larger than that in later crisis years. At Warfield a peak in 1303–4 was far larger than any found in the famine years and larger than the second pestilence of 1361–2. While most manors show a significant increase in the number of transfers at the time of the great famine around 1317, Waltham St Lawrence in north-east Berkshire does not, and in the neighbouring manors of Wargrave and Culham, as well as at Ivinghoe, further to the north in Buckinghamshire, the increase was very muted, suggesting that the dislocating effects of famine in this region were few. Any increase in transfers at Bishops Fonthill was barely perceptible. By contrast, the immediate impact of the Black Death was particularly great in the Wargrave region, and at Ivinghoe, Culham, West Wycombe and Warfield. So even this disaster had a varying impact on the land market.

Figure 5.2 supplies an overview of the number of entry fines across the estate from 1350 onwards, again without estimated adjustments for missing data. Although the first few years after the Black Death witnessed a high volume of transactions, chiefly because of inheritance and related effects following high mortality, and although there was another spike after the second pestilence of 1361–2, the trend for most of the period 1350–1415 was gradually downwards.[4] This decline is most readily

3. Page, 'Farnham', p. 167.

4. For the effects of these pestilences on the number of entry fines, see also Levett, 'Black Death', pp. 76–86; J. Mullan, *Mortality, gender and the plague of 1361–2 on the estate of the bishop of Winchester,* Cardiff historical papers (Cardiff, 2007–8).

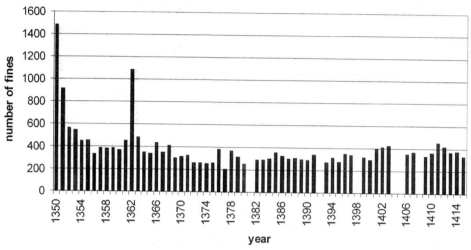

Figure 5.2 The number of entry fines in the pipe rolls, 1350–1415.

explained as the result of a falling number of peasant households following the epidemics of the mid-fourteenth century, although on some manors it continued a trend perceptible from the second quarter of the century. Whereas the number of annual transfers before 1348 was normally over 500, after that date there were usually fewer than 400 each year, and in the 1370s the number each year was usually below 300. These figures do not square well with some more optimistic interpretations of the 'Indian Summer' that supposedly followed the disaster of 1348–9 – a concept chiefly derived from the study of demesne agriculture. Between 1400 and 1415 there was a small increase in the number of transactions, probably transient, although its long-term significance is inevitably uncertain in the absence of later data.

As in the earlier fourteenth century, there were differences of experience between manors. At Bitterne, to the south of Hampshire, there was a noticeable rise in the volume of transfers from the early 1360s, a time of depression in transactions elsewhere. The general depression in activity during the 1370s was experienced differently in different places, and all manors did not necessarily experience a degree of recovery in the number of entry fines from around 1400. An increase in volume about this time is most strongly associated with the Taunton group and the manors of mid-Hampshire south of Winchester. It is also seen on some other manors across the estate – Twyford, Bishopstoke, Crawley, Marwell, Merdon, Bishops Sutton, Alresford and Cheriton. Yet there was no such recovery at Witney, Farnham, the manors of the Wiltshire group and other, especially smaller, manors.[5] Investigation of particular manorial characteristics in later chapters will help explain some of these differences. In fact, however, the general conformity to particular crisis years and long-term trends is more striking. Most manors showed peaks of activity in the early 1350s and in

---

5. Witney, Farnham, Bishopstone, Overton, Burghclere, East Knoyle, Ashmansworth, Beauworth, Wield, Culham and Warfield.

1361–2, a decline through the 1360s and 1370s bottoming out in the 1380s and 1390s, and then a mild recovery around 1400.

The changing level of average entry fines, 1263–1349

We know little about the changing levels of rent, since the sums owed are recorded only incidentally. Rents, however, were mostly conventional and subject to custom, and were less indicative of demand for property than the entry fines recorded in the pipe rolls, which were more open to negotiation.[6] It is true that entry fines are not straightforward indicators of economic rent, and A.E. Levett gave up the attempt to explain them except in terms of 'a rough reasonableness'.[7] Some fines, like customary rents, were governed by precedent, since there are examples of the same property paying the same sum over several transfers. The type of transfer also influenced the decision: fines for marriage to an heiress were often high, and so were fines for those who entered into property by marrying widows. On some manors, although not all, transfers between family members were dearer than extrafamilial ones, as we shall see in Chapter 6.

However, there was often an element of bargaining, reflecting case-by-case circumstances.[8] Sometimes the homage or other inquest adjudicated the details of a transfer, and may have had some input to what was an agreed and acceptable level of fine. And even precedent and custom were affected by real circumstances. Predictably, the size of holdings mattered. Virgate tenements often carried entry fines of around 13s 4d, whereas half virgates were charged half that sum, although comparisons are complicated by the varying size of virgates. Other influences at work reflected market forces. Periods and places of comparatively high fines indicate a comparatively high demand for well-positioned land of good quality and that the bishop, in taking full advantage of demographic and economic conditions, attempted to charge as much the market would bear. Many of the higher levels of fine are found in the regions we have identified as having an exceptionally active land market. They were high, especially before 1315, on the manors around Taunton, 'the granary of the west'.[9] Fines were also high on the manors of South Hampshire. At Witney and Wargrave, however, where much of the land in abundant supply was of mediocre quality, fines from customary holdings were exceptionally low. These variations will receive closer analysis in the following discussion.

Average entry fines for all manors and properties across the estate are graphed in Figure 5.3. The rising level of the late thirteenth and early fourteenth centuries is an indication of higher land values.[10] The price of wheat as well as other commodities, both grain and stock, reached new and unprecedented heights during the 1290s and

---

6. Miller and Hatcher, *Medieval England*, p. 46; Titow, *English rural society*, pp. 73–4.

7. Levett, 'Black Death', pp. 43–54.

8. L.R. Poos and L. Bonfield (eds), *Select cases in manorial courts 1250–1550: property and family law*, Selden Society, 114 (London, 1998), pp. lxxxix–xc.

9. Miller, 'Occupation of the land', p. 137; PRBW 1301–2, p. xxi.

10. Miller and Hatcher, *Medieval England*, p. 58.

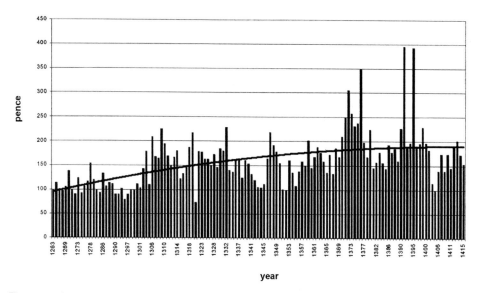

Figure 5.3 Average fines (pence) for all manorial and borough properties, 1263–1415.

early 1300s.[11] A population that had been increasing for some time reached a point at which competition for landed resources became acute, enabling the bishop to ask for higher fines in response to greater demand. However, there is no close relationship between high levels of entry fine and these economic variables, and it seems likely that to some extent the high fines were the result of more forceful bargaining by the bishop's officers. They were actively working in the first decade of the fourteenth century to lower the wages they paid to estate workers,[12] and it would be in keeping with this tougher regime to drive hard bargains over land values, since entry fines were a significant source of episcopal income. In the accounting year 1301–2, for example, £248 7s 3d out of an episcopal income of £4,121 came from fines, amounting to 6 per cent of the total.[13] Titow's calculations of total estate income between 1299 and 1308, although probably an underestimate, range between about £4,500 and £5,250 a year, towards which fines contributed somewhere between 3.5 and 10 per cent.[14]

Although we might expect to find regional and manorial variations in the value of land, a rise in annual average entry fines is perceptible on most manors in the late thirteenth century and the early fourteenth, even if starting from different bases. At East Meon, for example, the average fine for all properties in 1296–7 was 4s 4d but

11. Farmer, 'Prices and wages [1042–1350]', p. 734; J.Z. Titow, 'Evidence of weather in the pipe rolls of the bishopric of Winchester, 1209–1350', *Economic History Review*, 2nd series, 12 (1959–60), pp. 378–81; *idem, English rural society*, pp. 100–2.

12. Page, 'Challenging custom', pp. 39–48.

13. *PRBW 1301–2*, pp. xix–xxvi.

14. Titow, 'Land and population', p. 67; see also *PRBW 1301–2*, p. xxi, n. 4.

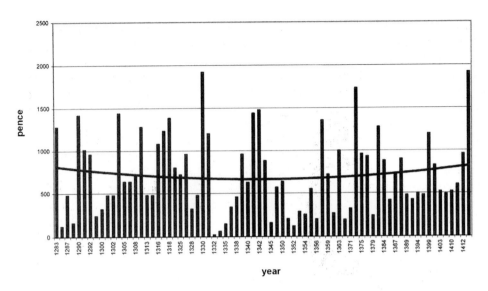

Figure 5.4 Average fines (pence) for half virgates at Holway.

the following year it rose to 9s 7d, a figure almost exactly matched in the two subsequent years. In 1302–3 the average rose to 19s 7d and by 1311–12 had risen a little further to £1 0s 2d, almost five times the level of fifteen years previously. At Bishops Waltham, to the west, fines before 1300 averaged 5s 11d, but dramatically jumped to 17s 0d in 1301–2 and to £1 8s 2d the following year. At Farnham, to take another example, the average fine between 1262–3 and 1298–9 was 5s 8d, but between 1299–1300 and 1338–9 it had risen to an average of 9s 2d. Similarly, at Twyford between 1262–3 and 1298–9 the average had already been high at 8s 7d, but it doubled to 16s 7d over the next twenty years.

Falling prices induced a reduction of entry fines across the estate in the 1330s and for most of the 1340s. Prices fell, chiefly because of a diminishing money supply, to a point where most were between 30 and 40 per cent lower than they had been three decades previously.[15] The average at Bishops Waltham, which had been 13s 1d between 1299–1300 and 1332–3, fell steeply over the next decade, and had almost halved to 7s 2d between 1333–4 and 1345–6. At Bishopstoke the average fine of the period 1296–7 to 1331–2 was 12s 9d, but this more than halved, to just 5s 2d, over the next twelve-year period. At Farnham the level in the second half of the 1340s was, again, almost half of what it had been over the previous four decades. Similarly, at Holway, in the Taunton group, fines underwent momentary collapse in the early 1330s after a period of exceptionally high levels (Figure 5.4).

15. Miller and Hatcher, *Medieval England*, p. 66; Farmer, 'Prices and wages [1042–1350]', p. 720; N.J. Mayhew, 'Money and prices in England from Henry II to Edward III', *AHR*, 35 (1987), pp. 125, 128–9; M.C. Prestwich, 'Currency and the economy of early fourteenth century England', in N.J. Mayhew (ed.), *Edwardian monetary affairs (1279–1344)*, British Archaeological Reports, 36 (Oxford, 1977), pp. 48–53.

Not all manors conform so easily to interpretation by reference to prices. The increase of the early fourteenth century was either non-existent or muted in manors where there had been heavy colonisation. At Witney, always a good manor for contrasts with the rest of the estate, there was no upward movement in the later thirteenth and early fourteenth centuries. With one or two exceptional years, which can be attributable to a few individual transactions, average fines there ranged between 3s and 4s. On other colonising manors the increase in levels of entry fine in this period was also muted, as at Wargrave and Ivinghoe. At Twyford an overall doubling of average fines in the first two decades of the fourteenth century owed much to a few exceptionally high individual fines in 1309–10, 1310–11 and in 1318–19. The faltering increase at Ivinghoe, Wargrave and Twyford, and its absence at Witney, are unlikely to mean that the bishop's officers were any less attentive to the bishop's interests here than elsewhere, and implies rather that much of the land on these manors was too poor to attract tenants.

The changing level of average entry fines, 1350–1415

After 1348 the abundance of vacant properties, the relaxation of services and the declining tendency for men to acquire land through marriage to widows all imply a fundamental shift in the availability of property. Yet, despite this evidence, average fines in this period do not show any long-term decline. Indeed, in the 1370s and 1390s the average fine rose to hitherto unseen levels, dropping back only at the turn of the fifteenth century.[16] Entry fines remained as important to the bishop's income as ever; in 1409–10 they contributed 7 per cent of the total £3,631.[17] This overall trend seems so poorly related to either the history of population or that of prices, and so divergent from changes in the total number of entry fines, that it demands explanation in other ways. Relatively high prices for agricultural produce between about 1350 and 1380 may have had a part to play in propping up demand for customary holdings during those decades, but cannot account for the overall movement of the later fourteenth-century figures.

One explanation with widespread relevance was the tendency for older holdings to become amalgamated so that the properties conveyed were on average larger than those of the past.[18] Large sums were often paid for accumulated holdings; at Holway in the Taunton group, for example, a fine of £50 was paid by Matilda Moor in 1390–1 to retain her husband's lands, which had once been twenty-two smaller separate properties. At Brockhampton John Milton paid £33 6s 8d for a marriage to Emma Burton that brought him four and a half virgates as well as cottages, tofts acres and a shop.

A simultaneous development, compounding the growing impact of larger single transfers of property, was the declining importance of cottages and smallholdings in the land market. Quite apart from what was happening to the individual fines, many such small properties became untenanted as the number of inhabitants fell.

---

16. This concurs with the observations of Levett, 'Black Death', pp. 122, 151.

17. *PRBW 1409–10*, pp. xxiv–xxvii.

18. This is discussed in greater detail in Chapter 9.

Table 5.1
Manors with falling average fines for virgate and half virgate holdings after 1349

Manor	Unit	c.1263–1348	1350–1415	% decrease
Witney	Virgate	£1 2s 11d	5s 1d	77.9
Wargrave	Virgate	17s 7d	6s 3d	64.5
Ivinghoe	Virgate	£1 14s 2d	14s 6d	57.6
Burghclere	Half virgate	18s 3d	8s 6d	53.4
Brockhampton	Virgate	£4 10s 1d	£2 3s 1d	52.2
Hambledon	Half virgate	11s 7d	5s 8d	51.1
Bishops Sutton	Half virgate	19s 8d	11s 2d	43.2
Twyford	Virgate	8s 9d	5s 5d	38.1
Merdon	Half virgate	14s 8d	9s 2d	37.5
Bishopstone	Virgate	19s 0d	12s 2d	36.0
Cheriton	Virgate	11s 0d	7s 5d	32.6
North Waltham	Virgate	6s 5d	4s 4d	32.5
Downton	Half virgate	18s 10d	13s 5d	28.8
Farnham	Half virgate	14s 1d	11s 5d	18.9
Staplegrove	Half virgate	£4 5s 0d	£3 9s 11d	17.7
Holway	Half virgate	£3 2s 7d	£2 16s 8d	9.5
Bishopstoke	Half virgate	19s 5d	18s 1d	6.9
Harwell	Virgate	£6 9s 7d	£6 4s 1d	4.2

Note: The units selected were the predominant customary holdings transferred on these manors. Virgates and half virgates with engrossments of any kind have been excluded. The data for 1348–9 has been excluded from the calculations in column 3.

Independent cottage holdings, in particular, were often abandoned, and then disappeared altogether from the property market.[19] The very fact that these small units were exchanged less frequently than in the past raised the level of average fines payable across the estate. High prices were often paid for the numerous small-holdings on the Taunton manors, including ferlings, cottages and other small parcels, but these were specially selected for some particularly advantageous qualities.

A true index of changing values in this period accordingly needs to rest not on the changing average of all fines, but on fluctuations in the fines charged for particular units, such as virgates or acres. This inevitably means that aggregates for the estate as a whole are ruled out by the absence of any common unit appropriate for such comparisons. Table 5.1 shows evidence from standard units on a number of manors before and after the Black Death, and confirms that the general tendency was downward, as expected.[20] It also demonstrates that, in this respect, as in the earlier

19. This is discussed in greater detail in Chapter 9.

20. Titow, *English rural society*, p. 75.

fourteenth century, there were wide differences of experience between different manors.[21]

The existence of variations is easier to demonstrate than explain. Soil quality was an important issue at a time of rising costs; rising wages after 1349 discouraged the cultivation of heavy, stony or impoverished soils that yielded a poor return to the labour expended on them. Fines remained well above average around Taunton, with its rich wheatlands on the core manors.[22] The drop in entry fines per unit at Holway and Staplegrove was conspicuously slight (Table 5.1). Late-fourteenth-century regional prosperity here can further be attributed to the good commercial opportunities presented by the borough of Taunton, which shared an urban boom with various other manufacturing and trading centres in this period. Taunton participated strongly in the growth of merchant-quality textiles, which were often exported through Exeter.[23] By 1524–5 Taunton's taxable wealth placed it in fortieth place among English boroughs.[24] The benefits of non-agrarian development in the Taunton region are analogous to those that, deeper into the South West, favoured high land values in parts of Devon and Cornwall.[25] Of the approximately 458 fines of £5 and over on the bishop's estates between 1349–50 and 1414–15, 247 were from the manors of the Taunton group. Holway regularly commanded the highest fines of all. In 1359–60, to select a year at random, £4 6s 8d was paid for a messuage and ferling, £4 for another messuage and ferling, £2 3s 4d for a ferling, £1 6s 8d for two acres of overland, £1 10s for a single acre of meadow overland, and £1 for an acre of overland. The average fine for a cottage holding at Holway across the later fourteenth and early fifteenth centuries was 10s 7d, whereas at Downton, where demand was far less and where there were rather fewer such transfers, the average stood at just 6s 1d. In the Taunton manors there was real competition for land. As the Holway evidence demonstrates, total entry fines remained consistently high, although fluctuating, all through the later fourteenth century (Figure 5.4).

The Taunton area was not the only part of the estate where local circumstances favoured a comparatively competitive property market. In the South Hampshire group of manors at Brockhampton, Bishopstoke and Bishops Waltham, and on the Hampshire Chalk Plateau at East Meon and Merdon, demand for land was well maintained. At Bishops Waltham entry fines increased slightly between the early fourteenth and early fifteenth centuries:[26] Figure 5.5 shows the chronology of fines for half virgates. The demand for land market in this region continued to be stimulated by commercial opportunities offered by Southampton and other south-coast ports.[27] Land values held up less well, although better than usual, at Farnham in Surrey, one of

---

21. For other evidence of strong regional variations in land values, corresponding to differences in regional economies, see J. Hatcher, *Rural economy and society in the duchy of Cornwall, 1300–1500* (Cambridge, 1970), pp. 130–3, 151–6.

22. Thornton, 'Arable productivity', p. 112.

23. M. Kowaleski, *Local markets and regional trade in medieval Exeter* (Cambridge, 1995), p. 95.

24. Dyer, 'Appendix', p. 766.

25. Hatcher, *Rural economy and society*, pp. 146, 151–2, 167–73.

26. *PRBW 1409–10*, p. xxvi.

27. Chapter 2, pp. 33–4.

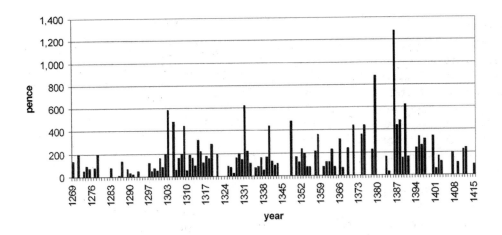

Figure 5.5 Average fines (pence) for half virgates at Bishops Waltham.

the bishop's largest manors, which benefited from the presence of a thriving borough.[28] Farnham was one of a number of small towns on main roads into London that increased their local prominence during the later Middle Ages. By 1524–5 it had come to rank sixty-third amongst English towns in terms of its taxable wealth.[29]

The pattern at Witney presents a striking contrast, despite the presence of a substantial borough there. There was an exceptionally severe drop in the total income from entry fines at this manor between the early fourteenth and early fifteenth centuries.[30] Analysis of the average fines for standard virgated tenements year by year illustrates the widespread decline in entry fines for customary holdings (Figure 5.6). Although the plague of 1348 temporarily undermined the demand for virgate tenements here, average fines for virgated units fell steeply only from 1360.[31] It was also at this time that a number of contractual leases with commuted services appear. In 1359–60 several entrants into virgates and half virgates were charged as little as 6d or 1s, and a holding of 1½ virgates was transferred for 1s. Such fines were a world away from those charged on the manors of the Taunton group or at Bishops Waltham, and speak volumes about the excess supply of standard customary holdings in these manors, which must in part at least be attributable to their poor quality. It is likely that assart in this manor at least was considered to be customary, although they owed money rents rather than labour services. Because the weak family attachment to such lands afforded greater than usual opportunities to treat them as marketable assets, more than three-quarters of entry fines for assarts in the later fourteenth and early fifteenth centuries were for extrafamilial transfers. Assarts and purprestures here

28. E. Robo, *Medieval Farnham: everyday life in an episcopal manor* (Farnham, 1939), pp. 173–91.

29. D. Keene, 'The south-east of England', in Palliser (ed.), *The Cambridge urban history of Britain, I: 600–1540*, p. 580; A. Dyer, 'Appendix', p. 766.

30. *PRBW 1409–10*, p. xxv; Ballard, 'Manors of Witney, Brightwell and Downton', p. 204.

31. For the Black Death and its aftermath at Witney, see also Ballard, 'Manors of Witney, Brightwell and Downton', pp. 195–204.

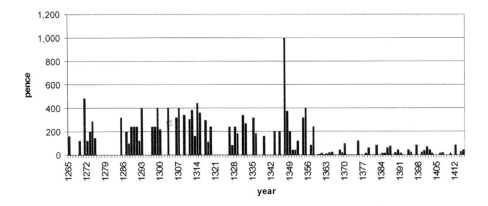

Figure 5.6 Average fines (pence) for virgates at Witney.

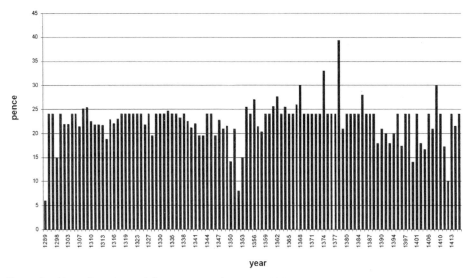

Figure 5.7 Entry fines (pence) for one acre of assart at Witney.

comprised only a small part of the vast number of tenements that fell vacant in the later fourteenth century; it was not until after the second pestilence of 1361–2 that untenanted assarts appear at all, and the entry fines they owed remained level, at 2s an acre (Figure 5.7).[32]

At the Woodland manor of Wargrave, similarly, there had been a decline in fines for standard virgates from about the first decade of the fourteenth century. A slight lift in the size of fines in the few years before 1348 was sustained for little more than a decade, but the earlier trend soon continued with almost no traffic in standard virgate holdings in the 1370s and 1380s and thereafter with fines a fraction of those of an

---

32. Titow, 'Some differences', p. 5; *idem*, 'Lost rents', pp. 109–12.

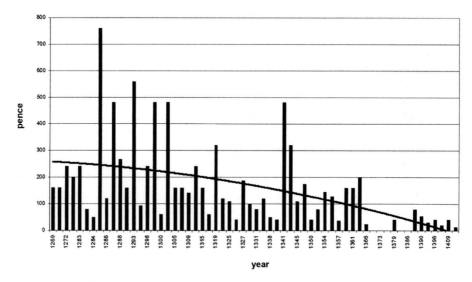

Figure 5.8 Average fines (pence) for virgates at Wargrave.

earlier period (Figure 5.8). As at Witney, large reductions in fines for virgated tenements coincided with a rush of contractual commutations. As at Witney, too, the presence of non-customary tenures exercised an adverse effect on the demand for virgated units. In contrast to the virgated units, purprestures, usually associated with a cottage holding, continued to command healthy entry fines, and in the later fourteenth century were frequently paying entry fines higher than at any time before. In 1362–3, Christine Fuller inherited a cottage with curtilage containing just a rood of purpresture for a fine of 10s, but in the same year Simon Piper paid only 1s 8d to enter into a customary cottage land. The tiny purpresture holding then commanded a fine several times that of its customary namesake. This is presumably explained by advantages of location that made such plots desirable for residence and, perhaps, trading.

Conclusion

In short, then, the number and level of fines charged by the episcopal administration on the uptake of property by new tenants supply important indicators of the changing value of land on the bishopric estates. The number of fines showed no upwards or downwards trend between 1268–9 and 1348–9, probably because there was little structural change in the amount of peasant land available or the number of units of tenure. Even the price depression of the 1330s and 1340s reduced the number of entry fines only on some manors, and had little impact on those where there was a heavy unsatisfied demand for property. After 1349, despite variation from manor to manor, the number of entry fines generally declined as a result of the smaller number of families entering the property market.

The average level of fines rose through the fourteenth century, but this does not correspond to the long-term movement of unit land values. In the early decades of the century this increase continued a thirteenth-century trend that mirrored rising commodity prices and increasing market demand for property. The stability of the average level of entry fines through the later fourteenth century was the somewhat arbitrary result of counteracting changes in the land market; the average unit value of an acre of land had fallen, but the average size of properties transferred was larger. There were more numerous transfers of large and composite holdings and fewer transfers of cottages and smallholdings.

Regional economic differences nevertheless affected the outcome in detail. The level of fines was higher in some manors, such as those of the Somerset region, because of regional prosperity that encouraged more competition for land than elsewhere. The generally higher land values of some manors in South Hampshire may similarly be explained by the greater opportunities for commercial farming in parts of the county near the coast. By contrast, at Witney and Wargrave the value of virgated tenures fell exceptionally severely in the later fourteenth century, chiefly because of the unwanted reserves of poor land on these manors. These variations confirm the very different circumstances of regions that, to judge simply from the number of entry fines per unit of assised rent, would have looked very similar.

Chapter 6

Families and their land

One of the most striking developments in the late medieval land market, and one which has been identified in the studies of several estates across England, is the increased proportion of transfers that conveyed property between families. Although the bond between families and their land was strong in the thirteenth and early fourteenth centuries, and ensured that the most transfers were by inheritance, extrafamilial sales and acquisitions became more common after the Black Death. While it is generally recognised that the extrafamilial market of land tended to be in smaller properties, often independent of standard virgated units, larger customary holdings also progressively began to move between families. This, however, was a development that showed considerable differences between manors.

Families and outsiders

Although custom in general protected hereditary rights in villein holdings, in certain extreme circumstances tenants were exposed to the bleak prospect of forfeiting their lands. Collective responsibility was imposed on local communities to make sure that lands were occupied, rents were paid and that tenants behaved responsibly, and those individuals who occasionally fell foul of this supervision could find themselves dispossessed. At Holway in 1298–9, the villeins asked the bishop to take into his possession a ferling of land in Otterford (ten acres, in this case), perhaps because of the unsuitability of the tenant. They then agreed to elect another tenant to hold the land, and also to stand surety for its satisfactory occupation. The consequences for a local community of allowing a tenant prolonged misuse of a property could be severe. At Downton in 1291–2 a property was forfeited to the bishop for default of rent and service and for neglect of the buildings. The entire tithing was taxed 10s, to be raised from the cultivation of the virgate in question, and the money was given to the tithingman to mend the ruined buildings. At the same time, William, son of William Stacy, was elected 'by the whole hundred' to hold the virgate, and he paid an entry fine of 2s. In 1297–8 Geoffrey Edmund of Bitterne fined for a ferling 'which he held of Nigel Shepherd which was taken into the lord's hands because Nigel wasted and destroyed the tenement, and it was let to him by election of the whole hundred'. Occasionally the record states explicitly that there was an element of compulsion in such elections. Again at Bitterne in 1297–8, Ascelina, daughter of Gilbert Snell, leased a ferling (eight acres) 'by election of the whole hundred and by compulsion'. The bishop had intervened because the previous tenant had wasted and destroyed the tenement. Other tenants were similarly compelled to take up devastated holdings at Bitterne at about the same time. The culpable mismanagement of property which these instances suggest appears to have occurred relatively rarely. No more than about twenty holdings were explicitly said to have been taken into the lord's hands because of waste or destruction, although the problem was acknowledged in the conditions of tenure demanded of other tenants.

At other times land was confiscated because of the incapacity of its tenant. Land could be forfeited if a tenant was incapable of performing the required obligations.[1] At Twyford in 1354–5 Isabel Dodde was compelled to surrender her holding because she was mentally ill (*demens*). At Bishops Fonthill in 1318–19 John Bagg gave up a messuage and half virgate because he was unable to maintain the buildings or perform the labour service. John, son of John Alwin, was elected by the tithing to take his place. At Harwell in 1370–1, Christine Morris was removed from her two holdings, a virgate and a half virgate, because she 'destroyed the tenement and wasted it through folly (*per infatuationem*) and forfeited it according the custom of the manor'. In the cases both of Isabel and Christine, individuals from outside the family took over the holdings. The courts were necessarily actively engaged in these procedures, which are likely to have been initiated by local jurors. Fines of these kinds were never numerous, and became even rarer in the later fourteenth century, when tenants were harder to replace.

Women were particularly vulnerable to losing their land. The forfeiture of land for fornication, which affected women exclusively, accounted for a quarter of all recorded forfeitures between 1285–6 and 1348–9. Both women and men might lose property for marrying against custom; of twelve cases recorded between 1298–9 and 1348–9, women forfeited in seven, men in five. At Wargrave at the very end of the thirteenth century, Reginald, son of Hugh Chapman, 'who ought to be heir according to his expectations', forfeited his right to claim the land of his deceased wife, Christine Siggers, because he remarried outside the manor.

Land could also be forfeited if it was illegally bought or sold.[2] A basic tenet of the peasant land market in customary land was that transfers were authorised by the lord, most commonly by the procedure of surrender and admittance.[3] The principal reason for trying to bypass this process was to evade paying an entry fine. The extent of illegal trade in customary land is, by its very nature, hidden from us; only when the perpetrators were caught do the documents reveal that the practice existed. At Witney in 1308–9 three properties were declared forfeit because the tenants had alienated them without first surrendering them to the lord. Since such illegal transfers depended upon extensive conspiracy their number was probably small. On other occasions the bishop stood to lose more than an entry fine. Some tenants sought to sell villein land by treating it as though it were free. At Bishops Waltham in 1331–2 Hugh Balhorn forfeited three acres which he had attempted to alienate by charter, 'to hold freely which before he held at the lord's will'. A similar case was recorded at Waltham St Lawrence in 1335–6, when John Prinkenham, who held his land at will, 'demised it by charter, disinheriting the lord, as was found by an inquest taken in the presence of John'. On only one known occasion was the illegal alienation of land subsequently condoned: at Bentley in 1313–14 Richard Archer paid 6s 8d to recover a house and curtilage that he had forfeited.

Two other uncommon occasions for episcopal discontinuation of tenure can be identified: transfer following the conviction of a felon, and transfers away from the

---

1.   Poos and Bonfield (eds), *Select cases*, pp. xciii–xciv.

2.   *Ibid.*, p. 29.

3.   Chapter 1, p. 3–4.

collateral heirs of bastards. In the first of these instances land was forfeited to the lord. A tenant convicted of felony had in most cases been hanged, although in a few instances he had fled and was outlawed. The tenant's land, in all but two instances, passed to a new tenant from another family, indicating that the claims of a felon's heirs were not normally recognised on the Winchester estate.[4] There are twenty examples of such extrafamilial transfers on account of felony between 1263 and 1349, and forty-nine between 1350 and 1415.

In cases where bastardy affected the heritability of property, the entry fine records that the tenant who had died was illegitimate and had died without heirs. Bastards, although unable to inherit, could receive intrafamilial gifts and could acquire property by purchase, but their only possible heirs, as prescribed by custom, were direct issue, collaterals being excluded.[5] The 113 cases between 1362–3 and 1414–15 in which the properties of bastards were forfeited to the lord at their death occurred chiefly during the higher mortality of the later fourteenth century, 22 of them after the plague of 1361–2.

All these cases of forfeiture could be equivalent to the death of a tenant without heirs, causing land to escheat to the bishop, who was then obliged to find a new tenant. In a small way they contributed to the development of the land market even before 1349 by making available land that would in different circumstances have been locked into a traditional pattern of family control.

Until comparatively recently the more usual conveyance of peasant property, whether between family members or *inter vivos*, has been interpreted as a response to the expansion and contraction of families and the corresponding incentives to redistribute resources among households. The peasant life cycle, it was argued, ensured there would be 'natural' sellers and 'natural' buyers, the former having more land than they could work, the latter having unemployed family members needing to be fed. This analysis, in which land was considered to be distributed to each according to his need, lent itself readily to an interpretation of family economy according to which parents provided for their children, or in which old people conveyed to family members land they were no longer capable of working. Peasant demography was therefore central to this analysis.[6] More recently, emphasis has been placed on the relevance of commercial considerations. These include the positive financial ambitions of families operating in a monetised economy with effective credit mechanisms.[7] Such analysis allows extrafamilial land transfers to be explained more in terms of a

---

4.   Practice varied in this respect: Poos and Bonfield (eds), *Select cases*, p. xcv.

5.   *Ibid.*, pp. clxxxiv–clxxxix.

6.   For an introduction to this model, see Smith, 'Some issues concerning families', pp. 6–21; P.R. Schofield, *Peasant and community in medieval England, 1200–1500* (Basingstoke, 2003), pp. 52–76.

7.   C. Briggs, 'Creditors and debtors and their relationships at Oakington, Cottenham and Dry Drayton (Cambridgeshire), 1291–1350', in P.R. Schofield and N.J. Mayhew (eds), *Credit and debt in medieval England, c.1180–c.1350* (Oxford, 2002), pp. 127–48; B. Dodds, *Peasants and production in the medieval North-East: the evidence from tithes, 1270–1536* (Woodbridge, 2007), pp. 153–8; J. Masschaele, *Peasants, merchants and markets: inland trade in medieval England, 1150–1350* (New York, 1997), pp. 33–54; J.A. Raftis, *Peasant economic development within the English manorial system* (Stroud, 1996), pp. 21, 24–5; Schofield, *Peasant and community*, pp. 138–49.

genuine land market, in which land was exchanged for money, or for the cancellation of debt, often with adverse implications for the seller.[8] The significance of commercial opportunity is accordingly considerable for the analysis of peasant families in relationship to the land.

In East Anglia a well-developed market in peasant land is evident in records of the later thirteenth century.[9] As early as the early 1290s at Martham (Norfolk), 80 per cent of sales and exchanges of land were between apparently unrelated villagers.[10] At Redgrave (Suffolk), a manor of the abbey of Bury St Edmunds, *inter vivos* transactions vastly outweighed transfers by inheritance by 1300, and this was associated with a steep increase in fines for extrafamilial transactions.[11] Elsewhere in England development was often delayed until the later fourteenth century. It was at this point that the bishop of Worcester's estates experienced increased activity in the land market.[12] A study of some Berkshire manors notes a steep rise in extrafamilial transfers from about 1349, and the turnover of land was greater in the last decades of the fourteenth century than at any previous time; at Brightwalton fines for transfers between families *inter vivos* constituted 44 per cent of the total in 1280–1300, 60 per cent in 1341–62, and 87 per cent in 1383–1402.[13] At Holywell-cum-Needingworth, formerly in Huntingdonshire, the family-land bond was 'overshadowed by non-family interests' by the early fifteenth century.[14] In the period 1377–1536, 64 per cent of fines on the Bedfordshire manor of Arlesey Bury were *inter vivos* transactions between different families;[15] and in the Welsh Marches the market in land was similarly busy by the final decade of the fourteenth century.[16] This tendency cannot be taken for granted as a universal phenomenon, however, and current studies imply wide local variation. At Halesowen in the West Midlands, extrafamilial transfers *inter vivos* in the period 1351–80 constituted only 32 per cent of all fines, and by 1381–1410 this had fallen to around 26 per cent.[17] On the estates of the abbot of Westminster, where an inter-peasant market developed slowly, larger family holdings were transferred chiefly by inheritance until well into the fifteenth century.[18]

---

8.   e.g. Schofield, 'Dearth, debt', pp. 1–17.

9.   Hyams, 'Peasant land market', pp. 18–31.

10. Williamson, 'Norfolk', pp. 75–6.

11. Campbell, 'Population pressure', pp. 87–134; R.M. Smith, 'Families and their land in an area of partible inheritance: Redgrave, Suffolk, 1260–1320', in *idem* (ed.), *Land, kinship and life-cycle*, pp. 135–95; Williamson, 'Norfolk'.

12. Dyer, *Lords and peasants*, p. 302.

13. Faith, 'Peasant families', pp. 89–91; R.J. Faith, 'Berkshire: fourteenth and fifteenth centuries', in Harvey (ed.), *Peasant land market*, p. 132.

14. E.B. DeWindt, *Land and people in Holywell-cum-Needingworth* (Toronto, 1971), p. 134.

15. Jones, 'Bedfordshire', p. 217.

16. R.R. Davies, *Lordship and society in the March of Wales, 1284–1400* (Oxford, 1978), p. 430.

17. Z. Razi, 'Family, land and the village community in later medieval England', *Past and Present*, 93 (1981), p. 17. Razi was able to find many family connections not apparent from the record of entry fines.

18. Harvey, *Westminster Abbey*, chapter ix.

To chart the developing market for customary land we need to examine changes in the numbers and proportions of transactions within and between families across the Winchester estate in aggregate, and explore chronological and regional variation. Typically, but by no means always, the pipe roll record of entry fines is sufficient to demonstrate whether peasant lands were transferred between family members or not, and whether the previous tenant was alive or dead. The former distinction allows us to classify transactions as intrafamilial or extrafamilial, and the latter distinction makes it possible to classify transactions as either *inter vivos* or *post mortem*. In recording intrafamilial transfers, clerks usually noted the family relationship between the partners to the transaction. Transfers have also been counted as intrafamilial for our present purpose if the surname of the parties to the transaction was the same: this decision accounts for 9.4 per cent of all intrafamilial transfers over the period of study (2,208 out of 23,444); in many of these cases a relationship can, in fact, be shown through subsequent fines. Where the surnames of the parties differ the transfer is counted as extrafamilial unless a family relationship is specified. Fines for surrenders, exchanges, recoveries and the like imply that both parties were living. Transfers of the property of tenants *post mortem*, whether to family members by inheritance or to someone in a different family, are analysed in the same way; the record of the incomer's fine normally states the name of the deceased tenant.

Analysis of the relative proportion of intrafamilial and extrafamilial transfers for the whole of the Winchester bishopric estate after 1320, decade by decade, shows a striking shift towards the multiplication of extrafamilial transfers (Table 6.1). Over the period as a whole, the inheritance of property accounted for the largest proportion of transfers. Extrafamilial transfers *inter vivos* constituted the second largest category. Acquisitions of land within families *inter vivos* and outside families *post mortem* represent comparatively smaller but still significant parts of the total. The figures demonstrate a contrast between the periods before and after the Black Death: whereas more than 59 per cent of all transfers between 1320 and 1349 were between family members (both *post mortem* and *inter vivos*), between 1350 and 1415 this proportion dropped to under 40 per cent. The reduction in the share of transfers within families *inter vivos* was particularly sharp. There was a corresponding rise in extrafamilial transactions, particularly following the death of tenants. This evidence points unequivocally to the growing proportion of transfers between families, as tenants who died were less likely to have heirs waiting to inherit. In the later fourteenth century, too, families were freer to dispose of property without the pressures occasioned by the needs of other family members.

The largest influence discernible from our data on both short- and long-term shifts from intrafamilial to extrafamilial transfers was the depopulation brought about by the Black Death. The earlier effects of the famine years of 1315–18 were significantly fewer; there was a huge temporary increase in the number of fines but only a small increase in the proportion of hereditary transfers and no significant shift towards extrafamilial transfers *inter vivos*. This suggests that mortality was not great enough in 1315–18 to destroy the cohort of heirs able and willing to enter vacant tenements. The pattern of transfers resembles that of the harvest-sensitive land market documented independently by Campbell and by Schofield on East Anglian manors.[19]

---

19. Campbell, 'Population pressure', pp. 110–20; Schofield, 'Dearth, debt', pp. 1–17.

Table 6.1
Proportions of intrafamilial and extrafamilial transfers by decade, 1320–1415

| | No. of rolls | Intrafamilial | | | | Extrafamilial | | | | Total |
		Inter vivos	(%)	*Post mortem*	(%)	*Inter vivos*	(%)	*Post mortem*	(%)	
1320–9	8	332	13.5	1005	41.3	1019	41.9	77	3.2	2433
1330–9	9	634	16.8	1371	36.3	1670	44.2	107	2.8	3782
1340–9	10	680	10.9	3357	53.9	1868	30.0	327	5.3	6232
1320–1349	**27**	**1646**	**13.2**	**5733**	**46.1**	**4557**	**36.6**	**511**	**4.1**	**12447**
1350–9	10	191	4.0	1623	33.7	1908	39.6	1094	22.7	4816
1360–9	10	147	4.2	1319	38.0	1637	47.1	371	10.7	3474
1370–9	10	97	4.3	756	33.4	984	43.5	426	18.8	2263
1350–1379	**30**	**435**	**4.1**	**3698**	**35.0**	**4529**	**42.9**	**1891**	**17.9**	**10553**
1380–9	9	137	6.5	622	29.7	986	47.0	352	16.8	2097
1390–9	8	140	7.2	680	35.0	785	40.4	337	17.4	1942
1400–9	7	172	9.0	603	31.5	819	42.7	323	16.8	1917
1410–15	6	144	7.9	580	31.9	796	43.7	300	16.5	1820
1380–1415	**30**	**593**	**7.6**	**2485**	**32.0**	**3386**	**43.5**	**1312**	**16.9**	**7776**

Table 6.2
Intrafamilial and extrafamilial entry fines, 1341–64

| | Intrafamilial | | | | Extrafamilial | | | | Total |
| | *Inter vivos* | | By inheritance | | *Inter vivos* | | *Post mortem* | | |
	no.	(%)	no.	(%)	no.	(%)	no.	(%)	
1341–48*	65.7	15.5	167.1	39.5	178.1	42.0	11.8	2.8	422.7
1348–9	77	3.2	1885	78.5	223	9.3	215	9.0	2400
1349–50	34	2.8	664	55.0	250	20.7	259	21.5	1207
1350–1	26	3.3	276	35.4	248	31.8	230	29.5	780
1351–2	14	3	139	29.6	204	43.5	112	23.9	469
1352–3	14	3.4	106	25.4	208	49.8	90	21.5	418
1353–4	15	4.3	91	25.9	170	48.3	76	21.6	352
1354–5	27	7.2	95	25.3	135	35.9	119	31.7	376
1355–6	10	3.7	54	19.7	153	55.8	57	20.8	274
1356–7	11	3.4	70	21.9	183	57.2	56	17.5	320
1357–8	22	7.1	54	17.5	182	59.1	50	16.2	308
1358–9	17	5.4	74	23.6	176	56.2	46	14.7	313
1359–60	14	4.6	64	21.2	170	56.3	54	17.9	302
1360–1	5	1.5	75	22.1	174	51.2	86	25.3	340
1361–2	25	2.8	577	65.1	212	23.9	73	8.2	887
1362–3	10	2.6	126	32.9	169	44.1	78	20.3	383
1363–4	16	5.9	63	23.1	140	51.3	54	19.8	273

* annual mean

The Black Death was different in scale, and consequently in its impact. Table 6.2 supplies a closer analysis of the years between 1341 and 1364 to demonstrate the changes in detail. Not surprisingly, the initial effect of the crisis was a sudden leap in the proportion of *post mortem* transfers, in which transfers by inheritance predominated. Within a few years, however, the land market had restructured. The proportion of intrafamilial transfers declined, whether by inheritance or transfer *inter vivos*, and the proportion of extrafamilial transfers correspondingly increased, most strikingly following the death of former tenants. The role of inheritance briefly reasserted itself after the second great pestilence of 1361–2, but extrafamilial transfers were rapidly re-established as the dominant type of transaction.

These figures, combined with the fall in number of transactions over the period, largely confirm what has been observed elsewhere. The declining take-up of inheritances is no doubt to be explained in some cases by the absence of an heir, but such an event would have been rare in a land-hungry population. It was more commonly the result of the facility with which heirs could obtain alternative and superior property following the mortality crises of the fourteenth century. Rosamond Faith has noted the greater ease with which a son could acquire land during his father's lifetime, and the weakening importance of the customary bonds between families and their land.[20] Christopher Dyer observed a decline in intrafamilial transfers on the midland manors of the bishop of Worcester,[21] and Bruce Campbell, in his study of Coltishall in Norfolk, observed developments amounting to 'an entirely new pattern of buying and selling'.[22] The evidence of the Winchester estates enables us to affirm the widespread significance of this observation throughout southern England. Table 6.2 demonstrates the long-lasting nature of these changes, which affected the composition of the land market into the fifteenth century.

Intermanorial and interregional variation

Although only a broad-brush analysis is possible with the sort of statistical evidence to hand, its implications for local variation are sufficiently robust to be important, and will no doubt suggest the appropriateness of more focused comparisons. The range of variation between the Winchester manors was at least as wide as the extremes suggested by existing studies from individual manorial archives. Table 6.3 records the share of extrafamilial fines on each manor in the period 1320–49. It shows that an extrafamilial market in property was already well advanced on a number of the estate's manors. There was also some regional patterning. Extrafamilial transfers were exceptionally important in two of the regions we have identified as having an exceptionally active land market – the Woodland manors of Witney and Wargrave and the Somerset manors. South Hampshire, the third of the regions identified in Chapter 2 as having an exceptionally lively land market, had a more mixed experience in this respect; the extrafamilial share was high at Havant with Brockhampton and at Bitterne, but not at Bishops Waltham, Bishopstoke and the other manors of the group.

---

20.   Faith, 'Peasant families', pp. 87, 92; *eadem*, 'Berkshire', p. 116.

21.   Dyer, *Lords and peasants*, p. 302; DeWindt, *Land and people*, p. 134.

22.   Campbell, 'Population pressure', p. 121.

Table 6.3
The percentage of extrafamilial fines on each manor, 1320–49 (estate average: 40.7)

Region	Manors (%)
Woodland	Witney (69.8), Wargrave (42.7)
Somerset	Holway (52.7), Poundisford (51.9), Kingstone St Mary and Nailsbourne (49.3), Trull and Bishops Hull (48.4), Staplegrove (45.3), Rimpton (33.3), Otterford (0)
South Hampshire	Havant and Brockhampton (54.9), Bitterne (48.6), Bishops Waltham (34.8), Fareham (34.4), Bishopstoke (14.1), Alverstoke (3.8), Gosport (0)
North Hampshire	Ashmansworth (46.8), Woodhay (28.6), Highclere (25.2), Ecchinswell (22.2), Burghclere (18.6)
Northern	Adderbury (58.4), Waltham St Lawrence (47), Brightwell (35.9), West Wycombe (32), Warfield (30.7), Harwell (30.3), Culham (29.8), Ivinghoe (26.4), Morton (6.1)
Wiltshire	Downton (37.4), East Knoyle (33.3), Upton (33.3), Bishops Fonthill (30), Bishopstone (21.9)
Hampshire Chalk Plateau	North Waltham (79.5), Crawley (44.0), Merdon (37.5), Overton (36.6), Twyford (36.2), Hambledon (33.9), Droxford (31.2), East Meon Church (27.9), East Meon (27.6), Bishops Sutton (25.5), Cheriton (25), Wield (25), Alresford (19), Beauworth (11.5), Marwell (4.5)
Eastern	Esher (51.2), Bentley (30.9), Farnham (24.8)

Table 6.4
The percentage of extrafamilial fines on each manor, 1350–79 (estate average: 60.8)

Region	Manors (%)
Woodland	Witney (81.1), Wargrave (60.3)
Somerset	Holway (69.7), Poundisford (60.7), Kingstone St Mary and Nailsbourne (70.4), Trull and Bishops Hull (63.1), Staplegrove (65.7), Rimpton (63.3), Otterford (65.3)
South Hampshire	Brockhampton (68.1), Gosport (63.6), Fareham (49.8), Bishops Waltham (49.6), Bitterne (44.3), Bishopstoke (33.8), Alverstoke (19.4)
North Hampshire	Ashmansworth (67.4), Burghclere (65.7), Highclere (60.0), Woodhay (58.2), Newtown (50), Ecchinswell (42.9)
Northern	Brightwell (64.7), Waltham St Lawrence (63.2), West Wycombe (61.6), Ivinghoe (61.5), Adderbury (56.1), Harwell (57.9), Culham (57.6), Warfield (48.3), Morton (33.3), Billingbear (16.7)
Wiltshire	Downton (63.5), East Knoyle (54.2), Upton (75), Bishops Fonthill (84.0), Bishopstone (73.9)
Hampshire Chalk Plateau	North Waltham (73.7), Merdon (68.1), Twyford (65.3), Beauworth (63.6), Cheriton (61.3), Marwell (61.2), Overton (60.0), Hambledon (59.4), Alresford (57.7), Crawley (56.9), Bishops Sutton (55.8), East Meon Church (55.4), East Meon (55.2), Wield (55.2), Droxford (50.0)
Eastern	Esher (67.7), Farnham (60.3), Bentley (53.0)

Table 6.5
The percentage of extrafamilial fines on each manor, 1380–1415 (estate average: 60.4)

Region	Manors (%)
Woodland	Witney (74.9), Wargrave (67.5)
Somerset	Otterford (85.7), Trull and Bishops Hull (68.6), Holway (64.7), Kingstone St Mary and Nailsbourne (64.4), Staplegrove (62.9), Poundisford (61.5), Rimpton (55.8)
South Hampshire	Alverstoke (100.0), Brockhampton (64.5), Gosport (63.6), Bitterne (54.5), Bishops Waltham (51.3), Fareham (49.1), Bishopstoke (46.5)
North Hampshire	Highclere (76.4), Burghclere (69.6), Ashmansworth (57.6), Woodhay (55.8), Ecchinswell (47.7)
Northern	Culham (100.0), Morton (100.0), Newtown (100.0), Brightwell (71.7), Waltham St Lawrence (66.3), Adderbury (66.2), West Wycombe (63.9), Ivinghoe (57.8), Warfield (52.4), Harwell (51.6)
Wiltshire	Bishopstone (76.0), Bishops Fonthill (75.0), Charlton (75.0), East Knoyle (73.7), Downton (70.2), Upton (66.7)
Hampshire Chalk Plateau	Easton (100), Overton (73.5), North Waltham (70.0), Twyford (64.6), Beauworth (64.3), Crawley (60.3), Alresford (58.5), Cheriton (58.7), Hambledon (57.9), East Meon (52.9), Bishops Sutton (52.1), Wield (50.0), Merdon (49.4), Marwell (48.9), East Meon Church (33.3), Droxford (30.6)
Eastern	Esher (75.0) , Bentley (56.6), Farnham (54.4)

Table 6.6
Extrafamilial fines post mortem *as a percentage of all* post mortem *fines on each manor, 1350–1364 (estate average 36.3)*

Region	Manors (%)
Woodland	Witney (35.2), Wargrave (20.6)
Somerset	Otterford (37.5), Rimpton (30.8), Nailsbourne (17.6), Bishops Hull (12.6), Holway (10.4), Staplegrove (9.2), Poundisford (4.9)
South Hampshire	Gosport (54.6), Alverstoke (27.8), Fareham (23.9), Bitterne (10.3), Bishops Waltham (8.4), Brockhampton (4.6), Bishopstoke (1)
North Hampshire	Burghclere (58.5), Ashmansworth (46.0), Highclere (33.3), Woodhay (26.6), Ecchinswell (25.9)
Northern	Brightwell (43.8), Culham (31.8), West Wycombe (29.8), Harwell (21.8), Morton (18.2), Waltham St Lawrence (16.7), Adderbury (15.7), Ivinghoe (13.7), Warfield (5)
Wiltshire	Upton (57), Bishopstone (54.8), Downton (33.3), Bishops Fonthill (33.3), East Knoyle (30.6)
Hampshire Chalk Plateau	Cheriton (52), Overton (50.8), North Waltham (45.5), Alresford (41.4), Beauworth (41.2), Crawley (34.4), Wield (33.3), Twyford (32.3), Bishops Sutton (32), Hambledon (25.2), Marwell (20.8), Droxford (10.5), Merdon (9.8), East Meon Church (5.8), East Meon (3.8)
Eastern	Farnham (29.3), Esher (22.7), Bentley (20)

The proportion was also high at Esher, which is interesting in view of the high proportion of fragmented tenures there. In the other regions the proportion of extrafamilial transfers was generally below the average for the estate as a whole – universally so on the Wiltshire manors – although there were high spots at North Waltham and Crawley on the Hampshire Chalk Plateau, at Ashmansworth in North Hampshire and at Adderbury and Waltham St Lawrence in the Northern group of manors.

Tables 6.4 and 6.5 show shifts in these patterns between the periods 1350–79 and 1380–1415. In the thirty years after the plague of 1348 there had clearly been an upward shift in the proportion of extrafamilial fines in nearly every manor. To judge from the Winchester evidence, the higher estimates of extrafamilial exchange among existing studies are more representative than lower estimates such as that from Halesowen. Already by 1350–79 extrafamilial transfers constituted over half the total on the overwhelming majority of episcopal manors, large and small, and this percentage was maintained during the period 1380–1415.

Although some of the differences between manors and regions may be the result of differing mortality in 1348–9 and subsequently, it seems likely that the differing commitment of families to their lands was ultimately more important. This might be affected by a number of variables, the relative ease of making a living from a particular holding being an important one. In the years immediately after the Black Death, the three regions of particular interest showed differences in the proportion of transfers *post mortem* that were extrafamilial (Table 6.6). The number of such fines was far below the average for the estate as a whole on the Taunton manors and on some South Hampshire manors: Bishops Waltham, Bitterne and Fareham. As Titow has shown, on these manors vacant properties were few after the Black Death; continuing family attachments excluded opportunities for potential tenants from new families.[23] On the Woodland manors of Witney and Wargrave the proportion was higher, although not outstandingly so; the high proportion of extrafamilial fines was more the result of families exchanging land *inter vivos* than of their abandoning land as unwanted. Elsewhere on the estate the commitment of families to their land seems to have been particularly weak at Burghclere and Ashmansworth in North Hampshire, at Upton and Bishopstone in Wiltshire, and at Overton and North Waltham on the Hampshire Chalk Plateau, as well as at the smaller manors of Cheriton, Alresford and Beauworth. These were manors that had high numbers of vacant tenements, relative to their size, in the 1350s. Downton bailiwick had one of the highest numbers of vacant tenements, totalling 861 acres in 1355–6.[24]

These differences in family commitment to inherited property can be demonstrated by examining what tenants were willing to pay by way of entry fines. There were conventional reasons why entry fines varied even for the same property. A virgate at East Meon in 1362–3 changed hands three times, on each occasion fetching a different entry fine: Juliana Read paid 10s to inherit it, Richard Berwick paid 6s 8d to acquire it by marriage to Juliana, and in the following fine, Richard surrendered the virgate to Adam Radesol for a fine of £1 3s 4d. Evidently particular properties did not

---

23. Titow, 'Lost rents', pp. 109–11.

24. *Ibid.*, p. 110.

have fixed customary levels of fine,[25] and it seems that different sorts of conveyance encouraged different charges. In this case the extrafamilial transfer incurred a significantly higher fine. But this relationship turns out to be variable both chronologically and geographically. Given the growing importance of extrafamilial transactions involving the take-up of vacant properties, it is initially surprising to find that in fact fines were often higher on transfers within families.

For many tenants, the descent of desirable property within the family continued to be important. Family members were often prepared to pay substantial sums for holdings they had worked for generations, and with which they felt some sense of identity. Many examples suggest a difference between the entry fines for intrafamilial and extrafamilial transactions, and imply that in some contexts the bishop's administration could take advantage of family attachments to particular properties. At Adderbury in 1386–7, for example, Agnes Rowse was charged 6s 8d for a messuage and virgate of villein land surrendered by Joan, the widow of Philip Jack. Meanwhile, in the same year John Dicken was fined £2 10s to enter into his inheritance of a property of the same description, a fine more than seven times the size. Similarly, at East Meon in 1366–7 a fine of £2 10s for an inherited virgate was levied on Christine Hook, whereas, in the same year, Alice Hond took up a virgate surrendered by Edmund Tyghale for a fine of £1. At Staplegrove in 1353–4 an inherited half virgate raised a fine of £4, another, in an extrafamilial transaction *inter vivos*, only £1 13s 4d.

The force of the family bond can be measured as the difference between average fines paid for intrafamilial transfers and those paid for extrafamilial transfers, many of which involved tenements that had escheated to the bishop. The premium on family continuity was likely to be highest on those manors, and in those regions, where families were most committed to continuity of tenure, presumably because tenures were more desirable than elsewhere. The family premium paid for inherited holdings may be expressed as a percentage of the average fine paid on *inter vivos* transfers (Table 6.7). At Wargrave, for example, the average fine for a virgate paid on *inter vivos* transfers was 3s 5d, but for virgates passed by inheritance it was 6s 4d; the family premium (the 2s 11d difference between these two sums) was 85 per cent. Manors on which fines for inheritance were higher were also manors with the highest fines in general. Across the whole estate nearly 70 per cent of entry fines over £5 were for the transfer of virgate and half virgate tenements, and, of these, 40 per cent passed by inheritance, 23 per cent by marriage, and 6 per cent by intrafamilial transfers *inter vivos*. The relationship between Tables 6.6 and 6.7 is far from close; they are not measuring the same thing, they relate to different time periods, and the sample sizes between different manors are very different. Nevertheless, Table 6.7 confirms that the bond between families and their land was particularly strong on the Taunton group of manors – most notably at Holway, Nailsbourne and Staplegrove. The strength of the family bond was not, of course, independent of the quality and location of the properties in question, since families were most likely to be attached to holdings they could not improve upon.

There was often a premium, too, on the intrafamilial transfer of smallholdings.

---

25. See, too, Titow, *English rural society*, pp. 186–8.

Table 6.7

The average family premium (the difference between average fines on transfers by inheritance and those on transfers inter vivos, expressed as a percentage of the latter), 1350–1415

Percentage	Manors
>150	Holway, Nailsbourne, Staplegrove, Gosport, Harwell
>66.67 to 150	Wargrave, Bishops Hull, Poundisford, Bishops Waltham, Brockhampton, Burghclere, Ecchinswell, Woodhay, Adderbury, Brightwell, Ivinghoe, Warfield, West Wycombe, Droxford, Marwell, Merdon, Bentley, Esher
>25 to 66.67	Witney, Bishopstoke, Ashmansworth, Highclere, Culham, Waltham St Lawrence, Bishopstone, Downton, Alresford, East Meon, Hambledon, Twyford
0 to 25	Taunton Borough, Bitterne, Bishops Fonthill, East Knoyle, Beauworth, Cheriton, Crawley, East Meon Church, Morton, Farnham
<0	Otterford, Rimpton, Fareham, Upton, Bishops Sutton, North Waltham, Overton, Wield

Although 60 per cent of the transfers of cottage holdings that had not been engrossed into larger accumulations were extrafamilial, the average fine of 11s 8d for a cottage tenement by inheritance was 40 per cent higher than the 8s 4d for extrafamilial transfers *inter vivos*. At Bishops Waltham in 1378–9, for example, Henry Bardolph paid £2 for a cottage he obtained by inheritance from his father William, for which William in 1351–2 had fined only 2s when he received it by extrafamilal transfer from John Seward. On the same manor in 1390–1 Thomas, son of Adam Cornmonger, was charged £8 to enter into his father's holding of two messuages with two curtilages and five acres of villein land in the tithing of Waltham. Adam, his father, had acquired the holding in 1352–3 by an extrafamilial transfer from Nicholas Boar for the significantly smaller fine of £1 6s. Inheritance fines for smallholdings were sometimes particularly high for heirs other than a widow or a son: in 1353–4 Richard Geoffery fined £2 to inherit his uncle's cottage in Adderbury; at Harwell in 1396–7, Thomas Fort paid £9 to succeed to a messuage and cottage of villein land that were his grandmother's; and in 1376–7 Henry Oyset paid £8 to have his sister's holding of a messuage, fifteen acres of villein land and twelve acres of overland at Poundisford. The fact that individuals were, on occasion, prepared to pay large sums to secure inheritances even during a time of relative land abundance confirms that there was a marked family attachment to some smallholdings as well as the more generously sized tenements. This is presumably because they had valuable rights attached to them, or because they were well sited for engagement in particular occupations.

Higher entry fines for intrafamilial transfers were associated with a general tendency for the bishop's income from intrafamilial transfers in the later fourteenth century to exceed that from transfers to new families. At Harwell, for instance, extrafamilial fines *inter vivos* brought in only a fifth of the revenue from inheritances, and this despite there being an almost equal number of each type of fine. On eighteen other manors the total revenue from inheritance was more than double that from extrafamilial transfers: as well as conservative manors such as Harwell and Bishopstoke, these included some of the more dynamic ones, such as Bishops Waltham, where an extrafamilial market was well developed and in which competition for land was sustained.[26] On most of the manors around Taunton extrafamilial fines *inter vivos* brought in only about two-thirds of the revenue from inheritances.

Significant premiums on intrafamilial transfers were not the universal experience, however. On some manors the family bond had weakened, either because holdings remained burdened with unattractive services, or more probably – given the estate administration's flexibility elsewhere – because of inferior location and agricultural potential. On such manors heirs were unwilling to inherit, and tenants abandoned their land in order to migrate. Such ambitions encouraged the extrafamilial land market and simultaneously affected the terms on which landlords could find tenants. Table 6.7, like Table 6.6, suggests the unattractiveness of tenements in Upton, Cheriton, Overton, North Waltham and Beauworth, and, to a lesser degree, in Bishopstone, Ashmansworth and Alresford. At Overton, which had an acute problem with vacant tenements, the difference in fines on abandoned and escheated standard virgate holdings and transfers within family was negligible, with both averages a little over 9s. There were comparatively few transfers within families on this manor in any case, and it is likely that family demand was so low that the administration was in no position to extract more. On some manors the fines on intrafamilial transfers even fell below those on extrafamilial transfers, as at Cheriton and North Waltham. These were small manors with exceptionally large amounts of vacant tenant land after the Black Death: at Cheriton 349 acres in 1355–6 and 499 acres in 1364–5, at North Waltham 370½ acres in 1355–6 and 562½ acres in 1364–5.[27] In such conditions the administration was unable to appeal to family sentiment in order to charge more, and was striving to retain families where possible.

On manors where the premium on family tenure was low, and especially where there was a large amount of untenanted land, the bishop's income from extrafamilial transfers was more likely to be superior to that from transfers within families. At Bishops Hull, unlike the normal situation around Taunton, inheritance brought in about 12 per cent less revenue than the extrafamilial market. At Witney, where there had been a busy market in assart tenements for some time, the number of extrafamilial fines *inter vivos* outstripped inheritance and brought in considerably more revenue. At Rimpton, North Waltham, Culham, Bishops Fonthill, Upton and Otterford a small number of inheritance transfers brought in only around half of the revenue of a larger number of extrafamilial fines.

These observations, for all the inconsistencies in the evidence relating to some manors, strongly suggest that the survival of bonds between families and land, with their accompanying implications for the strength and durability of kinship ties, was very variable between manors.[28] The sort of strength of family ties that Razi observes in Halesowen can be matched on some of the Winchester manors, but not on

---

26. Bishops Waltham, Adderbury, Beauworth, Bishopstoke, Billingbear, Bitterne, Bentley, Downton, Droxford, Ecchinswell, East Knoyle, Hambledon, Morton, Marwell, Warfield, Woodhay and West Wycombe.
27. Titow, 'Lost rents', p. 110–11.
28. For the general point, see, too, C. Dyer, 'Changes in the link between families and land in the west midlands in the fourteenth and fifteenth centuries', in Smith (ed.), *Land, kinship and life-cycle*, p. 309.

others,[29] and, not surprisingly, had to do with the desirability of cultivation or residence in particular locations relative to the attractions of migration and dispersion. It is likely that weakness of the family bond so remarkable on some manors was a transient phenomenon, dependent upon the specific economic circumstances of the period, rather than a permanent social transformation towards more commercial attitudes to land. In the west midlands, for example, the uptake of inheritances was particularly low in the late fourteenth and fifteenth centuries, but later increased.[30]

New tensions, new devices

The formation of an increasingly extrafamilial land market challenged the age-old primacy of customary inheritance as a means by which families were established on the land. The increased marketing of peasant tenures allowed increased opportunities for non-inheriting sons to acquire property, and for heirs to acquire land without waiting for the death of a parent. Meanwhile, the traditional expectations of heirs were called into question. Rosamond Faith found that in Berkshire 'changes in tenure were no longer only occasioned by the death of a tenant; land changed hands at random, governed only by the laws of supply and demand'.[31] The consequent weakening of custom was quickly countered both by new problems and by various strategies designed to ensure security of tenure and descent.

An increasing number of attempts to recover property from sitting tenants implies increasing discordance between inheritance custom and a developing extrafamilial market (Table 6.8). These actions – whose intention is expressed by the verb *recuperare*, or sometimes *rehabere* – are found throughout the estate, but a high proportion are found on the Taunton group of manors and at Bishops Waltham and Brockhampton in South Hampshire, parts of the estate where an extrafamilial land market had been established from an earlier date. A peak in their number during the 1320s and 1330s is not easily explained, but the bulge of the 1350s may be interpreted as a reaction to the loss of inheritances occasioned by disorder in the land market in the few years after 1348. A typical example is that of John Pook at Ashmansworth, who in 1358–9 paid 2s to recover a cottage with curtilage from John Bellet; John Pook's father William had been the previous tenant. Sometimes a claim to inheritance is implied rather than explicit. On the same manor, for instance, we learn that Richard Hern recovered a cottage with a few acres of purpresture from Richard Bolt on the grounds that the property was 'his right as a portion of his adjacent tenement'.

Throughout the period we also read of land recovered 'by inquisition', 'by inquiry of

29. Z. Razi, 'The erosion of the family-land bond in the late fourteenth and fifteenth centuries: a methodological note', in Smith (ed.), *Land, kinship and life-cycle*, pp. 295–304; *idem*, 'Family', pp. 25–7; *idem*, 'Intrafamilial ties and relationships in the medieval village: a quantitative approach employing manor-court rolls', in Razi and Smith (eds), *Medieval society and the manor court*, pp. 379–81.

30. C. Dyer, 'Changes in the size of peasant holdings in some west midland villages, 1400–1540', in Smith (ed.), *Land, kinship and life-cycle*, pp. 285–6.

31. Faith, 'Berkshire', p. 121.

Table 6.8
The number of actions of recovery on the Winchester bishopric estate, 1263–1415

	Number of years recorded	Number of recoveries	Annual average
1260–9	6	5	1.2
1270–9	27	8	3.4
1280–9	63	7	9.0
1290–9	41	7	5.9
1300–9	47	9	5.2
1310–9	59	10	5.9
1320–9	95	8	11.9
1330–9	106	9	11.8
1340–9	70	10	7.0
1350–9	81	10	8.1
1360–9	56	10	5.6
1370–9	46	10	4.6
1380–9	17	9	1.9
1390–9	8	8	1.0
1400–9	5	7	0.7
1410–19	1	5	0.2

the whole hundred', 'by twelve jurors of the homage', and so on. In the later fourteenth century recoveries began to be recorded as established by trial (*per actionem triatam*). Recoveries of land and the enforcement of customary rules of inheritance were not always straightforward, and a great many cases required local knowledge and considered judgement, especially where a case was unusual.[32] Inheritance could be a complex matter, and manorial custom could be ambiguous, particularly with regard to the claims of distant heirs. At Bishops Waltham in 1324–5 Henry Curr fined to recover a messuage and virgate in Woodcott as his right against Alice, widow of Richard Buckstock, who claimed a widow's customary life tenure of her husband's property. John Buckstock, Richard's heir, joined her in her plea. However, Henry pleaded a title that descended from his great-grandfather, and an inquest decided in his favour. Henry perhaps had a motive other than mere family attachment; custom could be used to gain desirable property regardless of any such sentiment. Sometimes in determining family rights manorial courts trespassed into issues properly belonging to ecclesiastical jurisdiction. At Bishops Waltham, again in 1324–5, Henry and Agnes Marshall lost two messuages and a curtilage and two acres when an inquest in the manorial court judged that Seyld, daughter of Richard and Agnes Woodrat, was born within wedlock. Her superior title had previously been passed over on the supposition that she was illegitimate.

Pleas for the recovery of land are just one indicator of a wider set of tensions

---

32. See Poos and Bonfield (eds), *Select cases*, p. ci.

concerning family rights. Families had long engaged in conveyancing techniques that sidestepped the restraints of hereditary custom, usually in the interests of providing property for children during their parents' lifetimes.[33] Such strategies allowed flexibility in the manipulation of descent so that, ultimately, lands were kept within families if it was so desired. However, especially from the later fourteenth century, we observe the use of various devices sanctioned by the manorial courts to make firmer and more secure family rights and, on other occasions, to claim back land that had been lost or alienated. Other new devices were designed to safeguard the title to newly acquired property from future claims by the family of an earlier tenant.[34]

Something of this tension between family claims and the increasingly unpredictable pattern of transfers can be seen in the reversionary clauses of inter-peasant leases. The inclusion of such a clause made a court-roll entry equivalent to an agreement between lord and tenant, and indicates the lessor's fear of losing control. Additional clauses to ensure that a property would be returned to the lessee in good condition also point this way. Although recorded inter-peasant leasing declined in the later fourteenth century, clauses designed to increase security of tenure became more common from the 1340s to the 1360s. Leases with reversion clauses became more numerous in the last quarter of the fourteenth century; the entry fines record seven in the 1370s, thirteen in the 1380s, fourteen in the 1390s, twenty-five in the first decade of the fifteenth century and nineteen in the five years between 1410–11 and 1414–15. Reversionary clauses were often employed for the purpose of excluding rival claims. At Warfield in 1389, for example, Matilda, daughter of John Rivers, and her husband, John Morse, paid a fine of £1 3s 4d for ten acres of purpresture in the tithing of 'Westende' surrendered by Matilda's father. The reversionary clause states that after the deaths of John Morse and Matilda the property should revert to Matilda's direct heirs. It is likely that John Rivers was providing a dower for his daughter and was concerned to rule out claims from other members of his family.

The Taunton group of manors, where the family premium was high, had a particular response to the tensions of the day. Here there are fines that allowed an individual to acquire part of a holding in expectation of eventually appropriating the remainder on the death of the sitting tenant.[35] All other claimants were now excluded from entry to the property. At Staplegrove in 1372–3, for example, John Winter paid 16s 8d as a fine for 'an acre in the croft called Hals on the western side, in the tithing of Pyrland, by surrender of Robert Winter his father, to appropriate the remainder when it should fall due, namely a messuage and half a virgate of villein land containing in total twenty acres'. John succeeded to his father's lands six years later in 1378–9, when he paid a fine of £6 13s 4d, the record noting that he had previously fined for one acre in expectation of his inheritance. Investment in a single acre was sufficient to stake a claim in most instances. This device does not occur before the 1340s, but its use increased over the following decades until by 1415 it was common; there are more than 400 such fines in all during this period.

---

33. This will be examined in greater detail in Chapter 7.

34. The use of these devices in the ten years after the Black Death is discussed in Mullan, 'Transfer of customary land', pp. 95–9.

35. This device occurs elsewhere on the bishop's estate only at Farnham in 1405–6.

These enrolled guarantees were themselves heritable. At Poundisford in 1400–1, for example, John Tough fined for half an acre of villein land from his mother in expectation of the eventual receipt of the whole holding of half a virgate and a daywork of overland. However, John died before his mother, and in the event in 1411–12 his widow Joan received both the half acre 'appropriating the remainder when it should fall due' and, in the following fine, the whole estate. The acre or other small plot might move between several parties to accommodate changing family circumstances. At Poundisford in 1350–1, Stephen Prout fined for 1½ acres of villein land from the estate of John Lamberd 'to appropriate the remainder [a messuage and half virgate] when it should fall due'. This was land that had once been held by Stephen's ancestor, Walter Prout. Stephen received the remainder in 1357–8. Ten years later he surrendered an acre from this same holding, again with a clause for later appropriation, to Agnes Baron, but in 1377–6 fined for the return of the same acre 'previously surrendered to Agnes Baron whom Roger Keen recently betrothed': it seems likely that some family plan had broken down, and that a decision had had to be reversed to prevent land being alienated from Stephen's family.

This device was not used only as a means for settlements within families; more than half of these fines at Taunton were for extrafamilial transfers. Small plots acquired on these terms could be bought and sold. At Holway manor in 1365–6, Roger Sevenoaks paid a 16s fine for an acre of villein land received from Gilbert Shoreditch 'appropriating the remainder when it should fall due': namely, a messuage, a half virgate of villein land and three acres of meadow overland. Nine years later, in 1374–5, Juliana Shaldew paid a fine of £1 6s 8d for the same acre, which her deceased sister, another Juliana, had had 'by surrender of Roger Sevenoaks who had had it by surrender of Gilbert Shoreditch, appropriating the remainder of the tenement of Gilbert when it should fall due'. Sometime between 1374–5 and 1388–9 this acre once more changed hands, this time by surrender to John Shaldew. Then finally, in 1388–9, and for the heavy fine of £10, John came into the remainder of the estate of a half virgate and three acres of meadow, surrendered to him by Gilbert Shoreditch. In other words, this customary acre with eventual appropriation passed through several hands over a period of about twenty-three years. It is likely that some at least of the extrafamilial contracts of this kind were the product of a kind of mortgage in which tenants either acquitted a debt, or borrowed ready cash, by conveying the reversion of their property to the creditor.

Besides these devices to secure future claims to property there were fines to protect individuals from future inheritance claims. Chief among these was the enrolment of an earlier remittance and release or quitclaim. At Bishops Waltham in 1395–6, William Frogg paid a fine of £1 10s to enter a toft and ferling for which John Woodlock's widow had refused to fine. In the following accounting year William fined a further 6s 8d to enrol a quitclaim to the property by Melchisar Woodlock, John's brother; in addition to the fine, William may have had to pay Melchisar. This sort of caution was also expressed within families. At Staplegrove in 1364–5, William, son of William and Edith Moor, fined 4s 4d to enrol his mother's quitclaim of her right in three ferlings of villein land and a half acre of overland previously occupied by her father, presumably part of her dower land. William may have feared that his mother would remarry and that her new husband would seek to re-enter the property. Within two years, in fact, she married Walter Moor, who fined for the marriage and the lands still in Edith's possession.

Some enrolments resulted from protracted disputes. There is more evidence for this in the later fourteenth and early fifteenth centuries than earlier. At West Wycombe in 1381–2, John Gransden paid 2d to enrol a settlement following a dispute whose details are well recorded. Earlier that year Richard Rammesmere had pleaded that John had unjustly deforced him of a messuage and a half virgate of villein land in Booker previously belonging to his kinsman Ralph Rammesmere. The holding, he said, had passed to Ralph's brother, and in turn to his brother's daughter, through whom he claimed his right. Richard was opening an old wound; nineteen year earlier, in 1362–3, John Gransden's uncle, Matthew Churchatch, had fined to enrol his right to the messuage and half virgate against the claims of Richard Rammesmere following a prolonged dispute. The origins of the dispute went back even further, at least to the second decade of the century, when – according to the jurors of 1381–2 – Walter Churchatch, Matthew's great-grandfather, had taken up the tenement as the lord's escheat after it had been in the bishop's hands for 2½ years.[36] It was at this point that any Rammesmere claims must have been deemed to have lapsed. Why the Rammesmere family was so persistent in the face of earlier defeat is not clear. In any event Richard's only option in 1381, when confronted with the earlier enrolment, was to allege that the jurors who had decided in favour of Matthew Churchatch had perjured themselves. A jury of attaint was summoned, with twenty-four jurors, but this too ruled against Richard and amerced him for making a false claim. John Gransden, as his uncle had done, had his triumph enrolled for future security, and the low fine he was charged implies that he had the sympathies of the court.

The purpose of these various devices was to protect titles to property, and the means by which they did so increased the tenants' dependence on written records that we observed in Chapter 4. Many were prepared to pay substantial sums to this end. Such fines – not all of which are for customary land – are found mostly on manors where an extrafamilial land market was well developed, especially on the Taunton manors, where actions of recovery and agreements for the later appropriation of estates were also common. They also occur at Bishops Waltham, East Meon, Brockhampton and Farnham; fewer than a handful are found elsewhere. Among the former colonising manors, where land was abundant even by later fourteenth-century standards, they are rare or absent. Few are found among the manors of North Hampshire or the Northern and Wiltshire manors.

Conclusion

Villager families in the later thirteenth and earlier fourteenth centuries showed a strong inclination to retain property intact from generation to generation. The difficulty of obtaining land at a time of high land values encouraged families to safeguard any claims they had. This was also in the common interest of estate officers because it supplied some guarantee that property would be well maintained and that services to the bishop and to the village community would be duly performed. In exceptional cases properties were confiscated when such expectations were not met, but even in

---

36. In 1273–4, Juliana, widow of Walter Churchatch, fined to retain her inheritance of a messuage and half virgate in her widowhood, and in 1309–10 Richard Churchatch, son of Walter, fined to receive the inheritance held by Juliana, his mother.

these instances family ties were usually respected except when tenements had fallen forfeit to the bishop on account of felony or bastardy.

The assumption of family continuity through inheritance was widely undermined by the depopulation of the fourteenth century. As a result of the greater availability of land, the development of a freer and more commercial attitude to family property and the need for landlords to find tenants for demesne land or land left empty by death or abandonment, there was an increase in the number of transfers of land between families, whether by transfers *inter vivos* or by new lettings made by the bishop. There was a particularly large decline in the proportion of transfers between family members *inter vivos*, and a particularly large increase in that of extrafamilial transfers *post mortem*.

On the other hand, manors differed greatly in the extent to which sitting tenants were prepared to give up their inheritances. These differences can be conveniently assessed by examining differences between the average fine paid by those inheriting property and those acquiring holdings by transfer *inter vivos*. In many cases the former was higher – sometimes considerably higher, as on some of the Taunton manors – suggesting that a core of tenants was prepared to pay a high premium for retaining inherited land of good quality or favourable location rather than moving to a new holding elsewhere. The pipe rolls also suggest that in the context of a more volatile land market there were new tensions in the later fourteenth century between former traditions of family continuity and the new world of a freer land market. Some families were taking additional precautions to protect their rights to property and rights of inheritance, either by including reversionary clauses in leases or by acquiring rights of reversion to family property during the lifetime of the sitting tenant.

Chapter 7

Transfers within families

Transfers of property between living family members rarely involved commercial considerations, and transfers by inheritance in particular were governed by customary rules and expectations. Between 1269 and 1349, 46.5 per cent of recorded land transfers on the Winchester estate were intrafamilial, and most of these (34.5 per cent of the total) were by inheritance.[1] Although on a few smaller manors, such as Culham, Morton and Otterford, inheritance came to be of small significance during subsequent generations, over the period and estate as a whole it remained important in the transmission of peasant property. Despite the rising proportion of extrafamilial exchanges, between 1350 and 1415 39.2 per cent of transfers across the estate as a whole were within families, again mostly (33.7 per cent of the total) by inheritance. The importance of transfers by inheritance on the Winchester estate was not unusual: before the Black Death inheritance was the single most important means of transferring villein property throughout England.[2]

Even where the number of extrafamilial transfers greatly outnumbered the intrafamilial in this period, as at Witney, the extended extrafamilial land market consisted primarily of small plots of non-customary land, such as assarts, rather than standard virgated holdings, which more usually remained within families and passed by inheritance or marriage. At Witney, out of 165 entry fines paid for virgated tenements between 1264–5 and 1348–9, 46 per cent were for intrafamilial transfers. The descent of property within families was nevertheless subject to numerous accidents of family history. Titow has observed that 'the notion of a family holding passing down from father to son, from generation to generation, belongs to the same brand of fiction as that of the typical manor'; he observed from his study of the Taunton manors how 'the family holdings had a way of wandering about'.[3] Continuity of title within families was particularly vulnerable to failures to generate a male heir, or to the remarriages of widows. Table 7.1 shows how common it was for properties to be inherited by relatives other than sons, and indicates that the proportion of such transfers rose in the later part of the period under study.

In general the variations to be found between manors in patterns of intrafamilial transfer do not conform to regional divisions, and are best discussed as intermanorial contrasts, often influenced by differences of manorial custom. Two aspects of inheritance custom, the rights of widows and those of sons, are worthy of particularly close attention. We shall examine some ways in which new techniques were developed to enable families to retain a greater control over their lands even within the

---

1. Page, 'Southern England', table 1, p. 317; *idem*, 'Estate', table 1, p. 63.

2. Whittle, 'Individualism', pp. 45–7.

3. Titow, 'Some differences', p. 7. For a similar comment, see J. Ravensdale, 'The transfer of customary land on a Cambridgeshire manor', in Smith (ed.), *Land, kinship and life-cycle* , p. 199.

Table 7.1
The number and proportion of relations inheriting land, 1269–1349 and 1350–1415

	1269–1349	(%)	1350–1415	(%)
Son[a]	4684	39.0	1852	31.1
Widow	4477	37.3	1827	30.1
Daughter[b]	1026	8.5	661	11.1
Brother	632	5.3	372	6.2
Sister	258	2.2	165	2.8
Grandson	127	1.1	131	2.2
Grand-daughter	54	0.5	47	0.8
Nephew	275	2.3	214	3.6
Niece	97	0.8	48	0.8
Other[c]	185	1.5	46	0.8
Kin[d]	194	1.6	597	10.0
Total	12,009	100	5,960	100

Notes: a including stepsons; b including stepdaughters; c grandparents, fathers, uncles and aunts, brothers- and sisters-in-law, cousins, sons-in-law, great-grandchildren, great nephews; d as deduced from same-surname evidence.

context of inheritance custom, before going on to examine intrafamilial transfers *inter vivos*.

Custom and inheritance: (a) widows

On the death of a male customary tenant, the custom of all the manors of the Winchester estate provided that the family holding would pass in the first instance to his widow, who would hold it for her life, although with many variations of detail. The widow's right to the whole holding was a more generous provision than that on many estates, where her portion was often a third or a half.[4] This custom delayed the descent of holdings to the next generation, in some cases for many years. For example, the father of Richard Hatch of Farnham died in 1316–17 leaving a messuage and 7½ acres of purpresture, but Richard did not inherit this property until twenty years later, in 1336–7, on the death of Alice, his mother. In some cases an heir had to await the death of a stepmother, since a woman who married a widower possessed the same rights as a first wife to retain her husband's holding on his death. If a widowed father married a young bride, his son might have to wait a long time for his inheritance. It is less clear that a child by a second marriage could inherit the family holding in preference to a child of the first. The terse accounts offered by the entry fines rarely provide any clues as to the marital history of an heir's parents, and family reconstitution can be a hazardous affair given the tendency of men, and particularly of second husbands, to adopt the surnames of their wives. A selection of reconstructed property histories from Taunton shows sons and daughters from second marriages

---

4.   J.M. Bennett, *Women in the medieval English countryside* (Oxford, 1987), p. 163.

Table 7.2
Remarriages of widows as a proportion of all marriages: 1263–1415

	Remarriages	Total marriages	(%)
1263–69	5	59	8.5
1270–79	47	208	22.6
1280–89	44	241	18.3
1290–99	108	289	37.4
1300–09	137	357	38.4
1310–19	157	439	35.8
1320–29	59	264	22.4
1330–39	86	422	19.9
1340–49	196	646	30.3
1350–59	60	542	9
1360–69	68	543	12.5
1370–79	70	298	23.5
1380–89	69	244	28.3
1390–99	34	222	15
1400–09	95	250	38
1410–15	51	184	27.7
Total	1286	5208	24.7

Note: Because the fines do not always specify the status of the woman, the figures for remarriage of widows are likely to be underestimated.

inheriting, thereby effectively switching the line of descent from one family name to another, but unfortunately it is not known in these instances if any children survived from the first marriage.[5]

In some cases delays led to inheritance by grandchildren, presumably because by this time the immediate heirs had died or established themselves elsewhere; fifty-one instances of this are recorded between 1350 and 1415, of which forty-four were inheritances by grand-daughters. The remarriage of widows might even alter the direction of descent altogether. Titow described the recurrent situation in which a younger man married an older widow as a means of access to land but, on her death, now relatively old himself, married a younger woman who in turn outlived him. She might still be young enough to remarry, perhaps more than once. With a young stepmother to outlive, the probability of a son's living long enough to succeed was reduced.[6] The incidence and pattern of the remarriage of widows is, therefore, a crucial aspect of both inheritance and of land pressure over time and space.

Table 7.2 is a decennial analysis of the number of remarriages by widows where

---

5. Titow, 'Some differences', pp. 12–13. In 1798, when a widow's right to her husband's customary land was still recognised on the Taunton manors, it was observed that 'it is no uncommon thing for a widow, on the death of her husband, having children by him, to marry again, and carry her estate into her second family, to the disinheritance of the first': Billingsley, *General view*, p. 268.

6. Titow, 'Some differences', p. 7.

Table 7.3
*Marriages to widows as a percentage of all recorded marriages on
Taunton manors, 1263–1349 and 1350–1415*

Manor	1263–1349 (%)	1349–1415 (%)
Otterford	70.0	0
Poundisford	43.5	18.4
Holway	43.4	18.8
Nailsbourne	39.7	13.8
Staplegrove	37.2	25.0

they are described as such in an entry fine. The figures show the proportional increase in the number of remarriages of widows between c.1290 and c.1310, confirming that widows were most keenly sought as marriage partners in this period of high land values. Conversely, apart perhaps from the 1260s – whose data are too imperfect for any sure conclusions – the lowest point for remarriage by widows was in the decade or so after the Black Death, when vacant land was readily available. In the later part of our period, predictably, the proportion of recorded marriages to widows declined in nearly all manors because of the increasing availability of land by other means.

The proportion of marriages to widows before 1349 was greatest on manors whose resources of land were in high demand; these were often also manors that had experienced an early fragmentation of holdings, had large proportions of smallholdings and had a more developed market in property. The rate of marriages to widows was high among the Taunton group of manors, as Titow observed, and declined steeply with the reduction of pressure on the land after 1349 (Table 7.3). Remarriage of widows was also more common on some manors practising ultimogeniture, as notably – besides the Taunton manors – at Downton, Bitterne, Rimpton and Bishops Fonthill, where elder sons stayed at home and added to the pressure on available property; marriages to widows here constituted respectively 71.5, 57.9, 56.3 and 53.9 per cent of all recorded marriages in the period 1263–1349, and 31.9, 13.9, 62.5 and 42.9 per cent between 1350 and 1415. The remarriage of widows was less likely, as Titow observed, where there had been a large measure of agrarian expansion onto new land during the thirteenth century. Witney, however, was exceptional in this respect: 43.3 per cent of recorded marriages there were to widows between 1263 and 1349, a proportion that fell to 20 per cent between 1350 and 1415. A peasant with only minor parcels of assart land had a precarious existence, so that marriage to a widow holding a customary tenement could be an attractive means to improve his circumstances.[7] Almost all marriages to widows here involved the transfer of virgates and half virgates, and none were for assart holdings. In 1310, for example, John, son of William Richard, fined for his inheritance of one acre of assart. The following year, however, he married Matilda, the widow of one Walter Losingrove, who brought him a messuage and full virgate.

A further telling feature of this distribution of marriage to widows is the incidence

---

7. Titow's explanation in terms of the timing of forest clearance on the manor is hard to grasp: Titow, 'Some differences', pp. 8–9.

Table 7.4
Inheritances from widows, 1350–1415

	Number	(%)
Son	296	29.5
Son/stepson	209	20.8
Daughter	137	13.7
Daughter/stepdaughter	43	4.3
Grandson	52	5.2
Grand-daughter	31	3.1
Nephew	54	5.4
Niece	15	1.5
Other	3	0.3
Kin	163	16.3
Total	1002	100

of widows remarrying more than once, which was almost exclusive to manors where land was highly sought. On the manors of the Taunton group examples are readily to be found in the early fourteenth century. A typical example is from Poundisford. Christine, widow of Richard Wyatt, married John Bradmore in 1314. In 1316, however, she was again remarried to William Bennet. At Holway in 1326 Eve Atmore fined to retain the land of William, her husband. In 1329 she married another William Atmore who, in turn, died by 1332. She then married Richard Moodey, the whole time retaining the estate intact. In the context of land hunger, widows often remarried speedily. At Downton manor in the early fourteenth century more than a third of widows were remarried within two years, the majority apparently immediately. Of 136 widows' marriages recorded at Downton before 1350, fifty had been delayed for a year or two after the widow had fined for her husband's property, being recorded in the next pipe roll or the one after that, but most came in the same year; the marriage fine was often recorded immediately after the widow's fine to enter her inheritance.

The degree to which a widow's occupation of a tenement might disturb a straight line of inheritance in the later fourteenth and early fifteenth centuries can be assessed by comparing inheritance by children and other younger family members in general to inheritance specifically from widows (Tables 7.1, 7.4). In some of these fines it is not clear whether the heir was a son or stepson, daughter or stepdaughter of the mother. A fine at Twyford in 1409–10, for example, records that William, son of John Smith, paid 1s for a toft and cotland that had belonged to John, his father, and for which Alice, John's widow, would not fine. It is, nonetheless, clear that stepsons and stepdaughters were more likely to inherit when their inheritance came through a widow. Although the proportions are quite small, there was also an increased possibility that more distant heirs, such as grandsons and nephews, would succeed.

On the other hand, widows' tenure did not jeopardise the integrity of holdings, or even the name of the family with which they were associated. In their concern to be associated with a particular holding husbands often adopted the surnames of the widows they married, as if the surname was conferred by the holding. On the manor of Alresford in 1284–5 Stephen Overton paid a fine of 2s for Alice Caldewell with her land. After Stephen's death in 1309–10 or a little before, Alice fined 1s for the land of a messuage and two acres of her late husband, named as Stephen Caldewell. A striking example of the way a family holding could be kept intact through widowhood is the case of the Colebrook family from the South Hampshire manor of Bishopstoke.[8] In 1342 Isabel, widow of Thomas Colebrook, fined to retain a virgate, half virgate, ferling and cottage in the tithings of East and West Horton. These were lands that Thomas himself had inherited from his father, Peter Winchesell. Peter had been the second husband of Dulcie Colebrook, who in turn retained them from her first husband, Robert, son of Richard Colebrook, in 1303. So Isabel had inherited an estate that had remained intact for at least thirty-nine years. The year following her widowhood, Isabel Colebrook married again, this time to John Bedwind, bringing with her the whole estate. However, John died the next year and in 1345 Isabel married for a third time, bringing the estate to William Middlington. Only in 1348–9 did Isabel relinquish a part of the holding, and then only a ferling, to her nephew. Such cases may be also found on the Taunton manors, as at Poundisford and Holway, and at Bishopstoke, but none can be found in the contrasting manors, such as Wargrave, where land was more easily acquired.[9]

Across the bishop's estate during the period 1269–1349, widows received 37.3 per cent of all recorded inheritances, as against 39 per cent received by sons and 8.5 per cent by daughters (see Table 7.1).[10] These figures in fact understate the extent of inheritance by widows because they do not include transfers for which no entry fine was due; widows were exempt from paying entry fines for their husband's land on nine of the Winchester manors: Adderbury, Bishops Fonthill, Brightwell, Crawley, East Knoyle, Harwell, North Waltham, Overton and Witney. For Overton the customary declared that 'a wife will not be allowed to fine after the death of her husband [but] will hold the land while single and chaste'.[11] There is no evidence that widows on these manors forfeited their land if they remarried, although the lord might then impose a fine on the new husband.

Custom and inheritance: (b) sons

There was variety in the rights of inheritance by sons. The evidence of the custumals is especially important on this point, since inheritance rules are rarely stated or even implied by the details of entry fines. Although the custumals do not cover every manor of the estate, they imply that primogeniture was the most common custom. However, the right of the younger son to inherit is to be found on the Somerset manors and most of the Wiltshire manors – at Downton, East Knoyle, Upton and Bishops Fonthill. It was the practice on several of the South Hampshire manors – at Bitterne, Bishops Waltham, Bishopstoke and, in more restricted circumstances, at Fareham – and among the Hampshire Chalk Plateau group at Droxford and Crawley. Ultimogeniture was chiefly applied to customary land, although, in some cases, as at Bishops

---

8.   M. Page, 'Lords, peasants and property: the effect of the Black Death on the bishop of Winchester's estate' (unpublished).

9.   This conclusion is based on searching the database for widows where the second husband adopted the widow's surname. There may be others where the widow adopted the surname of her new husband.

10. Page, 'Southern England', tables 3–5, pp. 322–4.

11. HRO, 11M59/E2/415808, fo. 71.

Waltham and Droxford, it also applied to purpresture lands annexed to customary land. At Fareham bondland passed to the youngest son but wasteland and purpresture to the eldest. The geographical distribution of ultimogeniture across the bishop's estate is in keeping with what has been observed elsewhere – it was practised on a broad band of manors extending through Surrey, Sussex, southern Hampshire and on westwards.[12]

Although in one respect primogeniture and ultimogeniture were alike – in that they secured property to a single heir – their effects upon family life were different. Inheritance by youngest sons encouraged older sons to remain in the household, helping to work the family holding after their parents' death, especially if the heir was a minor, unmarried or inexperienced. The resulting larger household size was more likely to set up pressures in the land market. Although very different in law from partible inheritance, ultimogeniture could therefore exercise some of the same effects in encouraging a higher density of population, a more vigorous market in land and the fragmentation of properties. For example, at Brockhampton, where according to the custumal ultimogeniture was practised, William Robiste in 1335 surrendered a house and plot in Havant to his elder brother Henry. There was a positive relationship between the incidence of ultimogeniture, the distribution of smallholdings, the fragmentation of properties, the proportions of extrafamilial transfers and the rapidity with which land was transferred. On the Taunton manors the right of the youngest son to succeed helps explain the large numbers of smallholdings, the high degree of fragmentation and the significant proportion of extrafamilial fines *inter vivos*. Similar developments at Rimpton were slower to show themselves, although they were well advanced by the mid-fourteenth century. The land market in the South Hampshire manors initially developed more slowly, but an extrafamilial market in virgated tenements at Bishops Waltham and Bitterne at least was very pronounced and the fragmentation of holdings there and at Fareham was also noticeably high. At Droxford and at Crawley, extrafamilial transactions, transfers of both virgated tenements and smallholdings and the fragmentation of older units were again proportionately numerous before the Black Death. It is interesting that ultimogeniture preponderated in two of the three regions for which we have identified a particularly active land market, although the fact that it also preponderated in the Wiltshire group of manors implies that the Winchester evidence gives only qualified support to the independent effects of ultimogeniture in the formation of a land market.

Over the whole period, 78.3 per cent of inheritance transfers to sons were through fathers rather than mothers, despite the high number of fines for widows. However, to some extent the documents are misleading. A number of entry fines which record the transmission of land from father to son fail to make any mention of the widow, who can be shown to have taken possession of the land on her husband's death several years before. The exact scale of this occurrence is unclear, but it certainly implies that our figures understate the number of transfers between a mother and her heir.

---

12. Faith, 'Peasant families', pp. 82–3.

The impact of epidemics

The Black Death was a major cause of transformation in the relationship between families and inherited property. Not only did inheritance decline in relative importance as a mode of transfer of property, but, as Table 7.1 illustrates, inheritance involved wider kinship groups. Zvi Razi noticed this development in much the same period at Halesowen, but he also demonstrated that reliance on same surnames as evidence of kinship led to a serious underestimate of the number of intrafamilial transfers. The Winchester evidence is more robust on this point because of the pipe rolls' consistent practice of specifying family relationships. We hear of many nephews whose name is different from that of their uncle or aunt, and of many sons and daughters with surnames different from that of their mother; this was often demonstrably because of the mother's remarriage. Fines that appear to be extrafamilial, but that turn out from the evidence of other fines to be wrongly classified, are sufficiently rare to be negligible, however.[13]

Epidemics had demonstrable effects on the pattern as well as the relative importance of heritable transfers. Table 7.5 demonstrates several developments. One was the sharp fall in the proportion of widows inheriting after the Black Death and through the 1350s. The relatively slight movement away from sons is not difficult to explain, given the failure of male heirs in many households. Daughters, brothers, sisters, nephews and nieces, as well as grandchildren and wider kin, all increased their share; the 'other' category includes uncles, aunts, fathers, mothers, and brothers- and sisters-in-law. Those described as kin may often be cousins or in-laws.[14]

The impact of the second pestilence of 1361–2 was different in one important particular. Several contemporary chroniclers remark upon a disproportionately high mortality among males: Ralph Higden's continuator notes that in 1361 there was 'a great pestilence of men' which began in London and spread through the rest of England 'killing many men but few women', and there are similar comments by Thomas of Walsingham and John of Reading.[15] To judge from the ratio of male to female heirs, higher mortality among males was more apparent in some regions than others – particularly on manors of the Somerset group, and on those of North Hampshire (Table 7.6). Disproportionate male mortality was great enough to affect the pattern of inheritance across the estate: the proportion of inheriting sons in 1361–2 was about half that after the first plague. Nor did brothers, nephews or grandsons make the increased appearance that they did in 1348–9. Accordingly, an unusually high proportion of heritable land – almost 60 per cent in 1361–2 – fell into the hands of women, so increasing opportunities for marriage to an heiress. The 11.7 per cent of total transfers going to widows outstripped even the relatively high proportion of 7.6 per cent in 1348–9, and no doubt more widows inherited on manors where they did not need to fine to do so. The proportion of sisters and daughters also increased over

13. For a discussion of this potential problem, see Mullan, 'Transfer of customary land', pp. 92–5.

14. *Ibid.*, p. 74.

15. C. Babington and J.R. Lumby (eds), *Polychronicon Ranulphi Higden monachi Cestrensis*, 9 vols, Rolls Series, 41 (London, 1865–6), VIII, p. 360; Thomas of Walsingham, *Historia Anglicana*, in H.T. Riley (ed.), *Chronica monasterii S, Albani*, 12 vols, Rolls Series, 26 (London, 1863–76), I, p. 296; J. Tait (ed.), *Chronica Johannis de Reading et Anonymi Cantuariensis* (Manchester, 1914), p. 150.

Table 7.5
The percentage of relations inheriting land, 1341–64

	Total	Son	Widow	Daughter	Brother	Sister	Grandson	Grand daughter	Nephew	Niece	Other	'Kin'
1341–8*	1328	36.5	42.3	7.9	5.3	1.4	0.8	0.5	1.7	0.9	1.0	1.7
1348–9	1825	34.6	19.4	12.3	8.8	3.2	2.4	1.7	6.6	2.3	2.6	6.1
1349–50	660	33.2	11.4	11.5	12.7	3.6	1.1	0.9	7.0	2.7	1.7	14.2
1350–1	270	30.0	13.4	12.2	8.9	3.7	3.7	2.2	6.7	0.4	1.0	17.8
1351–2	140	30.7	15.0	10.0	10.7	5.7	3.6	3.6	5.0	0.7	0	15.0
1352–3	105	34.3	13.3	8.6	13.3	6.7	2.9	2.9	9.5	0	1.8	6.7
1353–4	88	31.8	20.5	14.8	6.8	3.4	3.4	1.1	3.4	3.4	1.2	10.2
1354–5	93	36.6	18.3	9.6	0	4.3	2.2	0	6.5	2.2	0	20.4
1355–6	53	28.3	20.8	20.7	13.2	3.8	0	0	1.9	1.9	0	9.4
1356–7	72	26.4	29.2	9.7	2.8	2.8	4.2	2.8	6.9	1.4	0	13.9
1357–8	52	32.7	28.9	9.6	3.9	0	1.9	3.8	3.8	0	0	15.4
1358–9	75	34.7	38.7	5.3	4.0	0	2.7	0	4.0	1.4	0	9.3
1359–60	64	40.6	28.1	7.8	6.3	4.7	0	0	1.6	0	0	10.9
1360–1	75	36.0	26.7	13.4	6.7	1.3	1.3	0	1.3	2.7	1.3	9.3
1361–2	574	17.1	45.7	6.8	8.5	4.7	2.6	0.2	2.4	0.9	0.7	10.5
1362–3	122	31.1	22.1	10.7	9.8	4.1	1.6	2.5	0.8	2.5	1.6	13.1
1363–4	62	22.6	32.3	9.7	4.8	1.6	6.5	1.6	4.8	3.2	3.2	9.7

Note: The figures for sons and daughters include some stepsons and stepdaughters, since the entry fines do not make clear this distinction. Kin includes those named as kin as well as those sharing the same surname but for which no relationship is specified.
* annual average

Table 7.6
Heiresses as a percentage of the number of male heirs on each manor, 1361–2

	Manors (%)
Woodland	Wargrave (66.7), Witney (12.5)
Somerset	Rimpton (100), Taunton Borough (100), Bishops Hull (93.3), Staplegrove (78.6), Nailsbourne (70.0), Poundisford (69.7), Holway (65.7), Otterford (25)
South Hampshire	Fareham (66.7) , Bishops Waltham (65.1), Bitterne (57.9), Brockhampton (52.9), Bishopstoke (43.8)
North Hampshire	Ecchinswell (100), Woodhay (81.3), Ashmansworth (66.7), Highclere (50), Burghclere (50)
Northern	Ivinghoe (42.6), West Wycombe (37.5), Adderbury (36.4), Brightwell (35.9), Waltham St Lawrence (30.8), Warfield (29.2), Harwell (0), Morton (0)
Wiltshire	Downton (73.3), East Knoyle (0)
Hampshire Chalk Plateau	Alresford (81.8), Cheriton (75), Bishops Sutton (70.6), Hambledon (69.2), Merdon (69.2), Droxford (55.6), East Meon (50), East Meon Church (25), Crawley (0), Overton (0), Twyford (0), Wield (0)
Eastern	Farnham (73.9), Bentley (64.3), Esher (0)

Note: Beauworth, Marwell, Alverstoke, Gosport, North Waltham, Upton, Bishops Fonthill, Bishopstone and Culham record no fines for inheritance in this year.

previous years and a noticeable number of women entered property as kin. This created a greater likelihood that property would move to new families.[16]

Another significant effect of the plagues on inheritance patterns, particularly after 1348–9, was an increase in the number of under-age heirs. Over the whole period 1269–1415 there are 150 instances of a guardian fining for wardship of a minor; fifty-nine of these, almost 40 per cent of the total, were in the three years between 1348–9 and 1350–1. When, for example, young John, son of John Crudeshate, inherited his father's messuage, virgate and two acres of purpresture at Elstead, in Farnham, his wardship was granted for twelve years to a relative, Roger Crudeshate; two pledges undertook that he would manage the tenements without waste. However, such wardships do not feature any more significantly in 1361–2 than during the remainder of the century.

Ways of modifying custom

Even when widows remarried, their interests did not always negate those of male heirs. Probably, sons often continued to work the land for their mother and live off the proceeds. Pressure on sons waiting to step into their mother's shoes was also alleviated by the manipulation of custom through the manorial court. Widows, and in some cases fathers and other relatives, could pass on the family holding to sons, or sometimes daughters or other heirs, during their own lifetimes by simply 'refusing' to fine. At Bishops Sutton in 1371–2, for example, Richard, son of John Cobb, fined 10s for a messuage and two cotlands of villein land containing twenty acres in Sutton 'which Joan, widow of John Cobb, after the death of her husband refused to fine to retain'. Some widows were able to provide in this way for the sons of a first marriage even after they had remarried; at Bishops Waltham in 1349–50, Gregory, son of Richard Pigg, fined 4s for a messuage and a half virgate in Ashton tithing for which 'John Warmond, second husband of Agnes, who had been the wife of Richard Pigg, refused to fine'. There are around 330 such fines over the period, starting in 1324–5. A number appear in the difficult year of 1348–9, but they are chiefly found in the later fourteenth and early fifteenth centuries, perhaps because with the easing of widespread land hunger heirs-in-waiting could now be affordably provided for. They are found predominantly in the manors of South Hampshire and are rare elsewhere, especially in the Taunton group. One reason for this may be that on the Taunton manors widows had to fine only if they wished to remarry and therefore the usual legal formula was hardly necessary, but at Rimpton, where widows were compelled to fine, none declined to do so. A more powerful reason is, presumably, that where land was scarce, men who married a widow for her land were less likely to waive their rights in favour of children of her former marriage. In the South Hampshire manors widows had to fine if they wanted to retain the land of their deceased husband, and it was therefore necessary to give a refusal in order to accommodate an heir. Occasionally land was formally quitclaimed by the widow, most commonly to sons but sometimes to daughters and more distant kin.

There are also examples of brothers and sisters, as well as other kin, refusing to

---

16. This is discussed more fully in Mullan, *Mortality*.

fine, quitclaiming and releasing estates to other family members at the moment of their own inheritance. In some instances it seems likely that customary descent, whether primogeniture or ultimogeniture, was being modified. At Bishopstoke in 1342–3, Henry, son of Walter Bickbrook, fined 10s for 5½ acres and a further half acre and meadow that Robert, his elder brother, had just inherited from his father. Although ultimogeniture was the rule for customary land on this manor, purpresture unassociated with villein land went to the elder brother; one may accordingly deduce that these acres were purpresture, and that the elder brother was, in this way, providing for a younger sibling.

Intrafamilial transfers *inter vivos*

While rules of inheritance were often manipulated, it is through the intrafamilial transfers of property *inter vivos* that we see the most obvious attempts to satisfy family requirements. The largest share of intrafamilial transfers *inter vivos* before the mid-fourteenth century was to sons (about 46 per cent) and to daughters (about 29 per cent). The larger, although not overwhelming, share of such grants to offspring were surrenders by the father, but some were from widows to children and stepchildren. Most other transfers were to brothers and sisters or, less commonly, to nephews, nieces and jointly to daughters and their husbands.

Grants to sons were regularly substantial, often including a whole holding, although it was common for the parent to retain for life a part for his or her own use. Across the estate as a whole, in the first half of our period, nearly half of all transfers to sons mention a dwelling, and more than 20 per cent were of virgates or half virgates. This varied by region, however. These proportions are typical of the eastern manors of the Farnham bailiwick, but in the Bishops Sutton group on the Hampshire Chalk Plateau all the examples involved virgate or half virgate holdings. By contrast, in the Taunton group, where there had been considerable break-up of holdings, virgates were few but cottages numerous.

Daughters were more likely to be given land during their parents' lifetime than they were to inherit. The properties they received in this way were characteristically small, usually just a few acres or a cottage holding, and only rarely a virgate or its subdivisions. In Downton bailiwick between 1263 and 1349 there were thirteen *inter vivos* transfers to daughters, one of which was of a virgate, one of half a virgate, and the rest of only a few acres. These gifts often represented the father's responsibility to provide land for his unmarried daughter as a dowry, and there are many instances in which transfers of property to a daughter were followed immediately by a fine from the future husband. For instance, in 1310–11 Joan, daughter of Thomas Attwater, was given an acre of land by her father; the following recorded fine was paid by John Stoteville for taking Joan in marriage together with her acre.

Although the needs of family members were often met piecemeal over time, if and when it was possible to satisfy them, a more complicated family settlement often involved more than one land transfer at once.[17] On the manor of Nailsbourne in

---

17. For examples on other estates, see Miller and Hatcher, *Medieval England*, pp. 148–9; Razi, 'Family', pp. 7–8.

1344–5, William Haveling, the second husband of Edith Haveling, surrendered property by twelve separate transfers to nine sons and two daughters.[18] One of these, another William, may have been the expected heir (the youngest son on the Taunton manors), since he received slightly more than the others by two separate transactions. The others received adjacent properties, each of three dayworks of overland, in the tithing of North Fulford. Each grant carried the condition that the recipient should build a house. At Staplegrove in 1340–1 a widow parcelled out her estate to her children by six consecutive surrenders, while at Downton in 1340–1 Simon Marshall surrendered to his son Roger and to his daughter Isabel a few acres of bordland each; later that year Agnes, Simon's widow, fined to retain her inheritance. This suggests that Simon had sought to make settlement and provision for his children when his death was in prospect, knowing that the bulk of his property would remain with his widow. Where land was particularly in demand, as it was at both Downton and Taunton, these kinds of intrafamilial arrangements were more common.[19]

Parents often relinquished a holding, or at least part of it, to their heir. A number of fines record that a parent should retain for life a portion of a holding so alienated, usually a half. But there were sometimes alternative provisions to ensure parents a degree of tenurial security and domestic comfort in their later years. On the manor of Staplegrove in 1299–1300 Agnes, the widow of Adam Millane, who had just received her inheritance of a messuage and a half virgate, immediately passed it to her son, another Adam, with the condition that he should provide her with reasonable victuals and clothes. It further adds that if Adam is to marry she will have her own hall and chamber and half of all the corn grown, for which she will pay none of the costs of cultivation. Other agreements go into fine detail, specifying, for instance, the precise value and quality of items such as shoes, clothing and linen and the exact quantities of grain to be delivered at certain times of year. At East Knoyle in 1292–3, Geoffrey Herbert surrendered his virgate holding to his son John, who was required to provide his father 'with respectable victuals every year and the second-best house to live in, and every other year a tunic worth 3s. and every year two pairs of shoes and two linen sheets; and if he is unable to be at table he will also have, apart from the abovesaid, four quarters two bushels of grain at the four terms of the year, half of wheat and half of barley'. Although relatively small in number and chiefly between a parent and son, these more detailed arrangements tend, for some reason, to occur in the late 1290s and very early 1300s and perhaps represent an exceptional degree of pressure on parents in a period when land was hard to come by.

It is tempting to imagine that transfers were conducted in a spirit of intrafamilial altruism and in most cases the nature of a transaction leaves us little reason to suppose otherwise.[20] Nonetheless, some more detailed enrolments providing for the

---

18. Edith had inherited from her first husband Nicholas in 1327. In 1329 she married William Bret, who typically adopted his wife's surname. This brought him a messuage and five acres of villein land and an acre of overland.

19. See also, for example, Staplegrove 1337 (Cross), 1340 (Austen); Nailsbourne 1382 (Haveling), 1362 Holway (Ash). Several also occur at Witney, where good land was hard to come by. For example: 1342 (Stanlake), 1342 and 1343 (Poughley), 1344 (Parnell), 1386 (Hayward), 1390 (Denley).

20. Razi, 'Family', p. 7.

security of parents suggest a fear of possible friction. Even grants to brothers and sisters, where we might expect a degree of benevolence, sometimes have stringent conditions attached. Typical of these is a grant of a messuage in Havant by Petronilla Mill to her brother Robert 'on condition that Robert maintains his sister in victuals equal to his own while she lives, and provides her with a suitable chamber', but the enrolment goes on to say that 'if they are not able to agree together over food Robert will pay Petronilla 10s a year and a bushel of wheat a week'. There are also many examples of parents, siblings, even sons and daughters having to recover land from family members through the manorial court. Few of these intrafamilial recoveries can be related to an earlier transfer, which suggests that trouble had arisen from an informal agreement made without the authority of the court. In Bishops Waltham in 1276–7, for instance, William Free recovered land worth 9d 'which he had conceded to his brother'. Most of the fifty-three such intrafamilial recoveries are from the period before 1330, when tensions over available property were more likely.

Sometimes, if rarely, intrafamilial transfers resulted from the intervention of the court itself. At Twyford in 1302–3 Adam Whitewey was granted a half virgate because his brother Thomas 'was foolish and performed the rents and services incompetently'. Likewise at Ivinghoe in 1326–7 Adam Orpet was elected by the whole homage to take on a messuage and virgate 'on account of his brother's destitution'. Other cases, although small in number, are of lands said to be wasted or abandoned. Self-evidently, these instances of the intrafamilial transfer of property were attempts to resolve preceding family problems, but in character they belong with the types of intervention that were discussed in the previous chapter.

Marriage

One of the most common mechanisms by which land passed from family to family was through marriage, whether to an unmarried woman or to a widow, this being a significant way in which male tenants could acquire land of their own or augment what they already possessed.[21] Fines arising on such occasions are identifiable from the beginning of our period. A decennial distribution of marriage fines over the whole estate and period illustrates a gentle upswing in proportion, although the curve is less steep than that of the increasing proportion of extrafamilial transactions. Not surprisingly, the number of marriages varied very considerably from manor to manor, depending chiefly on the size of the resident population (see Table 2.7).[22]

Although transfers by marriage are classified as extrafamilial, they were for obvious reasons akin to intrafamilial transfers, and shared some of their characteristics. The nature of the properties acquired through marriage is especially noteworthy in this respect. The majority of these fines involved a dwelling with some land, and a high proportion included virgated tenements. We have already seen, in Chapter 3, that these had a higher propensity than other forms of property to be retained within families. The high incidence of the laconic term 'land' in the late thirteenth century

---

21. For a discussion of the manor court and marriage see Poos and Bonfield (eds), *Select cases*, pp. clxvii–clxxxi.

22. Chapter 2, pp. 25–7.

Table 7.7
Decennial distribution of for fines for marriage as a percentage of all fines, and the number associated with transfers of virgated holdings, 1263–1415

Years	Total fines recording transfers marriage (no.)	Marriage fines as a share of all fines (%)	Transfers at marriage with virgated holdings (no.)	Transfers at marriage with virgated holdings (%)
1320–9	267	11.0	135	50.6
1330–9	437	11.6	221	50.6
1340–9	663	10.6	326	49.2
1320–49	**1367**	**11.0**	**682**	**50.0**
1350–9	559	11.6	283	50.6
1360–9	575	16.6	259	45
1370–9	322	14.2	149	46
1350–79	**1456**	**13.8**	**691**	**47.5**
1380–9	257	12.3	114	44.4
1390–9	229	11.8	119	52
1400–9	253	13.2	128	50.6
1410–15	189	10.4	112	59.3
1380–1415	**928**	**11.9**	**473**	**51.0**

precludes any sure analysis until the early fourteenth century. When the evidence becomes reliable, about the 1320s, it is immediately apparent that the proportion of marriages that secured virgated tenements was much higher than the proportion of extrafamilial purchases that did so. In the period 1320–49, for example, while only 10.7 per cent of all extrafamilial fines secured a virgated holding, 50 per cent did so through marriage (see Tables 3.3 and 7.7). After the Black Death, although the number of marriages fell sharply (see Tables 2.7 and 2.8), the transfer of virgates at marriage remained as common as before, and the pattern was sustained through the last decades of our period.

Conclusion

Although customs governing the movement of property between family members were important for the transfer of peasant holdings in the late thirteenth and earlier fourteenth centuries, there was no common set of rules. However, customs across the Winchester estates were exceptionally favourable to widows, so that widows were frequently attractive as marriage partners because of the property in their control. The extent of this attractiveness varied according to time and place. Widows and their property were particularly desirable when land was hard to come by, as Titow demonstrated from the evidence of the Taunton manors; marriages to widows became less numerous as land became more easy to acquire by other means after 1349. Inheritance by widows frequently complicated the direct succession of holdings through the male line, delaying a son's succession sometimes to the point that the inheritance passed from the widow to a grandchild or a child of the second marriage. In some cases, however, it is apparent that a son continued to gain a livelihood from his father's tenement even though it was held in his mother's name.

Both primogeniture and ultimogeniture were to be found across the Winchester estate, and their effects upon the land market differed. Differences between individual manors are generally more striking than interregional contrasts, although the Taunton manors had a sufficient number of distinguishing features – land scarcity, fragmentation of holdings and inheritance by ultimogeniture – to stand out as a regional group. Ultimogeniture was characteristic of two regions of the Winchester estate where the land market was most active, namely the Somerset manors and those of South Hampshire, although it also preponderated on the Wiltshire manors. This suggests that ultimogeniture tended to encourage the development of an active land market, but that the strength of this stimulus depended upon other local circumstances. The operation of particular inheritance customs did not ensure that patterns of inheritance remained constant, however. The epidemics of the fourteenth century demonstrate well how crisis mortality and demographic change influenced the way in which property passed within families as well as between them, causing inheritances to pass to a wider range of kin than usual. In particular, the epidemic of 1361 can be shown to have caused particularly high mortality among potential male heirs.

The harsher consequences of inheritance customs could be modified by different forms of accommodation between family members. Sometimes widows waived their right to inherit in favour of sons by simply refusing to fine for properties to which they had a customary title. In other cases parents made over property to sons in exchange for an understanding that their livelihood would be guaranteed, whether by a private understanding or by a formal written agreement. Other family settlements were achieved by transfers of property *inter vivos*, which were eased by the greater availability of land after the mid-fourteenth century. Sons were often given property to support them by this means, and it was more common for daughters to be given property by their parents than for them to inherit. By marriage, daughters often transferred customary family property to the families of their husbands.

Chapter 8

Buyers and sellers

The implications of the fourteenth-century increase in the proportion of peasant property transferred outside of families, both between the living and *post mortem*, were wide-ranging. In particular, a higher proportion of transfers was motivated by principles other than family support, which suggests a shift towards more commercial considerations. This is most directly suggested by the increased share of extrafamilial transfers *inter vivos*. However, insofar as transfers of vacant land *post mortem* were to tenants exchanging or accumulating property, they too were primarily market transactions. The present chapter will examine buying and selling of land from the standpoint of those obtaining lands by processes of extrafamilial transfer, in some cases acquiring on new terms lands that had long been associated with particular families and particular customs.

An unpredictable feature of the growth of extrafamilial transfers was an increasing tendency to identify properties by naming them after their former tenants, families that, in many instances, had long disappeared. This was partly because the occupation of holdings was now more transient, often too brief for the sitting tenant's name to be a useful identifier.[1] Before about 1300 the names of holdings, where given in the rolls, predominantly relate to the location of the property or to some other physical characteristic. If a family name was in local use, as was probably often the case, it could have been deduced from the sitting tenant's name and was hardly worth recording. Increasingly during the fourteenth century, however, holdings were recorded with family names unconnected with either incoming or outgoing tenant, until, by the early years of the fifteenth century, this was exceedingly common. Between 1349–50 and 1354–5, a period in which there were a large number of transfers, there are about 280 family-named holdings mentioned, a number which rose to about 340 between 1360 and 1365 and to about 550 between 1410 and 1415. Both customary as well as other lands were subject to this form of nomenclature, which was more frequent on manors with a more active land market. Some of the families so memorialised in tenement names had disappeared from the holding many years before. In the 1390s there was a half virgate at Brockhampton called 'Mourhous', named from Adam Moor, who died before 1363, and a virgate called 'Rayes', named from John Ray, who surrendered it also in that year. The toft and cotland called 'Chaffynges' and acre of purpresture called 'Chaffyngeslade' in Woodhay in 1413–14 had belonged to Geoffrey Chaffing, who had died during the Black Death, over sixty years earlier. The increased tendency during the fourteenth century for tenants to accumulate several holdings led to a breakdown of the one-to-one association between traditional units and occupying families and meant that a single tenant's lands might retain the names of more than one former occupant. The composite estate of John Cous at East Meon

---

1.   Harvey, *Westminster Abbey*, p. 319.

in 1396, made up solely of cottages and tofts, included a toft called 'Chepman', named after Richard Chapman who surrendered it in 1365, and another called 'Hugheslond'. Although it may always have been common in everyday practice to give family names to holdings, the increased recording of those names in the pipe rolls was a feature of the weakening of traditional bonds between families and their land.

Transactions between families *inter vivos*

Most extrafamilial transactions *inter vivos* were simple surrenders of property by one peasant to be transferred through the manorial court to the use of another. The fines themselves sometimes demonstrate that, as we should expect, such transactions had a history before they reached the court. At Bishops Waltham in 1271–2, for example, Andrew Claille fined for a licence to 'hold three acres of the lord's tenement which he had bought from Henry Ballaster', and in Merdon in 1297 a fine legitimised the transfer of 1½ acres that had been sold by the previous tenant. An entry fine for land transferred at East Meon in 1299 records that Matilda, wife of Walter Digg, 'was examined within the bar because that land was her right, and she was granted that the said sale be confirmed'. Such examples are uncommon, however, and we usually know nothing of the terms of transfer. As that implies, the pipe rolls do not record the prices paid by those buying land through manor court procedures.

Something of the administration's attitude to a burgeoning market may be implied by the formulaic wording of fines. Before 1297 they were usually said to be 'by concession' (*ex concessione*) of the outgoing tenant, but from then on they were normally 'by surrender' (*ex redditione*); the latter expression, which first occurs in the pipe rolls in 1291, was not instantly adopted as a standard and was employed only infrequently during the following six years.[2] The terminology of *redditio* was more specific to the conveyance of unfree tenures, since it emphasised the requirement that the tenant of such property should surrender it to the lord before it could be granted to another tenant; the term *concessio*, which could be used equally readily of freehold conveyances, had no such special significance. Similar changes in conveyancing practice on other estates from the middle of Edward I's reign have been observed not only on the manor of Redgrave in Suffolk but also on the estates of St Albans Abbey, the manors of the abbot of Crowland and on several Norfolk manors.[3]

Analysis of the careers of many thousands of tenants indicates a more conservative picture of the land market than we might have expected. We can compare the holdings of deceased tenants, identifiable through fines for transfers *post mortem*, with their earlier involvement as buyers of land. On the small manor of Esher in Surrey, where a relatively busy market was in existence from a comparatively early date, *post mortem* fines give us the names of twenty-two deceased tenants between

---

2. The expression *sursum reddere*, commonly found on other estates, is rarely employed in the pipe rolls.

3. R.M. Smith, 'Women's property rights under customary law: some developments in the thirteenth and fourteenth centuries', *Transactions of the Royal Historical Society*, 5th series, 36 (1986), pp. 176–80; see also Williamson, 'Norfolk', p. 58; F.M. Page, *The estates of Crowland Abbey, a study in manorial organisation* (Cambridge, 1934), pp. 336, 346.

1350 and 1415, of whom only eight can be shown to have acquired land from other families during their lifetime. This suggests that even here a majority of tenants never acquired land in this way. On many manors where we have more names the proportion was higher still: 76.5 per cent at Holway, 77.5 per cent at West Wycombe, 79.7 per cent at Nailsbourne, 79.8 per cent at Downton, 88 per cent at Bishopstoke and 90.7 per cent at Bitterne. This implies both that only a minority of tenants bought land, and that the majority of buyers were not existing tenants at all but rather non-inheriting children and migrants who sought property through the market. At Esher there were, further to the eight buyers of non-family land who were established tenants of the manor, sixty-eight who seem to have had no holding of their own other than that secured outside of the family lands. High mortality had created greatly improved opportunities for those who had not inherited family property or who wanted better.

Buyers and sellers

Various studies have drawn attention not only to the steady increase in the proportion of extrafamilial transactions over the period but also to the varying proportion between the numbers of buyers and sellers, which can provide further insights into the dynamics of the market. Not only were some manors more heavily involved in an inter-peasant market in land but some individuals within manors were more active in buying and selling than their peers.

Table 8.1 demonstrates a general decrease from about 1370 in the proportion of tenants who either acquired or sold property by extrafamilial transactions on more than one occasion. The decrease is especially marked among buyers. The absence of this effect during the 1350s and 1360s corresponds to the sudden burst of new opportunities for acquiring good property that was created by the epidemics of 1348–9 and 1361–2, but from then onwards the market was characterised by fewer buyers and sellers and a smaller proportion who were actively engaged.[4] The table also shows that the proportion of buyers to sellers increased slightly after the Black Death. This was presumably caused by the accumulation of holdings by a minority of tenants, a feature in the development of the market to be discussed at greater length in Chapter 9.

Aggregates here, as in other contexts, conceal local variation in the propensity to trade property. On some manors – notably those in the regions identified in Chapter 2 as having an exceptionally active land market – we find significantly more active buyers and sellers than on others. At Witney the proportion of buyers who bought more than once – trafficking chiefly in small pieces of assart land – was nearly 35 per cent of all buyers between 1320 and 1349 and 33 per cent between 1350 and 1379. Between 1325 and 1349 the vicar of Witney, Richard Dormer, occurs as a buyer twenty-seven times and as a seller eight times. On the Taunton manors, too, busy buyers were common. Between 1350 and 1379 29 per cent of buyers at Holway appear more than once; on this manor between 1327 and 1349 Richard Polruan occurs nineteen times as a buyer of land and as a seller only once. A similarly high

4.   The same phenomenon has been observed at Coltishall (Norfolk) over a similar period: Campbell, 'Population pressure', pp. 109–10.

recurrence of buyers is to be found at Esher.

Most of those involved in buying land with some frequency are found selling also, as in the case of the vicar of Witney, suggesting that they treated property as a marketable asset. At Witney several borough families – the Lamberts, Herings, Abingdons and Stanlakes – engaged vigorously in extrafamilial traffic in assart holdings. In the 1270s many of the manor's assart had been in the hands of around seventy-six burgesses, in particular those of an elite of around a dozen men. Robert Hering, for example, who in 1278–9 held eleven houses and forty-five acres of assart, was a wool merchant who also rented demesne and fulling mills. The lay subsidy roll of 1327 confirms the later existence of this elite, several of whose members were from families prominent six decades earlier. Richard Stanlake, the wealthiest, belonged to a family involved in no fewer than 159 transactions in assart between 1263 and 1349: the busiest family for these lands in this manor. Frequent buyers and sellers occur elsewhere on the bishop's estate. Between 1350 and 1367, John Cleps of Holway is found in four fines as a buyer of property and in seven instances as a seller. And from 1350 to 1379 Adam Moor of the same manor bought and sold on four occasions each. There are hundreds of similar examples.

Some tenants bought and sold on more than one manor. Common names and shared names among kin make it impossible to measure this reliably, but such activity may reasonably be deduced when transactions involve unusual names and property on neighbouring manors. Thomas Billing purchased land in Holway in 1324–5 and at Bishops Hull in 1330–1, and later sold parcels of both. But such intermanorial activity is more commonly found in the later period of this study: Thomas Bacot – probably a single individual, since there is no other occurrence of this surname – was involved in several extrafamilial acquisitions and sales of lands between 1395–6 and 1408–9 in the manors of Holway and Staplegrove as well as in the borough of Taunton; these were chiefly small parcels, but included two messuages and 2½ virgates at Staplegrove. Nicholas Chilliswood was active in the market between 1354–5 and 1390–1 on the manors of Bishops Hull, Holway and Otterford. In the early fifteenth century Walter Deneby traded parcels of land in Holway, Bishops Hull, Poundisford and Taunton borough. Possibly because of the history of the Taunton manors as one federated unit such intermanorial activity was more common there, but the main reason for the quality of our evidence is surely the contiguity of these manors. Such examples are less easily found elsewhere. In South Hampshire in 1351–2, Roger Cupping acquired a messuage and a half virgate of villein land in Droxford and in 1357–8 is found selling a toft and half virgate in East Meon a few miles to the east. John Plaistow traded parcels in Hambledon, East Meon and Bishops Waltham.[5] Evidence of such intermanorial interests, although inevitably restricted because of the scattered nature of the Winchester manors, suggests that it was not uncommon for more active buyers to be dealing across manorial boundaries, and this may have occurred even when the manors in question belonged to different lords.

Women, too, were involved in this developing property market as buyers and sellers (Table 8.1). Their marital status is usually unrecorded, but between 1320 and 1349 45 per cent of women buyers for whom we are given any status are described

---

5. For comparable East Anglian evidence from 1491, see R.H. Britnell, 'Tenant farming and farmers: eastern England', in *AHEW* III, p. 616.

Table 8.1
The number of recorded extrafamilial transfers inter vivos *on the Winchester manors:*
buyers and sellers, 1320–1415

Years	No. of transfers	No. of buyers	No. of women buyers (% in brackets)	No. of buyers more than once (% brackets)	No. of sellers	No. of women sellers (% in brackets)	No. of sellers more than once (% in brackets)	Ratio of buyers to sellers
1320–9	1019	814	146 (14.3)	142 (17.4)	831	223 (26.8)	120 (14.4)	0.98
1330–9	1670	1036	243 (14.6)	230 (22.2)	1317	316 (24.0)	233 (17.7)	0.79
1340–9	1868	1479	362 (19.4)	285 (19.3)	1518	427 (28.1)	268 (17.7)	0.97
1350–9	1908	1564	183 (9.6)	253 (16.2)	1508	254 (16.9)	220 (14.5)	1.04
1360–9	1637	1320	158 (9.7)	236 (17.9)	1290	213 (16.5)	191 (14.8)	1.02
1370–9	984	869	83 (8.4)	103 (11.9)	815	111 (13.6)	97 (11.9)	1.07
1380–9	986	825	74 (7.5)	118 (14.3)	766	113 (14.8)	114 (14.9)	1.08
1390–9	785	684	50 (6.4)	67 (9.9)	642	91 (14.2)	92 (14.5)	1.07
1400–9	819	716	59 (7.2)	97 (13.5)	675	94 (13.9)	79 (11.7)	1.06
1410–15	796	750	51 (6.4)	81 (10.8)	696	113 (16.2)	75 (10.8)	1.08

as daughters, so were presumably unmarried. Most of the remainder acted jointly with their husbands; only a handful were widows. Between 1350 and 1415 the proportion of female buyers described as daughters fell to 10.5 per cent as a result of a large increase in the number of purchases made jointly by husband and wife. Widows remained a tiny minority, but were proportionately more significant as sellers in this period. Of those instances where we have information about the status of women selling land, 40 per cent are described as widows and only 15 per cent as daughters.[6]

Although we have separately examined intrafamilial and extrafamilial transfers of property, many hundreds, if not thousands, of individuals were engaged in acquiring and releasing properties both within and between families. Such was Thomas Dawe of Poundisford manor who, in 1349–50, inherited a messuage and ferling in the tithing of Leigh. The following year he surrendered a cottage to someone outside his family, and at about the same time secured a vacant messuage and half virgate following the death of another tenant. In 1352–3 he inherited half a cottage from his brother, but sold it again outside his family the same year. Two years later he surrendered the ferling he had inherited in 1349–50, but in 1355–6 secured a few further acres, again following another tenant's death. His active engagement in the market, using inherited properties as commercial assets and buying land that had previously belonged to other families, is representative of many commercially active peasants at this time. Many went on to create large composite holdings, a phenomenon to be examined in Chapter 9.

6. For women in the land market, see Bennett, *Women*, pp. 110–14, 160–8; M.E. Mate, *Daughters, wives and widows after the Black Death: women in Sussex, 1350–1535* (Woodbridge, 1998), pp. 109–16; Poos and Bonfield (eds), *Select cases*, pp. clxxviii–clxxxi.

Reasons for selling

At a time when the holding of land was all-important as a measure of security and wealth, it is pertinent to ask why a tenant might wish to let his holding pass outside the family. In the vast majority of such transactions the fines give no explanation, but in some instances the reason is evident.

A small number of fines tell us that the outgoing tenant was surrendering property on account of poverty or destitution. At West Wycombe in 1326–7, for example, John Nichol the younger fined 2s for a messuage and virgate to which he was elected by the whole homage of the manor because Philip Cake 'refused to hold and surrendered in court into the lord's hands on account of destitution, nor did any of Philip's kin want to fine for it'. Similarly, in 1351–2 Nicholas Caerwent fined 1s for a messuage, virgate and 6½ acres of moor and heath in Farnham 'which Robert Foghelesbrook was unable to hold by reason of poverty and surrendered it into the lord's hands'. Sometimes this explanation was linked to the poor quality of the property in question. At Bishops Fonthill in 1331–2 John Pointel secured a messuage and a half virgate that Robert Cook refused to hold on account of poverty and the weakness of the land. Most transfers where poverty is cited as an explanation involved larger customary tenements, virgates, half virgates and a few ferlings. The episcopal administration was perhaps concerned to record the reasons for the surrender of these holdings as a memorandum of why a family's hereditary interests were forfeited.

There were fewer grounds to record the reason for transfers of smaller holdings and assarts. Among tenants of these properties, too, poverty could create problems calling for extreme measures.[7] It is difficult otherwise to account for the increased number of extrafamilial transfers during famine years when poorer families needed to raise cash for food.[8] Hugh Cartdean, who acquired four separate half acres of assart and a further acre and rood of land at Witney in 1312–13 and 1313–14, sold them all in 1316–17 and, now presumably landless, never appears in the records again. Some tenants were in debt to others and were forced to sell when they could not repay. The rolls are almost silent on this, but in a rare instance at Witney in 1330–1 John Hedlow fined for a plot that he held by virtue of a writ of *eligit* for a debt that Simon Bear owed him upon recognisance. This writ, introduced by statute in 1285, gave creditors upon a recognisance the option of taking half the creditor's land, as well as half of his goods other than plough beasts, until the debt was settled.[9] At Merdon in 1291–2, Roger, son of Christina Thorn, fined for a messuage which his mother had acquired from William, brother of Simon Burley, by virtue of paying Simon's debts.

Some fines record the transfer of property because of the former tenant's incapacity, which presumably implies old age or poor health. At Bishops Waltham in 1273–5, William Carpenter fined 2s for a cottage and five acres of villein land that had been surrendered by Lucy Durrand 'because she was incapable'. And at Wargrave in 1297–8, Walter Frances sold out to Agatha Ackerman 'because he is blind'. As we

---

7. M. Bailey, 'Peasant welfare in England, 1290–1348', *Economic History Review*, 51 (1998), pp. 223–51; Campbell, 'Population pressure', pp. 107–20; Schofield, 'Dearth, debt', pp. 1–17.

8. Page, *Medieval bishops*, p. 19.

9. T.F.T. Plucknett, *Legislation of Edward I* (Oxford, 1949), pp. 149–50.

have seen, some tenants were forcibly dispossessed by manor courts for similar reasons.[10] Occasionally property was sold in exchange for a maintenance contract, the new tenant undertaking to provide for the former tenant in some way. Such surrenders are akin to the intrafamilial maintenance contracts discussed in the previous chapter. A number of such transactions arranged to accommodate the former tenant on the holding, usually in a house but sometimes in a room; others make provision for victuals and clothes. There are in all thirty-two such agreements, distributed across the estate, of which twenty-seven are from the period 1263–1349 and only five from a later date. A number of them give details of the maintenance to be expected. For example, at Hambledon in 1297, Maynard Scott surrendered his messuage and half virgate to Simon Sharp on condition that he should provide Maynard and his wife with a house for life, together with various quantities of grain, ½d a week and 6d for shoes every two years. Ralph Gander, who acquired a messuage and half virgate from Adam Standfast in Staplegrove in 1297, was required to provide Adam with 'a room on the south side of the hall' with food and clothing, and also to 'acquit him of all rents, dues and services incumbent on the said land'. Some examples explicitly comment on the infirmity of the former tenant. At Bishopstone in 1347, Thomas, son of Walter Uphill, secured a messuage and two virgates from Edith Gale 'who is blind, old and decrepit', but in return she was given accommodation in the house. At Wargrave in 1297, Agatha Ackerman took over a messuage and three acres from Walter Frances on condition that she should provide for him because he was blind. These provisions, which in effect were annuities for the life of the former tenant, were probably the means by which the incoming tenant paid for the land. In the great majority of extrafamilial transactions, however, no such provisions are stated and it is likely that a simple cash payment, with the ratification of the court, was sufficient to secure a holding.

The exchange of lands was often also mutually beneficial as a means to rationalise holdings, especially in manors where there had been much fragmentation of former units. There are more than 700 examples of exchanges between 1260 and 1415, spread more or less evenly over the period. Most involved small parcels; of the 381 exchanges before 1350, 265 were of three acres or less, most of the remainder being plots, 'lands' and, on the Taunton manors, dayworks. Exchanges of larger customary holdings are very rare; only one full virgate and ten half virgates were exchanged between 1263 and 1415. Until the 1290s it was usual for inter-peasant exchanges to be dealt with in a single transaction, but, from that time, probably as a means to increase the bishop's income, they required two separate but sequential fines. As a result, the 705 fines for transfers of this kind actually equate to a little over half this number of exchanges. A typical example is from Holway in 1312–13, where Robert Shoreditch fined 1s for a half acre of overland surrendered by Thomas Leach in exchange for an equivalent half acre elsewhere. The following transaction records Thomas's acquisition of a matching property from Robert. Such exchanges might be subject to public scrutiny. In 1302–3, again at Holway, an exchange of an acre between Edmund Parker and Roger Halliwell took place only after 'it was found by the two neighbouring tithings of Ruishton and Henlade that it is to the profit of Roger and

---

10.   Chapter 6, pp. 84–5.

Edmund'. At Ivinghoe in 1305–6, half acres were exchanged between Henry Dodedean and Gilbert Seybrook 'because it is to the advantage of the lord's villeinage'. Many, if not most, exchanges were local; it was common for the clerk to note that the properties in question were in same tithing, place, meadow or even furlong, and phrases such as 'beside his land', 'near his land' and 'opposite his tenement' are frequent. Some examples indicate a precise purpose for the exchange, as at Ivinghoe in 1305–6 where one half acre was exchanged for another 'for building on'.

There was considerable regional variation in the propensity to exchange, and the principal observable differences were maintained throughout the period. They do not correspond closely with other indices of high activity in the land market, although around 60 per cent of exchanges took place among the manors of the Taunton group. The fact that on these manors exchanges continue in considerable volume throughout the fourteenth and early fifteenth centuries indicates that they were the result of some enduring regional characteristic. By contrast, at Twyford, where there were fifty-eight exchanges, forty-three of these took place in 1314–15, and all involved Walter Woodlock. In the Woodland and Northern groups of manors to the north of the estate – at Witney and Wargrave but also at West Wycombe, Ivinghoe and Warfield – exchanges were particularly rare, with only a dozen over the whole period. The existence of lately colonised land seems to have made exchanges less necessary or desirable on these manors. But this cannot be the whole answer because in other regions, such as Wiltshire, where resources were more restricted, exchanges are also very few. Since the wish to exchange land arose from a utilitarian need to rationalise the layout of individual holdings, it is likely that the reasons for intermanorial differences relate to features of agrarian topography that have yet to be explored on the Winchester estate.

A developing market in property also allowed tenants to dispose of land that was surplus to requirements as a ready way of raising cash. Numerous entry fines recording a surrender of property obtained through marriage note that the wife 'was examined in court'. There are more than 600 such extrafamilial transfers of a wife's holdings over the period 1263–1415; before 1300 there was rarely more than one a year across the whole episcopal estate, but they become more numerous over the following decades to reach a dozen or so a year in the 1340s. This accords with evidence elsewhere that the procedure of examination, designed to protect a married woman's dower, became more common from the late thirteenth century.[11] In the aftermath of the Black Death their number fell to single figures with the slackening demand for non-family land in general, but by the 1360s the numbers were back to a dozen or more and in line with the overall increase in extrafamilial transfers. Lands acquired by marriage were not necessarily close to the husband's lands and may often have been difficult to manage; having acquired them, many couples preferred the cash they would raise, so they were surrendered outside the family soon after the marriage. It is likely that the prospective sale of such lands was an expected outcome of many marriage settlements. At Merdon there were twenty-eight extrafamilial surrenders of a wife's property between the Black Death and 1415, mostly in the 1360s and 1370s, implying that perhaps as much as 30 per cent of wives' property

---

11. Smith, 'Women's property rights', pp. 182–4.

was surrendered after their marriage.[12] In thirteen of these instances, mostly before the 1370s, the marriage is traceable through a settlement of the bride's marriage portion recorded in the pipe rolls, and in nearly all cases the disposal of the property took place within a year or two of that event. At Bishops Waltham, in the later part of our period, surrenders of a wife's land followed about one in four marriages. However, Merdon and Bishops Waltham were manors on which such transfers were particularly numerous, together with East Meon, Witney, Fareham, Farnham, and to a lesser extent some manors of the Wargrave group. They were much rarer in Bishops Sutton and the surrounding manors, and almost entirely absent on manors in the western part of the estate, in Wiltshire, Somerset and north-west Hampshire.

Extrafamilial transfers *post mortem*

In all periods, the bishop's officers intervened through manor courts to fine new tenants for holdings that had escheated to the lord. The significance of transactions of this sort for the land market was different from those transferred *inter vivos*, in that their extrafamilial status was mediated more actively by the lord. Instead of a tenant requesting in court to transfer property in his own interest, in these cases the lord or an agent on his behalf transferred to new families properties that were vacant by death, rejection or forfeiture; the former tenant therefore gained nothing by the transaction. They may be thought of as 'indirect' extrafamilial exchanges. This difference from transfers *inter vivos* is important, as we saw in Chapter 5, in accounting for the terms on which *post mortem* transfers were negotiated.

Until around 1300, and in many instances beyond, fines tell us little, if anything, about why a property moved outside a family on the death of a tenant. At the turn of the century, however, it became more common to state this cause, which was at that time often simply that the deceased tenant had left no heirs. In Farnham in 1299–1300 Richard the doctor (*medicus*) and Cassandra his wife fined for a cottage 'which came into the lord's hands as his escheat through the death of Herbery Porcher who died without heirs'. Thereafter this wording, or variants on it, becomes usual in such circumstances. Describing a holding as an escheat in the Winchester pipe rolls implied the lord's authority to choose a successor, but in practice a new tenant was often chosen by local juries. Escheats so described were usually standard customary holdings, whose descent engaged greater interest from the episcopal administration.

Transactions *post mortem* resulting from the refusal of heirs to fine constitute another distinct category, and one particularly indicative of changing pressures in the land market. Such cases were fewer in the earlier part of our period, when land was hard to come by and the prospect of inheriting land was often the sole hope of obtaining it. An early example, from Bishops Sutton in 1335, is one of the most explicit. Roger Haywood paid a fine of 1s for a messuage and land in Ropley containing one virgate 'which remained in the hands of various bishops of Winchester

---

12. It seems apparent that not all marriages resulted in a fine. For instance, of the twenty-eight fines at Merdon in which the wife is examined in court, in six cases, all from 1372 onwards, no earlier fine for marriage can be found. Some may, of course, occur in missing rolls but this cannot be the whole explanation since no rolls are missing between the 1330s and 1380–1.

Table 8.2

The number of elections to holdings on the Winchester bishopric estate, 1283–1349

1283–9	1290–9	1300–9	1310–19	1320–9	1330–9	1340–9	1283–1349
1	6	6	29	14	43	18	117

for a long time as devastated and abandoned because none of the kin of John and Thomas wanted to fine for the same although a proclamation was made concerning it at many law-days'. Roger took the land 'as the lord's escheat for want of kin'. Commonly lands were said simply to have been abandoned, as in this case, but sometimes the reasons for tenants' reluctance to take up property were developed a little further. Poverty or destitution were sometimes a stated cause for the abandonment of holdings, just as they sometimes explain their transfer to new tenants, and the poor quality of a tenement could also be a reason. At Milton in East Knoyle in 1330–1, William Breakbatt refused to hold a messuage and virgate on account of his own poverty and the weakness (*debilitas*) of the land; indeed, the land was so poor that no one wanted it. In such circumstances manor courts were often expected to supply a tenant by compulsory 'election'. Following William Breakbatt's refusal, Walter Aylward was elected by the homage, although reluctance on his part is suggested by the fact that the bishop pardoned him an entry fine.[13]

Elections to holdings did not occur on every manor of the estate, nor were they spread evenly over time (Table 8.2), which implies that courts varied in their practice. Geographically, they were most numerous on manors in central Hampshire: two-thirds (78) of the 117 recorded elections took place on fifteen manors in Hampshire, 39 of them on the three manors of Bishops Sutton, Cheriton and North Waltham in the Hampshire Chalk Plateau region. The remaining third were on twelve manors scattered across the rest of the estate. The concentration at Bishops Sutton, Cheriton and North Waltham was due primarily to the abandonment of holdings there and the reluctance of tenants to fine for them. Entry fines at Cheriton and North Waltham for virgated holdings were among the lowest for any manor of the estate, suggesting a lack of demand. Yields of wheat were not high on any of the three manors, those for Bishops Sutton being very low indeed. Chronologically, the bulk of elections occurred during the period of the Great Famine in the mid-1310s, and there was another very large concentration during the 1330s.

In the later fourteenth and early fifteenth centuries a larger proportion of extrafamilial transactions *post mortem* were the result of the property having escheated to the bishop, but this was not simply because tenants had died without heirs. It is commonly recorded in this period that a tenement 'came into the lord's hands as an escheat because no one of the kin cared to fine, although a proclamation was made according to the custom of the manor'. These fines indicate that an heir of some description was thought to exist but that he or she had found some preferable alternative. Predictably, escheats of this kind occur mostly on manors that had the largest numbers of vacant holdings as a result of depopulation, such as those of North Hampshire and Wiltshire. Land here was now so easily available that even surviving

---

13.   For some examples in the aftermath of the Black Death, see Levett, 'Black Death', pp. 46, 51, 85.

family might safely reject their patrimony in favour of something better. Between 1350 and 1415, three-quarters of the 497 extrafamilial transfers *post mortem* of holdings described as tofts, most of which were customary tenements, were available because 'no one of the kin cared to fine'.

The transfer of land to new families was most in evidence on manors where the reservoir of unclaimed land was large. At Downton in 1355–6, thirty-three tenements containing 448 acres were vacant, and by 1382–3 the situation had actually worsened; the forty-three holdings then vacant contained about 480 acres. On this manor, nearly 60 per cent of all land transfers in the decade after 1348–9 were *post mortem* transactions in which the property moved to different families.[14] The contrast with the pre-plague situation could not have been more complete, for on this manor in the years before the Black Death extrafamilial transfers of property *post mortem* constituted fewer than 5 per cent of transfers. Similarly, between 1320 and 1349, only 24 of 518 transactions at Downton were extrafamilial and *post mortem*.

Leases

Another indication that tenants saw their holdings as potential marketable assets is evidence for inter-peasant leasing. The terms of recorded transactions are not always spelled out in sufficient detail to distinguish a lease from a fee-farm (a sale reserving a rent charge), but leases are clearly revealed whenever fines for transfers *inter vivos* note that the property was to be held for a period of years or for life.[15] Peasant leasing is known to have been widespread in some contexts, even in the thirteenth century,[16] being perhaps most common where there were most obstacles to outright sales.[17] As a response to temporary incapacity or poverty it was often preferable to permanent alienation.[18] Leases were sometimes a way of providing for old age, since they supplied the lessee with a regular income while protecting the interests of his heir.[19] Some had a reversion clause, often with the stipulation that the lessee should surrender the property at the end of his term in the same state as he had received it. Such leases do not occur before 1270–1, but between then and 1348–9 there are about 340 of them. But the recorded instances of leasing do not correspond to the true number of leases. Lessors and lessees could agree short-term contracts without the necessity for a formal record, and inter-peasant leases before 1270 may be poorly documented simply because nobody saw any reason to enrol their ephemeral details. An oral agreement in the presence of witnesses was sufficient.[20] Even where there

---

14. Titow, 'Lost rents', pp. 109–12.

15. Levett, 'Black Death', pp. 125–6.

16. Homans, *English villagers*, pp. 202, 212; R.H. Hilton, *A medieval society: the West Midlands at the end of the thirteenth century*, 2nd edn (Cambridge, 1983), pp. 161–3; Schofield, *Peasant and community*, p. 20; Williamson, 'Norfolk', pp. 53–4.

17. M.K. McIntosh, *The royal manor of Havering, 1200–1500* (Cambridge, 1986), p. 123.

18. Harvey, *Westminster Abbey*, pp. 214, 320.

19. Levett, 'Black Death', pp. 126–7.

20. Harvey, *Westminster Abbey*, p. 320.

Table 8.3.
Numbers of recorded inter-peasant leases, 1271–1415 (excluding the Brockhampton leases after 1352, whose number is given in brackets)

1271–9	30	1320–9	23	1370–9	43 (14)
1280–9	27	1330–9	55	1380–9	53 (13)
1290–9	70	1340–9	111	1390–9	41 (15)
1300–9	29	1350–9	76 (41)	1400–9	42 (27)
1310–9	15	1360–9	64 (15)	1410–15	49 (31)

was a written contract, there was no necessity for the pipe roll to record it.[21] The pipe roll account for Holway in 1271–2 records a lease between two individuals 'as contained in the writing made between them', yet the contract is not formally enrolled. The rise in the number of recorded leases over the earlier fourteenth century may have been shaped by a growing desire to record the conditions of lease as a precaution against subsequent dispute, in which case it is a further example of the growing tendency for lords and tenants to put more faith in the written record of the pipe rolls.[22] Recorded inter-peasant leases declined in number after the Black Death, especially after 1370 (Table 8.3).

Despite some inevitable uncertainties about the chronology of leasing, given the partial nature of our evidence, entry fines can still be employed to illustrate some differing patterns in the peasant land market across the estate. Before the Black Death, recorded leases are most numerous where extrafamilial dealing was most energetic – at Witney in the Woodland group, and in the Somerset and South Hampshire groups. They are also often to be found in the south-eastern part of the Hampshire Chalk Plateau – especially at East Meon – at Adderbury in Oxfordshire, and, to a lesser extent, on the Buckinghamshire manors. On most of the Chalk Plateau of central Hampshire, as in the North Hampshire region, they are rare. After 1349, while leasing continued to be relatively common at East Meon and Bishops Waltham, it noticeably declined in Taunton bailiwick and at Adderbury. It continued to be rare in those manors where it had been unusual or absent before 1348–9.

The properties concerned in leases are more often smaller acreages of arable and meadow lands, although in a few instances they are larger customary holdings; fifty-one holdings of a virgate or half virgate were leased between 1270–1 and 1348–9. After the Black Death larger customary holdings constituted a larger proportion of all leases, in line with the overall trend in the extrafamilial land market. The fifty-two full virgates, other larger holdings and half virgates recorded in leases between 1349–50 and 1414–15 are about as many as those recorded before 1349, despite the overall decline in the total number of recorded leases. A large proportion of recorded leases

21. Poos and Bonfield (eds), *Select cases*, p. lxxxv; J.A. Raftis, *Tenure and mobility*, Pontifical Institute of Medieval Studies, Studies and Texts, 8 (Toronto, 1964), p. 239.

22. The number of leases is calculated by those transactions recording grants for years or for life with reversion clauses. For the importance of the enrolment of the terms of a lease on other manors see Faith, 'Berkshire', pp. 111, 124.

are for life – 215 out of the 340 known from before 1349, and almost all those subsequently – presumably because these were contracts for which memory alone was not reliable in preventing disputes. The remaining known leases were most usually for between three and ten years, although sometimes for as long as twenty or thirty years. The small number of those for only a single year suggests that such short-term lets were not usually recorded.

Sometimes the pipe rolls record the rent due from the subtenant. At Overton in 1342–3, Robert Cole leased from John, son of Henry Edward, three acres of purpresture for which he was bound to perform the services due to the lord and to pay John 4d a year. At Hambledon in 1349–50, John Diggle paid a large fine of £5 to lease for life a messuage and virgate, together with a further ten acres of customary land and thirteen acres of purpresture, for a rent of £1 10s a year at two terms. Some life leases where the rent was substantial were probably the equivalent of extrafamilial maintenance agreements. At Downton in 1335–6, Alice Hakehood fined to lease a messuage and virgate from Robert Salaman on condition that she paid £3 a year in silver during Robert's lifetime. Other examples record more complex provisions. John Burret's lease to Adam Bythewood of a croft of three acres at Hambledon for twenty-four years from 1340–1 was on condition 'that if John's tenement become vacant by death or surrender during the said term, Adam should contribute to the fine made by the heir or tenant for his portion'. But such examples are rare.

Some of the lord's tenants were frequent lessors of property. At Adderbury leases are most numerous in the earlier part of our period: Robert Andrew, for example, surrendered nine holdings of between two and four acres of arable and meadow there between 1309–10 and 1329–30, seven of which were specifically leases for life or for a term of years. A more outstanding example from the same manor is that of Alexander Jenner, who in 1308–9 received an inheritance from Richard Jenner, who was probably his stepfather or uncle. Over the course of the next thirty years he surrendered properties on more than seventy occasions, nearly all leases of a few acres and mostly for life. These leases were chiefly in the tithing of Bodicote. Towards the end of his life his leases were more substantial; in 1340–1 by two separate leases he parted with a 'hall and court house', and with the principal dwelling, cellar and solar within his enclosure. This implies that he gave up his own house to retire elsewhere. The leases sometimes provide that services should be performed by the subtenant. In 1338–9, for example, Alexander leased out a cottage with curtilage on the condition that the lessee should mow five swathes and do two harvest boon-works 'at Alexander's expense in victuals'. In several instances he surrendered properties with subtenants in place; in 1339–40 he transferred to Richard Goldwell 3½ acres in Bodicote, of which 2 acres were held by Edith and Ralph Woolmonger and 1½ acres by Denise Goldwell. These latter had, therefore, become tenants of subtenants. The scale of leasing by Robert Andrew and Alexander Jenner was atypical; their activities alone accord Adderbury an exceptionally high proportion of leases in these years.

Comparable evidence of recurrent peasant subletting at Brockhampton in the South Hampshire region is, unlike that from Adderbury, from after the Black Death. Property surrendered there from one peasant to another is often said to be 'from the tenure' of a third party. In 1355–6, for instance, Isabel Punfeld surrendered a cottage and curtilage to Walter Arnald 'from the tenure of John Hall'. This wording, which indicates the existence of a market in sublet property, is unique to Brockhampton, presumably because of some peculiarity of manorial custom. There are more than 200 such transactions from 1352 onwards, and no other form of leasing appears in the fines for the manor. Most of these surrenders were of cottages, but they also included many tofts, crofts and small acreages. The lessees concerned were presumably poorer tenants. Those from whom the holdings in question were sublet were relatively few in number, but these few were exceptionally active; between 1353 and 1391 John Hall appears in this role twenty-nine times, Simon Jordan sixteen times, William Arnald twelve times, and John Burton six times. These were not, as might be thought, long-deceased holders of now disintegrated larger holdings, but men currently active as buyers and sellers of property. Nor were they freeholders, but rather some of the manor's wealthier customary tenants. At his death, in or before 1393, John Hall left to his son and two daughters two customary virgates with messuages and two cottages. Unfortunately, no conditions of such subleases are included in these fines.

Conclusion

The sum of evidence indicates that there was an increasing tendency, particularly during the fourteenth century, for holdings on the Winchester estate to be viewed less as hereditary family resources and more as marketable assets. This was in part, at least, because of the increased availability of land after the Black Death, and the greater ease with which tenants could pick and choose among alternatives. While poverty was often a reason for the surrender of a holding, tenants were increasingly sensitive in the course of the period to the quality of land. Tenants had occasionally declined to inherit land for that reason before 1349, but such refusals became very much more common after 1349, and account for significant intermanorial differences in the vigour of the land market and the ability of the bishop's officers to find new tenants.

The increased availability of land created many opportunities for those with capital and commercial acumen, but only a minority of tenants were very actively engaged in the land market; most transfers were to non-inheriting children or migrants, and tenants by inheritance were usually content with what they had. However, a significant minority *were* actively involved in buying, selling and leasing land, occurring more frequently in regions with an active land market, particularly in the Somerset and Woodland groups of manors. It is demonstrable from the Taunton manors, with some support from elsewhere, that this more active group was not constrained by manorial boundaries but bought and sold property on several manors. Besides transfers of land 'by surrender', other forms of transfer, such as exchanges and leasing, tell us that these men saw their holdings as something to be remodelled, when the opportunity presented itself, in the interests of rationalisation and profit. The breakdown of links between family and property created new problems of identifying property, and led to a greatly increased use of fixed tenement names in the pipe roll record of transfers. These names often perpetuated the name of some long-deceased tenant.

Leases of property by customary tenants were more numerous than the pipe rolls imply, because it was not the normal practice to record them. Most of those about which we know were for life. The pipe rolls nevertheless show that tenants could, and sometimes did, manage their properties by means of leases, and at Brockhampton such leases appear to have been negotiable.

Chapter 9

Accumulation

The development of a land market allowed the enterprising peasant greater opportunities to accumulate properties of all sizes. This phenomenon has been recognised on many manors across England, chiefly in the late fourteenth and fifteenth centuries.[1] Our evidence allows broader comment on both the incidence and the consequences of this development up to 1415. The high mortality of the Black Death and subsequent epidemics, with the associated changes in the availability and price of land, increased the ease with which holdings could be amalgamated, and 1348–9 can consequently be regarded as a turning point. However, even before this period there had been accumulation on some manors, and these early accumulations had a lasting effect on intermanorial differences. The present chapter will first examine what can be deduced about the earlier history of accumulation as a prelude to a more extended study of the distribution of land after 1349.

Before the Black Death

Opportunities for accumulation before the Black Death were locally very variable. To some extent they depended upon custom regarding virgated tenements, whose amalgamation, as we saw in Chapter 3, was often disallowed by manor custom. The tenants of Bishops Waltham were more actively engaged than most in the accumulation of customary land. Titow calculated from the rental of 1332 that the 705 tenements in the rental were held by only 363 tenants, and that the holdings of 19 tenants together included about 70 dwellings.[2] Before 1348 there were about twenty recorded transactions on this manor involving multiple holdings in which a virgate or half virgate had become associated with another customary holding. A core holding, usually a half virgate, is often found attached to a half or third part of a ferling, which suggests that fragmentation had been a precursor to later accumulation. In 1309–10, Thomas Ford of Bishops Waltham paid £5 to inherit a messuage, a half virgate and an additional ferling in the tithing of Durley. In 1327–8 Isabel, the widow of John Cangeler, fined £3 6s 8d for her former husband's messuage and half a virgate, a messuage and ferling, and twenty-six acres of land. An interesting feature of these composite customary holdings is that they were not necessarily close together. Isabel Cangeler's inheritance was divided between Durley, Parkhurst and 'Lykstede'. This feature of accumulation is corroborated by the rental of 1332, which shows that forty acres or

---

1. J.L. Bolton, *The medieval English economy 1150–1500* (London, 1980), pp. 208–15, 218–20; M. Keen, *English society in the later Middle Ages, 1348–1500* (London, 1990), p. 66. For other manors demonstrating an increase in the size of holdings as well as a polarisation in the size of tenements, see P.D.A. Harvey, 'Conclusion', in *idem* (ed.), *Peasant land market*, pp. 340–3. This issue is discussed region by region by the contributors to the chapter 'Tenant farming and tenant farmers', in *AHEW* III, pp. 596, 600–1, 617–18, 636–8, 662–4, 703–7, 723–6.

2. Titow, *English rural society*, p. 86. It also uses material from Page, 'Lords, peasants and property'.

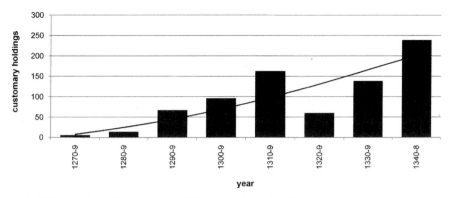

Figure 9.1 The number of customary holdings transferred with purpresture and assart, 1270–1349.

more held by Geoffrey Clerk were distributed between four tithings, and that sixty acres, three cottages and other properties of John Everard were located in six. Given the difficulties of farming such scattered holdings from a single centre, they are probably further indications of the peasant leasing that we observed in Chapter 8.

Besides Bishops Waltham, the accumulation of customary holdings was found most prominently on the manors of Brockhampton and Fareham in the South Hampshire region and at East Meon and Twyford, the larger manors of the south-east part of the Hampshire Chalk Plateau. At each of these four manors between eight and a dozen such holdings were transferred over this period. Accumulation of customary holdings is exceptional on manors elsewhere at this time. There are only about a dozen examples in the bailiwicks of Taunton and Wargrave before 1348, and only three examples of accumulated customary holdings can be found in the large manor of Farnham. Elsewhere examples are rarer still: the bailiwicks of Downton, Highclere and Witney yield only a single example each.

Accumulation before the Black Death could more easily take alternative forms across the estate's manors, involving property whose tenure was not regarded as customary. Ultimately the differences depended on the properties and customs of any one manor. Tenants on some manors built up composite holdings from a range of smallholdings or from assart and purprestures. Despite the fact that many properties are poorly categorised before 1300, the chronological trend is striking. The evidence of Figure 9.1 has been assembled by counting virgates (and their subdivisions), ferlings and cottages associated with assart and purpresture land, and involves 804 transactions across the estate.

The appropriation of purpresture by customary tenants characterised accumulation on the Eastern group of manors at Farnham and its neighbour Bentley, and to a lesser degree at Twyford and Merdon on the Hampshire Chalk Plateau, on the North Hampshire manors, and at Wargrave. It was uncommon elsewhere.[3] These were all manors noted for earlier colonisation and, except at Twyford, the amalgamation of

---

3.   Of the 804 transfers of a customary holding and assart or purpresture prior to 1350, 214 were at Farnham and 39 at Bentley. There were about 150 each in the bailiwicks of Twyford, Wargrave and Highclere.

customary holdings was rare before 1349. By contrast, there are fewer than a handful of examples of customary tenants accumulating purprestures on the Somerset and Wiltshire manors.

The acquisition of purpresture by customary tenants at Farnham was clearly exceptional.[4] This development began before the mid-1280s; the first occurrence of such a transfer was in 1284–5, when William Oak inherited a half virgate and four acres of purpresture from his father. From that time the fines reveal an increasing incidence of such amalgamations, corresponding to the implications of Figure 9.1; by the mid-1330s virgated tenements without attached purpresture were in the minority. There was little extrafamilial transfer of such lands. Customary holdings were relatively compact, and the addition of consolidated plots of purpresture was better adapted to the local system of farming. The terms of customary tenure were particularly favourable because labour services had been entirely commuted in 1257, the only example of complete commutation on the estate in the period before the Black Death, so that bonds between families and their land were especially strong. There were also relatively few smallholders to compete for available purpresture. The net effect of local conditions meant that the acquisition of purpresture by customary tenants here gave no scope for an extrafamilial market in assart land.

A comparable situation is found in several of the Taunton group of manors, where overland, owing money rents, was perhaps equivalent to purprestures elsewhere. Its attachment to customary holdings can be found at Poundisford, Holway, Staplegrove and Kingstone St Mary, which was part of Nailsbourne manor. This process of small-scale accumulation began about 1310, and may be somehow linked to the administrative reorganisation of the Taunton manors between 1307 and 1309.[5] At Poundisford, for instance, before 1348 there are 118 recorded transactions involving a customary holding, usually a virgate, with attached overland; all except 5 of these were from after 1310–11. At Holway, Staplegrove and Kingstone St Mary an accelerated incidence of this sort of engrossment comes rather later, in the 1330s and 1340s. Nonetheless, attached overland was usually of small acreage, often even measured in dayworks. While this sort of accretion was common on these manors it did not become standard practice to hold overland in addition to a customary holding as was the case with purpresture at Farnham. At Holway before 1348–9 about 80 transfers of virgate and ferling holdings had attached overland, as against around 180 without. Similarly, of the 98 standard smallholdings containing a messuage with five acres transferred before 1348–9, only 21 had plots of attached overland. Besides the overland attached to customary units, there was some free-standing overland available to be transferred between families. The apparent severe land shortage at Taunton kept much of the overland in the hands of smallholders. A market in these properties represents a development midway between the experience of Farnham, where assart devolved through inheritance by its attachment to customary holdings, and that of Witney, where the market in customary land was more clearly distinct from that in assarts.

---

4. For this and the remainder of the paragraph, see Page, 'Farnham', pp. 174–6.
5. See Thornton, 'Arable productivity', pp. 112–15.

At Witney, the most demonstrably colonising manor of the estate in the thirteenth century, the situation was very different from that at either Farnham or Taunton. Here there were accumulations of assart land by 1349, as we saw when we examined the practices of a number of sub-leasing burgesses there. But transfers of land involving an additional customary holding were rare and there were virtually no transfers of a customary tenement with an assart holding. Disallowing the accumulation of standard tenements perhaps extended to discouraging customary tenants from acquiring these properties too; of the 156 virgates transferred before 1348, only eight conveyed additional property and only one had attached assart, and that was less than an acre.

It has already been noted that the accumulation of customary holdings was unusual on many manors of the bishopric before the Black Death; the same observation may be made of the accumulation of assart and purpresture by customary tenants. The accumulation of holdings, although advanced at Bishops Waltham and quite frequent on some other manors, was absent, or almost absent, on others. Virgaters, half virgaters and holders of ferling tenements and cottages at Bishops Sutton, Beauworth, Cheriton and Wield, manors in the Hampshire Chalk Plateau group, engrossed very little property, almost entirely confined to a few acres of purpresture. There were 231 transfers of standard holdings at Bishops Sutton before 1348–9 of which only 15, all virgaters or half virgaters, had purpresture lands attached; none had engrossed a customary holding of any kind. There was some limited accumulation on Twyford manor, but it was absent from nearby Crawley and Merdon. The situation was similar at Bishopstoke in South Hampshire, most of the North Hampshire group of manors, the Wiltshire group and in many of the Northern manors of Buckinghamshire and Berkshire.

What brake was at work on these manors? In addition to any customary restraint on accumulation, it seems that the small size of some manors hindered accumulation of holdings because of the small number of properties available. These smaller manors include Crawley, Cheriton, Beauworth, North Waltham, Overton, Ecchinswell, Upton, Bishops Fonthill, Bishopstone, Culham and Esher. In all these not only was there no accumulation of customary holdings by customary tenants, but also no acquisition of purpresture. A sluggish development of an extrafamilial land market also held back accumulation, as in the Bishops Sutton group of manors especially; before the Black Death over 60 per cent of land transfers within this bailiwick were intrafamilial. On these smaller manors there was also very little, if any, fragmentation of customary holdings.

Small size was not the only explanation for lack of accumulation, however; it does not explain the institutional conservatism of the Wiltshire manors. At Downton there was barely any accumulation, despite the release of a relatively large amount of demesne and bordland in the first half of the fourteenth century.[6] For much of the earlier part of our period this bordland was held by smallholders with no other property. In the 1340s a small number of the customary tenants of this manor began to enlarge their holdings with added parcels of former demesne, but such land became more strongly associated with virgate holdings only after the Black Death.

---

6.   See also E. Miller, 'Tenant farming and tenant farmers: the southern counties', in *AHEW* III, p. 704.

Often held on short-term leases, demesne properties were hardly to be considered in the same way as the rest of a family's inheritance. Across most of the estate, and most notably at Witney, assarts and purprestures were evidently considered inappropriate additions to customary holdings.

Throughout the estate, the relatively small number of short-term leases of demesne land in this period meant that it was rarely attached to standard holdings for very long. Before the Black Death there are only ten examples of tenants holding demesne land in conjunction with customary holdings at the time of their death.

After the Black Death

The plague of 1348–9, and subsequent outbreaks, created new opportunities for the accumulation of large composite holdings. A sharp reduction in the number of households lowered the demand for peasant holdings and so made it easier for those who wanted more land to acquire it. This effect was augmented by reduced entry fines, the commutation of labour services and the leasing of manorial demesnes. The most cursory of glances at the pipe rolls, particularly towards the turn of the century, shows that accumulation had become more widespread and that composite holdings had become more complex in their composition, even on many manors where there had been none before 1348.[7] At Bishops Fonthill in Wiltshire, for example, where there had been no amassing of property in the early fourteenth century, the pipe roll for 1410–11 records Walter Golie's marriage to Agnes, widow of William Dany, which brought him 'a messuage and virgate of villein land containing twenty-four acres, two acres of bordage land and a messuage and half a virgate of villein land containing eleven acres'. At Bishops Sutton, where there had, similarly, been little previous accumulation, a number of tenants began to build up holdings composed of multiple customary holdings from the 1370s.

Increasing accumulation of property across the whole bishopric estate can be assessed by analysing the proportion of transfers of standard virgated holdings, virgates, half virgates, ferlings or cotlands, with additional properties (Figure 9.2). The additional properties in question were from the whole range of standard tenements, fractions of such tenements, and acres of villein land, assart and purpresture. An unambiguous increase in such composite standard tenements is apparent from the first and second decades of the fourteenth century, and the upward trend continued inexorably over the later fourteenth century. Although these results are clearly significant, they are also crude, since they ignore intermanorial differences, accumulation by lesser customary tenants and changes in the scale and complexity of such composite holdings.

Table 9.1, which sets out the intermanorial distribution of virgated standard holdings transferred with some kind of additional property, shows wide intermanorial variation. The number and quality of properties available on any one manor ultimately explain this distribution, although the varying local effects of mortality and migration also contributed. Four broad types of manor may be distinguished: first, there were

---

7.   For more general comment on these developments, see Bolton, *The medieval English economy*, pp. 237–42; Postan, *Medieval economy and society*, pp. 139–42.

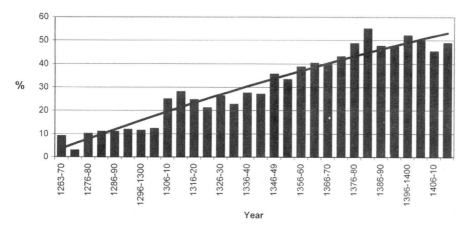

Figure 9.2 Entry fines for virgated tenements augmented with additional properties, as a percentage of the total number of entry fines on the Winchester bishopric estates, 1263–1415.

manors in which accumulated holdings were frequent, often being constructed from a larger virgated tenement to which more virgated tenements and other properties were attached; secondly, there were manors whose tenants aggregated holdings from a range of smaller customary holdings; third are those in which assart and purpresture continued to be important additions; and, finally, there were manors where amalgamations of property remained unusual.

Outstandingly large composite holdings across the estate were mostly constructed by those customary tenants, chiefly virgaters and half virgaters, who acquired additional virgated holdings and often smaller properties as well. Table 9.2, which records the proportion of virgated tenements that had accumulated other virgated holdings, shows differences from Table 9.1. With the exception of some smaller manors, such as Culham and North Waltham, which had few composite holdings in any case, the accumulation of further standard holdings by tenants of virgated tenements was largely a feature of the South Hampshire manors. It belonged, in other words, in a region where accumulation had been prominent in the earlier period.

The long-term consequences of accumulation on this scale can be observed by comparing the Bishops Waltham rental of c.1332 with a later one from 1464. The earlier rental, as we have seen, gives evidence of considerable accumulation, but this was much more accentuated in the later one. The number of properties listed in 1464 is broadly comparable with that in the earlier rental, but they were now held by 164 tenants, fewer than half the 363 tenants of 132 years earlier. There was an impressive development in both the number of engrossed tenements and the extent of subtenancy. Smallholders of ten acres or less now constituted only 33 per cent of all tenants, and most of these were resident in the town. Of the other tenants, 29 per cent held between ten and forty acres, but 38 per cent now held forty acres or more. In the tithing of Ashton, thirteen tenants held the twenty-eight virgated tenements previously held by twenty-five. Some of this concentration of occupation had occurred since the end of our study period in 1415, but the trend was strongly in evidence long before that date. A large accumulation of property held by William Stake in 1409–10 was itself composed of several more ancient accumulations, but it had become part of an even larger tenement when brought together by Robert Crisp in the 1450s; it was

Table 9.1
The intermanorial distribution of standard holdings transferred with accumulations, 1350–1415

Range (%)	Manors (number of standard holdings/percentage with accumulations in brackets)
75–100	Woodhay (105/90.5), Bentley (76/82.9)
50–74.9	Farnham (613/70), Warfield (52/63.5), Ashmansworth (56/58.9), Burghclere (133/55.6), Highclere (68/54.4), Merdon (291/54.3), Wield (37/54), Poundisford (380/52.6), Bishops Hull (205/51.7), Brockhampton (183/51.4), West Wycombe (165/50.3), Beauworth (30/50), Esher (14/50)
25–49.9	Twyford (154/47.4), Bishopstone (114/46.5), Wargrave (92/45.7), Staplegrove (240/44.6), Bishops Waltham (679/43.9), Holway (361/43.5), Nailsbourne (167/42.5), Bitterne (45/42.2), Waltham St Lawrence (107/40.2), Cheriton (114/38.6), Marwell (291/38), Ecchinswell (101/37.6), Fareham (238/36.6), Droxford (193/35.8), Hambledon (104/33.7), East Meon (392/33.4), Morton (24/33.3), Downton (246/31.3), Adderbury (153/30.7), Brightwell (104/28.9), Bishops Sutton (197/27.4), Alresford (144/25.7)
0–24.9	Otterford (87/24.1), East Meon Church (43/23.3), Crawley (124/22.6), Rimpton (68/20.6), Harwell (69/18.8), Ivinghoe (157/18.5), Bishopstoke (206/16.5), Witney (134/15.7), Culham (8/12.5), Overton (90/11.1), Bishops Fonthill (56/10.7), East Knoyle (65/9.2), Alverstoke (6/0), North Waltham (49/4.1), Gosport (0/0), Upton (5/0)

Note: Standard holdings include virgates, half virgates, ferlings and cotlands.

Table 9.2
The intermanorial distribution of standard holdings transferred with additional virgated tenements, 1350–1415

Range (%)	Manors (number of composite virgated holdings/percentage with further virgated tenements in brackets)
75–100	Bishops Fonthill (5/100), Culham (1/100), North Waltham (2/100), Overton (10/80), Bishopstone (53/75.5), Brockhampton (94/75.5), Crawley (28/71.4)
50–74.9	Wargrave (42/57.1), East Knoyle (6/50), Fareham (87/50.5), Harwell (13/53.9), Ivinghoe (29/51.7), Marwell (46/50)
25–49.9	Adderbury (47/46.8), Droxford (69/44.9), Nailsbourne (71/43.7), Alresford (37/43.2), Warfield (33/42.4), Beauworth (15/40), Bishops Waltham (298/40.6), East Meon (131/38.2), Hambledon (35/37.1), Bishops Sutton (54/35.2), Ecchinswell (38/34.2), Bitterne (21/26.3), Twyford (73/26)
0–24.9	Merdon (158/23.4), Waltham St Lawrence (43/23.3), Rimpton (14/21.4), Ashmansworth (33/21.2), West Wycombe (83/19.3), Bentley (63/19), Witney (23/19), Holway (157/18.5), Cheriton (44/15.9), Staplegrove (167/15), Bishops Stoke (34/14.7), Otterford (21/14.3), Brightwell (30/13.3), Woodhay (95/10.5), East Meon Church (1/10), Wield (20/10), Farnham (429/7.5), Bishops Hull (106/3.8), Highclere (37/2.7), Downton (77/2.6), Burghclere (74/1.4), Poundisford (200/1), Esher (7/0), Gosport (0/0), Alverstoke (0/0), Morton (8/0), Upton (0/0)

Note: Standard holdings include virgates, half virgates, ferlings and cotlands.

Table 9.3
The intermanorial distribution of standard holdings transferred with assart, purpresture and overland,
1350–1415

Range (%)	Manors (number of composite virgated holdings/percentage with assart and purpresture in brackets)
75–100	Poundisford (199/99), Highclere (38/97.3), Bishops Hull (205/97.1), Staplegrove (102/95.3), Burghclere (133/94.6), Farnham (397/93), Woodhay (88/92.6), Holway (143/91.1), Wield (18/90), Twyford (65/89), Warfield (28/84.8), Ecchinswell (32/84), Bishops Sutton (43/79.6), Cheriton (34/77.3), Waltham St Lawrence (33/76.7), Merdon (121/76.6)
50–74.9	West Wycombe (62/74.7), Beauworth (11/73.3), Otterford (15/71.4), Bitterne (13/68), Alresford (25/67.7), Bentley (60/64.5), Nailsbourne (42/59.6), Bishops Stoke (17/50), Harwell (13/53.9)
25–49.9	Bishops Waltham (139/46.6), Droxford (69/44.9), Marwell (20/43.5), Rimpton (6/42.9), Wargrave (17/40.1), East Meon Church (4/40), Esher (2/28.6)
0–24.9	Ashmansworth (33/21.2), Hambledon (7/20), Fareham (17/19.5), East Meon (19/14.5), Crawley (4/14.3), Ivinghoe (3/10.3), Overton (1/10), Brockhampton (5/5.3), Witney (1/4.4), Brightwell (1/3.3), Adderbury (0/0), Alverstoke (0/0), Bishops Fonthill (0/0), Bishopstone (0/0), Culham (0/0), Downton (0/0), East Knoyle (0/0), Gosport (0/0), Morton (0/0), North Waltham (0/0), Upton (0/0)

Note: Standard holdings include virgates, half virgates, ferlings and cotlands.

then an enormous eleven-virgate holding of over 290 acres.[8] Elements of this holding can be traced back to small-scale accumulations as early as the mid-thirteenth century.

The propensity of tenants of full virgates to create the largest accumulated holdings can be illustrated from the bailiwick of East Meon. Analysis of the entry fines suggests that already by the early 1360s about a third of full virgates had some kind of accretion of property, but that the number of such holdings increased to 40 per cent or more after 1380.[9] The size of such accumulations also grew; properties described as a messuage and two virgates, often with smaller pieces of land attached, became increasingly common. The reasons for East Meon's particularly high level of accumulation must lie at a local level, and cannot be fully explained within the range of information supplied by entry fines. The quality of the soil was good, and the village was within reach of the Winchester market; the demesne was occasionally able to sell grain in bulk.[10] But Meon also had extensive downland pasture, and the attraction of accumulating land may relate closely to the importance of pastoral husbandry in the village, either because former arable could be put down to grass or because it carried with it valuable rights of common.[11]

At Fareham, similarly, an increasing number of multi-virgated composite holdings were transferred over the period, especially after 1400. Only nine virgaters and half

8. HRO, 11M59/B1/190; 11M59/Bp/BW/68, 81; Page, 'Lords, peasants and property'.

9. Mullan, 'Accumulation and polarisation', figure 11.6, p. 189.

10. Chapter 2, Table 2.5; Farmer, 'Marketing', pp. 348, 351, 361.

11. Miller, 'Occupation of the land', pp. 138; M.M. Postan, 'Village livestock in the thirteenth century', *Economic History Review*, 2nd series, 15 (1962), pp. 234–5, reprinted in *idem, Essays on medieval agriculture*, pp. 231–2.

virgaters transferred holdings with additional virgated tenements in the forty-five years between 1350 and 1399, but a further seven did so between 1400 and 1415. Over 70 per cent of these larger accumulations based on customary units were transferred within families following the death of a tenant, implying a strong family commitment. Their increased complexity can be illustrated from the holding that Walter Mayle of Fareham inherited from his father in 1409–10, which comprised a messuage and half virgate of villein land, a further messuage and eight acres of villein land in the tithing of 'Catisfeld', a toft and half a virgate of villein land in Dene and a toft and a further half a virgate of villein land in the tithing of Cams ('Cammoysbusshop').

Composite holdings based on ferling and cottage tenements were, not surprisingly, of a lesser order. On the manor of Bishops Waltham, where ferling-holders formed a large proportion of the manor's customary tenants, there were a few large composite ferling holdings immediately after the Black Death; Thomas Everard's inheritance in 1349–50 comprised 'a messuage and a ferling, a cottage, half an acre, an acre of meadow, a cottage with curtilage, half an acre, a cottage, a ferling, a messuage and three acres of villein land, a messuage and two acres, one acre and half an acre'. Smallholders found themselves more frequently able to accumulate after about 1385, and from then on they did so in a proportion comparable to that of tenants of larger standard holdings. Across the whole estate about 417 ferlings are recorded to have been transferred between 1384–5 and 1414–15, of which 17 per cent had engrossed either another ferling, a cottage, a croft, or a significant acreage of purpresture or overland.

On several manors there was a good deal of accumulation of properties other than virgated holdings. Composite holdings, from whatever base, here tended to be engrossments of smaller units of land, a phenomenon identified on manors outside of the bishopric estate.[12] This pattern of accumulation corresponded to the nature of properties available; it was especially prominent on manors that abounded in ferlings, cottages, crofts, messuages with smallholdings, and unattached acres of land both customary and free. A distinction may be made between manors where smallholdings became the chief unit of accumulation and those where a history of colonisation provided plentiful assarted land and purpresture. Assarts and purprestures were a variable ingredient in the acquisitions of customary tenants, and this is reflected in the distribution of such holdings across the estate (Table 9.3). The trend for standard customary holdings to acquire small non-customary additions became more usual in the later fourteenth century, to a point where nearly all tenants of virgated holdings held such additional land. There was a very high incidence of such appropriation on the manors of North Hampshire and the Taunton group and on a sprinkling of others elsewhere. However, on some notably colonising manors, such as those of the Woodland group (Wargrave and Witney) and some in the Northern group (Ivinghoe, Culham), the appropriation of purpresture and assart by customary tenants remained unusual, even though such properties continued to be bought and sold independently.

The distinction between virgated units and other types of property long remained significant. In manors of the Taunton group there was little amalgamation of virgated units after 1348. Demand for such land remained high, and a large proportion of standard holdings remained within families. The few vacant virgated tenements from

---

12. Jones, 'Bedfordshire', p. 220; Harvey, 'Conclusion', p. 343.

the 1348 plague were taken up again in the 1350s and the section of the pipe roll that listed rents in default quickly disappeared from the accounts of these manors.[13] The level of fines for some types of customary holding actually rose over the course of the later fourteenth and early fifteenth centuries; the average fine for a messuage and ferling without any engrossment at Bishops Hull was 15s 6d in 1350, 18s in 1354–5, £1 6s 8d, in 1364–5, £1 10s in 1367–8, £2 10s in 1383–4 and 1389–90, and £3 6s 8d in 1398–9. This was a local phenomenon that supports the view that there was exceptional economic development in the Taunton area through the later fourteenth century.[14] However, among the tenants of the Taunton manors there were hundreds of accumulations of smaller composite holdings made up of small acreages, dayworks, cottage holdings and overland, to the point that the land market was dominated by the transfer of such small units. At Poundisford, for example, only 1 per cent of composite holdings contained two virgated units, but 198 of the 200 virgated properties with accumulations transferred between 1349–50 and 1414–15 had acquired cottages, messuages with a few acres, a few acres of overland and fragmented customary acres without a dwelling. The pattern of accumulation was substantially the same at Bishops Hull, Holway, Nailsbourne, Staplegrove and Otterford. The property that Nicholas Bost acquired at Holway in 1357–8, by marriage to Matilda Chaffing, is typical of many others: it comprised a messuage and five acres of villein land, half an acre of overland, a further three acres and three roods of overland and pasture for one beast.

As before 1350, the tenurial horizons of accumulating peasants were not necessarily limited to one manor. Among those tenants who can be identified in different contexts more securely than most because of their unusual names was John Gaburdel of Staplegrove, who had created a composite holding in that manor of a messuage and virgate together with two cottages and curtilages and parcels of overland. He also held four properties on Nailsbourne manor; these were mostly of one or two acres, but one was of a messuage and twenty-five acres of villein and ten acres of overland. Examples away from the Taunton manors include that of John Cottel, who inherited a cottage in Burghclere in 1350–1. Over the next few years he acquired a number of further holdings on the manor, all from outside the family, and all properties that had come into the lord's hands for want of willing heirs. In 1354–5, through a refusal of the outgoing tenant's family to fine, he entered into more than thirty-three acres of purpresture in the neighbouring manor of Highclere and then, in the following year, a further 9½ acres in the same manor.

On a number of manors the rarity of accumulation observable before the Black Death continued in the later fourteenth and early fifteenth centuries. These differences cannot easily be explained in regional terms since some manors with little accumulation lay in some instances close to others with a great deal. Bishopstoke in South Hampshire, only three miles from Twyford, is a case in point. This was a manor with little land outside the virgated customary tenures, and the land was sufficiently good to command family loyalties, so the obstacles to accumulation that had operated

---

13. Titow, 'Lost rents', pp. 109–12.
14. See also Chapter 5, p 79.

in the earlier period were still present,[15] and the two holdings made vacant by the Black Death were soon reoccupied.[16] Of the 121 virgate and half virgate holdings transferred there between 1349–50 and 1414–15, only two full virgate and thirteen half virgates had attached properties, and most were no more than an acre or two of purpresture or a cottage holding. The subsection of the annual account recording defaults of rent as a result of the plague, common to most manors, never appeared here. The number of fines, generally well maintained, increased from the 1390s; the yearly average of 4.5 transactions in the 1370s and 1380s had doubled by 1400–10. Marriage to widows remained frequent, and the proportion of transactions within families remained unusually high. The smallness of the manor and the absence of empty holdings seems to explain the absence of accumulation on some other manors, such as Brightwell, Esher, Culham, Upton and Morton.

If absence of vacant land held back accumulation on some manors, it was inhibited on others by the failure of demand for unattractive land. In contrast to the manors mentioned so far, there were several, some of them large, where vast acreages of customary and some non-customary holdings were abandoned after the plagues: notably Witney, Downton and North Waltham. At Witney the vacant acreage over the course of the later fourteenth century ranged somewhere between about 1,200 and 1,600 acres; at Downton it was between about 450 and 1,000 acres; and the smaller manor of North Waltham had between about 360 and 600 acres.[17] At North Waltham, where soils were poor, the episcopal administration had struggled to fill full virgate tenements even before the Black Death; in 1336–7, Richard, son of John Smith, paid an entry fine of 3d for a messuage and virgate which 'for a long time remained in the lord's hands as abandoned'. There had been little aggregation or fragmentation of tenements before the Black Death, and afterwards there was a precipitous fall in the number of transactions on these manors. The bishop's officers had sometimes to compel tenants to occupy vacant property. In all three manors, extrafamilial transfers dominated the market, often following either the death of a tenant who had no kin willing to take on the tenement or the abandonment of unwanted property. Although abundant vacant land created easy opportunities for engrossment on these manors, incentives were few. The most sizeable accumulation at Downton, for instance, was a forty-acre virgate associated in 1402–3 with an additional cottage and curtilage and three acres of bordage land.

Large accumulations

Analysis of single fines does not always present us with the full scale of an individual's holdings. Larger multiple holdings are usually revealed through inheritance fines and fines for extrafamilial transfers *post mortem*, but many large holdings may have been sufficiently ephemeral in character to have been dispersed prior to a tenant's death. By building up the evidence relating to individual tenants we are occasionally able to see the existence of such larger holdings. At Bishops Waltham in 1409–10, William Stake

---

15. Page, *Medieval bishops*, pp. 18–19.
16. Titow, 'Lost rents', pp. 109–12.
17. *Ibid.*

Table 9.4
The number and distribution of composite holdings over 60 acres, 1350–79 and 1380–1415
(arranged by region)

Region Manor	Before 1380	After 1380	Total	Region Manor	Before 1380	After 1380	Total
South Hampshire				**North Hampshire**			
Brockhampton	24	31	55	Woodhay	4	2	6
Bishops Waltham	13	11	24	Ecchinswell	1	0	1
Fareham	3	4	7	Burghclere	0	2	2
Hampshire Chalk Plateau				**Woodland and Northern**			
East Meon	9	19	28	Warfield	5	1	6
Bishops Sutton	5	3	8	Wargrave	3	3	6
Beauworth	2	3	5	Harwell	2	0	2
Cheriton	1	2	3	W. St Lawrence	1	3	4
Alresford	0	2	2	Adderbury	1	2	3
Twyford	2	3	5	West Wycombe	1	0	1
Merdon	0	7	7	**Wiltshire**			
Marwell	2	6	8	Bishopstone	0	7	7
Droxford	1	3	4	**Somerset**			
Eastern				Poundisford	0	1	1
Farnham	1	1	2	Staplegrove	1	1	2
				Holway	0	1	2

Note: The figures from East Meon and Brockhampton include holdings of two or more virgates, most of which occur after 1380.

fined £6 to marry Agnes, daughter of William Mortimer, who brought him three messuages and a toft, 2½ virgates, a ferling with three acres of purpresture, and an additional five acres. In the same year he also fined for a messuage, two tofts, and half a virgate of land, three ferlings and four acres of purpresture from Henry Mortimer, no doubt a relative of Agnes. His total holding amounted to about 173 acres.

Large accumulations are nevertheless more easily identified when many properties are conveyed by a single fine. Between the mid-fourteenth and the early fifteenth centuries we can identify across the episcopal estate about a hundred such fines concerning holdings of sixty acres or more, or composed of an especially large number of smallholdings (Table 9.4). As one may expect, they occur most frequently where accumulation was more common anyway, as at Bishops Waltham, Brockhampton, East Meon, Merdon and Fareham. These examples are noteworthy for their own sake, since they represent the enterprise of an upper echelon of wealthy peasants who figure large in the agrarian history of the fifteenth century as a new rural elite.[18]

18.   e.g. DeWindt, *Land and people*, pp. 110–15; C. Dyer, 'Were there any capitalists in fifteenth-century England?', in J. Kermode (ed.), *Enterprise and individuals in fifteenth-century England* (Stroud, 1991), pp. 18–19; Harvey, *Westminster Abbey*, pp. 288–90; R.H. Hilton, *The economic development of some Leicestershire estates in the 14th and 15th centuries* (Oxford, 1947), pp. 105, 129; Miller, 'Tenant farming and tenant farmers', pp. 704–6, 714–16.

One of these accumulations was a large composite holding at East Meon in 1399–1400: as described in the record of an entry fine, it is representative of a widespread feature of half a century of change:

> And 106s 8d from Nicola, widow of Thomas Knoller, to retain one messuage and one virgate of villein land in Comb', one toft one garden, 4 acres of villein land called Spyghtes in Meon', 3½ acres of wood in Hyden', 8 acres of old purpresture in Comb', a piece of meadow in M[...], one cottage 10 acres of villein land called Budellond in Meon', lately of John Parker', one toft, 2 crofts of villein land containing 8 acres lately of Richard Couk', and 40 acres from the lord's demesne in Selescomb', from Thomas Knoller her husband.

This holding was made up of at least ten separate units totalling over 100 acres drawn together from a variety of sources, and dispersed about the manor. It was not the whole of Thomas's accumulated wealth: although his widow, Nicola, received the bulk of his property, his son, another Thomas, inherited a further two cottages with curtilages of purpresture, four acres of purpresture and three acres from the lord's demesne. There were varied tenures within Thomas's legacy: not only did it contain customary holdings, some with a decayed appearance, but also purpresture and a large portion of former demesne. Some portions were held by customary inheritance, and others, such as the demesne, were probably leased; no doubt, Nicola owed a variety of rents, services and other dues. An analysis of the manner in which Thomas Knoller had been able to construct this large composite holding can serve as a helpful basis for approaching some general features of this widespread aspect of late medieval rural society.

In 1348–9 Thomas had inherited from his mother, Alice, a messuage and virgate that were apparently the core of what he still possessed in 1399–1400. He started acquiring additional property soon afterwards; his first fine was for four acres of villein land acquired in 1351–2 following its surrender by the previous tenant. In 1357–8 he fined for a messuage and ten acres from John Parker and in 1361–2 for a toft and ten acres of villein land from Richard Cook, both having been surrendered by the outgoing tenant; he retained both properties until his death. His largest acquisition, also in 1361–2, was an extensive composite holding surrendered by John, son of Nicholas Bere, in the townships of Combe, Meon and Hyden, for which he paid an entry fine of £6. These are all properties to be found in the inheritance he left his wife. He paid a fine of 13s 4d for a forty-acre portion of demesne with pasture taken up directly from the lord in 1369–70, this being one of three fines by which he acquired parcels of demesne land, one of which 'lay between his cottage and the barn'. Most of these fines were for lands obtained by extrafamilial transactions *inter vivos*. Other properties, demesne as well as customary land, were acquired over the period, most of which made up the holding that his son inherited independently. In the course of his recorded career he was involved in thirteen land transactions, but surrendered property only twice. His last transaction was in 1396–7.

Thomas Knoller's example suggests that one desideratum for a would-be accumulator of land was longevity. Among the manors of the East Meon group several wealthier tenants had been active in the land market for more than twenty-five years. John and Emma Burton's holding at Brockhampton, comprising three messuages, four and a half virgates, four and a half acres, two curtilages, a toft, a cottage and a shop, was built up over thirty-nine years between 1350–1 and John's death in 1389–90. John Sole from East Meon, who had, by the time of his death in 1400–1, built up an estate of a messuage and toft, two virgates, a water mill and two acres of purpresture, seems to have been active from 1351–2. Other long-lived accumulators of property were John Neng at East Meon (from 1365–6 to 1392–3), John Forcombe at East Meon (from 1348–9 to 1383–4), Henry Napier at Brockhampton (from 1350–1 to 1394–5), Walter Mayle at Fareham (from 1356–7 to 1409–10) and John Cous at East Meon (from 1351–2 to 1395–6).

With regard again to Thomas, a long-standing family connection with East Meon and East Meon Church is another relevant consideration. The name Knoller can be traced back on the manor of East Meon to the late thirteenth century and the family, or at least branches of it, also had interests as virgaters in the neighbouring manor of East Meon Church. In 1271–2, at East Meon Church, an earlier Thomas Knoller had fined for land in 'Oxenbourne'. At East Meon in 1290–1, John, son of Thomas Knoller, had secured a messuage and seven acres from Elias Telfer. In 1316–17 in the same manor Thomas, son of Thomas Knoller, had obtained two acres in East Meon from outside the family. The long-established presence of the family in these manors was an influential factor in the formation of a later large holding. Among other things, it presumably indicates that the family identified strongly with the place, the land and the village community and had a high status there.

Status could only operate effectively, however, if backed by finance. A striking feature in the formation of these large properties was the ability of peasants to pay large entry fines. Thomas Knoller paid a total of £15 10s 4d in fines over the course of his career. Individual fines such as the £6 he paid in 1361–2 were exceptional, but featured quite often in the transfer of exceptionally large units. Thomas Molin of Brockhampton paid £12 for the composite holding of Clement Bachesmere in 1362–3, and his nephew paid £10 when he succeeded to the estate in 1391. John Langrish paid £16 to succeed to his father's lands in 1355–6, and his son in turn fined £10 to secure his inheritance. Perhaps the largest fine of all was the £50 paid by Matilda, the widow of Adam Moor, at Holway in 1390–1 for an accumulated holding made up of a great many smaller holdings characteristic of the form of engrossment in the Taunton manors. The size of these weighty fines bears an obvious relationship to the large size of the holdings, but even multiple smaller fines could add up to a large commitment over a lifetime. Henry Napier, who, as we have noted, built up his estate almost entirely from small properties and entirely by extrafamilial surrender, paid nineteen fines totalling £7 14s 4d. One can only speculate about where such sums might have come from. One possibility was surely the accumulated proceeds of subleasing through which wealthier peasants could draw rents; this must have been a normal way of managing large and often disparate properties. But it is likely that some accumulation was financed by borrowing, since it is now clear that the credit market in medieval villages was able to serve the needs of prosperous peasants.[19]

Thomas Knoller's acquisition in 1361–2 of an already existing composite holding, distributed between three townships, represents another common aspect of large accumulations. Although most large holdings were formed after about 1380, their origins often lay many years earlier. In 1412–13 William Loneway of Warfield manor paid a fine of £10 to have the estate of Thomas Rothwell deceased. This consisted of

---

19. Briggs, 'Creditors and debtors', pp. 136–41.

two messuages and 14½ virgates, two additional acres of customary land, forty acres of purpresture and £1s 0s 2d rent. This amounted to more than 330 acres of land and was easily the largest holding on the manor. Thomas Rothwell had acquired the estate by marriage in 1378–9 from the Joliff family for a fine of £20. Roger Joliff in turn had fined in 1350–1 for the core of this property, consisting of a messuage and seven virgates, after the death of William Newnham. Earlier still, in 1290–1, William's ancestor, John Newnham, had held the same holding but with an additional 49 acres of purpresture. Similarly, the 173-acre property brought together by William Stake at Bishops Waltham in 1409–10 had composite elements within it that can be traced back to much earlier accumulations. Although the rental of c.1332 records that the seven-virgate tenements and purpresture of this estate were in the hands of at least six different tenants, four of these virgates or fractions of them were already held by one man, William Buss, and in 1259–60 William's ancestor Richard Buss had held two of them.[20] Early accumulation on this manor had facilitated the later creation of exceptionally large properties.

Yet the most significant opportunities for one such as Thomas Knoller lay in the changes in the nature of the land market occasioned by the Black Death and the second great pestilence of 1361–2. The sudden greater availability of land created obvious opportunities. Surplus land did not necessarily encourage accumulation, as we saw in the case of Witney, since some of what came onto the market was unattractive for one reason or another. But the presence of land surplus to the requirements of other families, to be taken over by agreement or after it had been abandoned, and often for a relatively low entry fine, was undoubtedly in some contexts a major stimulus to the emergence of a new peasant elite. Some of the most significant steps towards the creation of these large composite holdings took place within a short time of the plagues of 1348–9 and 1361–2. Thomas Knoller's acquisition of 1361–2 was almost certainly an indirect result of the second pestilence, for John, son of Nicholas Bere, had himself only inherited the estate the same year through the death of his father and for one reason or another was willing to part with it quickly. Similarly, John and Emma Burton's first apparent foray into the land market began with a messuage and three acres from one John Stakes, who had died in 1348–9. The roll for the following year records that John and Emma fined for further lands in Brockhampton: another messuage with one and a half virgates from Adam Moor and a messuage and virgate from John Ray. All three of these acquisitions were from deceased tenants for which no kin could be found who cared to fine for the holdings. This was a common feature of *post mortem* transactions in the years after the plagues, a circumstance through which peasants such as the Burtons were able to extend their enterprises.

Thomas Knoller's career also demonstrates how the accelerated formation of an extrafamilial land market after 1349 facilitated access to property. Many wealthier tenants secured most of their lands, particularly the smaller ones, by direct purchase. Henry Napier, active on Brockhampton manor from 1350–1 until his death sometime between 1387 and 1395, was involved in no less than nineteen transactions as incoming tenant and every one of these was an extrafamilial transaction *inter vivos*.

---

20. Page, 'Lords, peasants and property'.

John and Emma Burton also built up their holdings at Brockhampton by transactions of this kind. Some of the few accumulating cottagers built up their estates in the same way. John Cous, also from Brockhampton, who accumulated an unusual holding comprising several cottages, tofts and irregular acreages, acquired them exclusively by extrafamilial transfer *inter vivos*. Even some of the composite holdings that became part of still greater conglomerations were by surrender of the outgoing tenant, as in the case of Thomas Knoller's acquisition of John Bere's estate in 1361–2. Similarly, Thomas Molin of Brockhampton, who on his death in about 1389–90 left an estate stretching over three tithings, made a particularly large acquisition in 1362–3 of a messuage, a virgate, a cottage and several other pieces surrendered to him by Clement Bachesmere. Lands acquired *inter vivos* were presumably often of better quality than those for which heirs were unwilling to fine.

The developments in the practice of the manorial courts on the bishopric estate that we have already examined also served the turn of tenants of composite holdings.[21] There are numerous fines by which these wealthier tenants sought to preserve their gains. Thomas Knoller, for example, fined for an enrolment to make good his claim of one and a half acres of land in Combe after an earlier quitclaim. The provision of such extra-customary devices helped to combat the overall fragility of these disparate holdings. Larger peasants were able to take advantage of other developments in manorial practice. Those who sublet property for lengthy terms were glad to make use of the possibility of establishing the reversion of their property through manor courts. John Langrish of East Meon, who built up a considerable estate of cottages, surrendered a grove and two crofts to William and Nicola Morton 'with reversion after their deaths'. John Sole and his wife similarly conceded their water-mill and two acres in the Forcomb tithing of East Meon to Robert and Isabel Baker for their lives with reversion. There is also an element of speculation in the acquisition of some smaller holdings. William Hook of East Meon, who had built up a multi-virgated tenement with crofts and cottages from 1349–50, surrendered a cottage and croft to Joan Hatch with the stipulation that the tenement would revert to William on Joan's death, yet William had only fined for the property earlier that year.

There is no reason to suppose that Thomas Knoller's accumulation of property depended upon any exceptional influence he was able to exercise in East Meon by virtue of an official position, or indeed that such institutional power was common among successful accumulators. It is true that on the Winchester manors, as elsewhere, the chief officers can sometimes be shown to be those who held large tenements. Several of those named as reeve or farmer in the pipe roll of 1409–10, for example, had accumulated significantly large composite holdings. Richard Monk, reeve of Holway manor near Taunton, had, since 1364–5, acquired two messuages and two half virgates, a cottage and several free-standing acres. Edward Cleeve, reeve of Brockhampton, was also a man of this type; in the first years of the fifteenth century he assembled by marriage and purchase a holding of three and a half virgates as well as cottages and other smaller pieces of land. Other reeves who held large composite holdings in 1409–10 were Nicholas Basset of Cheriton, John Wixi of Woodhay, Thomas Arnold of Brightwell and John Farnham of Warfield. However, this

---

21. Chapter 6, pp. 97–101.

phenomenon was not universal across the estate, and any benefits of local power and influence were more likely to be gained informally than through administrative office. Despite the oft-quoted notion that reeves were in a unique position to peculate a manor's resources, successful entrepreneurs were as likely to eschew office as to seek it: among the entry fines are more than a dozen instances where individuals paid to be released from manorial offices. They begin in the later fourteenth century with William Fry's release from office in 1386–7 on the manor of Bishopstone. In 1390 William Pophull of Bishops Waltham paid the large fine of £2 'in order that he is able to be excused from the office of reeve for the term of his life'. He was a successful participant in the local land market. In the 1390s he acquired two messuages, a virgate and a ferling of villein land and a croft, and at his death in 1414–15 he left his son a further two messuages, a plot, a toft, twenty-seven acres of purpresture and three other acres of unspecified character. Licences to avoid office occur most commonly in the first few years of the fifteenth century. Nicholas Kirkby of Twyford, who was released from manorial offices in 1402–3, was heavily involved in the manor's land market from 1364–5 until his death in 1408–9. His inheritance, which amalgamated the tenancies of five other families, was substantial, consisting of two messuages, two tofts, four half virgates of villein land, four sets of purpresture of two and a half acres each and a small plot measuring a rood. Men such as these were significant holders of customary land within their own localities, with substantial agrarian enterprises of their own and doubtless with subtenants to oversee. It is hardly surprising that they should not always welcome the taxing responsibilities of manorial administration.

The polarisation of land tenure

The acquisition of amalgamated properties by a minority of tenants inevitably implied a widening gap between them and those who did not accumulate. Hilton observed this polarisation on the estates of Leicester Abbey, and derived from it implications that were far from optimistic concerning the welfare of the peasantry: 'on the one hand richer peasants would build up farms above the size of the "normal" virgate holding of 20 or 30 acres, and on the other hand the poorer would lose what land they had and tend to become labourers'.[22] This interpretation, which transfers back into the fifteenth century agrarian developments traditionally associated with more modern times, implies that the gains of the minority were at the expense of the majority. The growth of larger units of production among the peasantry implies the emergence of an elite more dependent than their forefathers on the employment of wage labour for the cultivation of their extensive holdings. This, Hilton's argument implies, both required and caused the expansion of a rural working class, and so signified the development of a sort of peasant capitalism.

In fact this representation of the late fourteenth and early fifteenth centuries has severe flaws; it implies a conflict of interests that was not, in fact, characteristic of the period. It is true that a peasant elite emerged, but not true that this caused the impoverishment of lesser tenants, since it overlooks the flood of tenant and demesne

---

22. Hilton, *Economic development*, p. 100.

land into the land market after 1349. Nor is it true that the accumulation of land by the few contributed to the formation of a rural class of labourers. Such a class was already in existence, in large numbers, before the Black Death, working on demesne lands that were increasingly leased, and often broken up, towards the end of our period of study.[23] So, far from growing, the class of rural labourers shrank considerably between 1350 and 1415. Because of fourteenth-century depopulation, cottagers and smallholders, who constituted much of the labour force of the medieval countryside, were less numerous than in the past and were able to command increasingly high wages.[24] The employment opportunities both for men and women were bright, particularly near some of the late-fourteenth-century towns, whose trade and industry was expanding to satisfy new markets.[25] If cottagers continued to work on the land, and on the holdings of larger tenants, it was for good wages, and unlikely to be for want of other opportunities.

Evidence for the abandonment of cottages, implying a reduction in the number of cottagers, is widespread. At Bishops Waltham there are fourteen instances after 1348–9 of peasants abandoning their land, and nearly all of these were cottagers and smallholders; only one had as much as a half virgate. In the Taunton group of manors nearly all holdings specifically said to have been abandoned were cottages, small plots and half ferlings. Cottage holdings, and to a lesser extent ferlings, were often absorbed into the property of virgaters and half virgaters because they had been so abandoned; many virgated tenements engrossed more than one such cottage as well as other small parcels of land. At Bishops Hull in 1393–4, for example, Juliana, widow of William Shaldow, paid the large fine of £8 for a half virgate and 5½ additional acres of land that also included five cottages. In some instances these may have been used to house farmworkers,[26] although such accumulations were often the incidental effect of absorbing formerly independent tenements – the cottages may have been either derelict or converted to other purposes. The impermanence of cottage tenure was apparently closely related to changes in the character of the cottager class, and in particular to its diminished numbers and increased spatial mobility. The evidence, all

---

23. D.L. Farmer, 'The *famuli* in the later Middle Ages', in R. Britnell and J. Hatcher (eds), *Progress and problems in medieval England: essays in honour of Edward Miller* (Cambridge, 1996), pp. 207–36; Harvey, *Medieval Oxfordshire village*, pp. 75–86; N.S.B. Gras and E.C. Gras, *The economic and social history of an English village (Crawley, Hampshire), A.D. 909–1928* (Cambridge, Mass., 1930), p. 67; Page, 'Challenging custom', pp. 39–48; M.M. Postan, *The famulus: the estate labourer in the XIIth and XIIIth centuries,* Economic History Review supplement II (Cambridge, 1954); Robo, *Farnham,* pp. 41–5.

24. W.H. Beveridge, 'Wages in the Winchester manors', *Economic History Review,* 7 (1936–7), pp. 22–43; C. Dyer, 'Changes in diet in the late Middle Ages: the case of harvest workers', *AHR,* 36 (1988), pp. 21–37, reprinted in *idem, Everyday life in medieval England* (London and Rio Grande, 1994), pp. 77–99; D.L. Farmer, 'Prices and wages, 1350–1500', in *AHEW* III, pp. 467–94; J. Hatcher, 'England in the aftermath of the Black Death', *Past and Present,* 144 (1994), pp. 3–35.

25. R.H. Britnell, *Growth and decline in Colchester, 1300–1525* (Cambridge, 1986), pp. 95–7, 149; P.J.P. Goldberg, *Women, work and life cycle in a medieval economy: women in York and Yorkshire, c. 1300–1520* (Oxford, 1992), pp. 280–304.

26. H.S.A. Fox, 'Servants, cottagers and tied cottages during the later Middle Ages: towards a regional dimension', *Rural History* 6 (1995), pp. 136–43.

told, probably indicates that changes in employment opportunities had encouraged cottagers to move. Abandoned homes and high mobility are the most prevalent features of improving opportunities for cottager families, many of whom could improve their lot more rapidly by securing steady employment in Winchester, Southampton, Salisbury or Taunton than by acquiring property piecemeal.

At East Meon and Bishops Waltham, despite the development of some large accumulated holdings, smaller tenements were more stable than usual rather than less. Local employment opportunities for cottagers were perhaps protected here rather than threatened by the accumulations of their wealthier neighbours. A few cottagers in both these manors created composite smallholdings towards the end of the century. For example, at East Meon in 1395–6 Richard, son of John Cous, inherited his father's cottage with a curtilage containing one acre, five acres of purpresture, and two tofts with two ten-acre holdings of villein land. The independence of the cottagers was apparently exceptionally well assured here, as only a small proportion of virgaters had acquired cottage holdings; between 1349–50 and 1414–5 only seventeen virgated tenements at East Meon and nineteen at Bishops Waltham had done so.

We do not know in detail what happened to smallholders who abandoned their cottages. On the manor of Nailsbourne in the Taunton group the rolls identify the former tenants of 108 out of the 110 cottages transferred between 1349–50 and 1414–15. Of these 108 names, fewer than a fifth later fined for any sort of holding, and even this proportion is doubtless an overstatement; identifying tenants from names alone is problematic because of intervening time gaps – over twenty years in some cases. Our knowledge of the economy of late-fourteenth-century and early-fifteenth-century England debars a generally pessimistic interpretation of the disappearance of cottagers from our records. Their gains were differently achieved, by migration and wage-bargaining rather than by accumulation; the pipe rolls record what they left, but not where they arrived.

Conclusions

Before 1348 the freedom to accumulate was tightly circumscribed by manorial custom. Although the courts, in the bishop's name, sometimes condoned the accumulation of traditional holdings, this was rare, and the accumulation of property by any significant number of tenants depended upon locally distinctive customs, which appear to account for the exceptional level of accumulation already in evidence at Bishops Waltham and some other southern and eastern Hampshire manors by the 1330s. Even the availability of significant areas of assart, purpresture or overland did not universally lead to the addition of further properties to virgated tenements. Such accumulations are to be found at Farnham and the Taunton manors, but not on some of the most actively colonising manors where they might be most expected, such as Witney. It seems that the force of custom was able to separate the two categories of land – virgated tenures and assarts – in such a way as normally to inhibit the process of accumulation by customary tenants even where newer land was relatively abundant.

Between 1348 and 1415 the accumulation of holdings became much more common across the bishopric estate, but local differences remained as strong as before 1348. There remained on many manors a distinction in practice between virgated lands and land of other sorts, and the presence of extensive assarts, as at Witney, did not inevitably arouse the acquisitive ambitions of customary tenants. The accumulation of property became much more frequent than before 1348–9, however, chiefly because of an abundance of land available on good terms. A minority of tenants accumulated large and complex holdings, for which they were prepared to pay large entry fines. These accumulators tended to come from long-established families and benefited, in particular, from the availability of untenanted land, which they often accumulated gradually over the course of a long lifetime. It is likely that they usually sublet property, although such sublettings are only occasionally in evidence. Despite their wealth, the relationship between this peasant elite and the tenure of manorial office was weak, implying that official roles on the bishop's manor gave no significant advantage to a would-be accumulator.

The propensity to accumulate was more marked, unsurprisingly, among larger tenants than among smallholders and cottagers, so that the distribution of landed wealth became more polarised between the Black Death and 1415. The implications of this for welfare are not obvious, however, since this was a period when the employment opportunities and wage levels available to labourers and artisans were significantly improving, probably faster in fact than returns to landed property. The accumulation of property by a minority was made possible by taking up lands vacated by death or abandoned by former tenants, and not by expropriation. It did not imply the impoverishment of the majority. The large numbers of abandoned cottages in the later fourteenth century, some of which were absorbed into larger holdings, impy that the cottager class had considerably contracted rather than grown, and this is incompatible with the view that a rural working class was in the process of formation.

Chapter 10

Conclusions

There is undoubtedly scope for further study of the land market on the bishopric of Winchester estates in the light of our findings, particularly to define more clearly the local context of individual manors and the bearing that that had on the balance between traditional and commercial attitudes towards property. Our approach to the problem through the comprehensive collection of entry fine data has nevertheless provided a number of conclusions, some of which seem barely contestable while others will benefit from further testing and refinement. Because of the large and scattered character of the estate, these conclusions are best divided into three categories: those of general relevance to the whole estate, those of regional significance, and those relating to differences between individual manors.

The estate as a whole

Because all the manors of the estate were under the lordship of the bishopric of Winchester, the wide variety of experience across the estate encourages the conclusion that local custom was of greater relevance in understanding the development of the land market than seigniorial fiat. Episcopal officers, because they presided over manorial courts, were no doubt involved on some occasions in the interpretation or relaxation of custom, as we saw in discussing restrictions upon the amalgamation of customary tenures. Yet matters of such importance as inheritance rights varied locally to an extent that implies independence of central law-giving. Even the question of whether virgated units could be subdivided was subject to local variation, despite the administrative interest the bishop's men might have in maintaining such units intact. Some of the bishop's manors were of recent acquisition, notably the south-coast manors of Havant with Brockhampton and Alverstoke with Gosport, which were acquired from the monastery of St Swithun, Winchester, in 1284, for settling a dispute about the monks' liberties.[1] The similarities between the development of the land market on these manors and on those nearby that were already under the bishop's lordship imply that their separate management had not been a dominant determinant in their development. However, the episcopal estate as a whole had enjoyed considerable continuity since before the Norman Conquest, so the bishops had had ample opportunity to standardise practice across the estate had they had the will and power to do so.[2] All in all, the ability of the bishops to regulate the land market according to any systematic set of principles seems to have been weak.[3]

Across the whole estate the development of a land market in customary land was

---

1. Doubleday *et al.* (eds), *Hampshire and the Isle of Wight*, III, pp. 123–5, 203.
2. Great Domesday Book, fos. 31, 40–40v, 58, 65v, 87v, 143v, 155.
3. See C. Dyer, 'The ineffectiveness of lordship in England, 1200–1400', in C. Dyer, P. Cross and C. Wickham (eds), *Rodney Hilton's Middle Ages: an exploration of historical themes*, Past and Present Supplement 2 (2007), pp. 69–86.

significantly slower to emerge than in East Anglia, notwithstanding greater activity in some manors than in others before the Black Death. The pipe rolls show that before the Black Death there were strong feelings in most of the bishop's manor courts against either the fragmentation or amalgamation of virgated units. The precise reasons for this difference are not easily isolated; East Anglia was more populous, more commercialised and in aggregate wealthier than the part of England in which the bishop had his estates,[4] and there was also more partible inheritance in eastern England.[5] In this respect the impression given by the bishopric estates is in line with those of other historians concerning the southern English counties, so it seems likely that the relatively conservative practices of manorial courts were a rational response to the needs and interests of village leaders. As yet, apparently, the relative security of custom was worth more to them than any benefits of the greater freedom that its abandonment would bring. On the other hand, the Winchester evidence shows that a market in assart land and purpresture was already well developed before the Black Death on those manors where such land was available, and suggests that this land was to some extent subject to a different structure of demand – and perhaps different customary expectations – than that affecting the transfer of virgated tenements. As these comments imply, the peasant land market before 1349 was dominated by dealings in small parcels of land rather than in virgates and half virgates.

Because our observations do not advance beyond 1415 they do not allow us to comment on some developments that are more strongly associated with the fifteenth century. They nevertheless register a definite change in the operations of the land market during the fourteenth century, and particularly after the Black Death. There was a marked decline in the number of transactions: between the periods 1320–49 and 1350–79 the number of entry fines on the bishopric estate fell by about 15 per cent, and it then declined more steeply by a further 26 per cent between 1350–79 and 1380–1409 (see Table 6.1). These figures exaggerate the contraction of business, however, as the average size of transactions increased; larger units of property were being transferred, and it was increasingly common for formerly independent units to be combined. Although the average size of fines tended to increase (see Figure 5.3), this is compatible with the likelihood that the unit value of land was declining, particularly after 1380. These changes were in turn associated with a relaxation of former inhibitions concerning the transfer of customary units and their amalgamation into larger tenures. By 1415 there are numerous examples of wealthy peasants, often with deep roots in their respective communities, who had accumulated substantial complexes of property.

Across the estate there is also good evidence, despite variations to be considered shortly, that the bond between land and family weakened in the late fourteenth century (see Table 6.2). Much of the increase in the proportion of extrafamilial to intrafamilial transactions after the 1340s was the result of tenements falling vacant at the death of tenants, and it might be argued that this represents the dying-out of

4.   Campbell and Bartley, *England on the eve of the Black Death*, maps 17.2, 17.3, 18.3, 18.6, pp. 194k, 305–6, 326; R.S. Schofield, 'The geographical distribution of wealth in England, 1334–1649', *Economic History Review*, 2nd series, 18 (1965), pp. 504–7; R.M. Smith (ed.), 'Human resources', in G. Astill and A. Grant (eds), *The countryside of medieval England* (Oxford, 1988), pp. 196–202.
5.   Faith, 'Peasant families', pp. 81–2; Homans, *English villagers*, pp. 116–17.

families rather than the weakening of bonds between families and their land. But although an inevitable effect of crisis mortality was to reduce the number of potential heirs, it was simultaneously true that younger peasants wanting land were less dependent than in the past upon inheritances. The failure to take up inheritances was in large part the result of heirs declining to do so because they could find a superior alternative, especially when the property available by inheritance was on difficult land or in an isolated location. The swing of extrafamilial transfers across the estate from 40.7 per cent of all transfers in the years 1320–49 to 60.8 per cent in 1350–70 and 60.4 per cent in 1380–1415 represents the effects of a greater availability of land and reduced dependence of peasant families upon hereditary claims. In spite of this trend, the role of family connections in the transfer of property remained very considerable to the end of our period, and in some manors it was still the dominant consideration into the fifteenth century. It is likely, too, that, as on the Worcester bishopric estates, family attachment to land grew stronger again after 1500.[6]

Regional differences

The bishopric manors nowhere constitute more than a small sample from any single definable region, and some of the regional divisions we have used are too large, and too weakly represented, to allow any certain conclusions to be drawn. Our Northern group of manors, which comprises manors in Berkshire, Oxfordshire and Buckinghamshire, has no definite regional characteristic, and must be regarded with suspicion. The bracketing together of Esher and Bentley, both small manors, gives equally unreliable evidence of any regional characteristics. However, some groupings of manors have better justification and provide the basis for conclusions about the scope for and foundation of regional variation in the medieval land market. The principal contrasts, as identified in Chapter 2, distinguish three regions where transactions were particularly numerous in relation to the level of assized rents. These were the Woodland manors of Witney and Wargrave (defining a type of region rather than a particular region, given the distance between the two), the Somerset manors and the manors of South Hampshire.

The most definite conclusion to emerge from a comparison of these regions is that there was no single environmental characteristic that they shared. There is no simple explanation as to why transactions were more numerous in some regions rather than others. In the case of the Woodland manors a decisive influence was the large amount of land reclaimed from forest that lay outside the more closely regulated customary holdings. In a period of high land values, like the late thirteenth and early fourteenth centuries, this land was good enough to attract buyers even though it was poor. By contrast, the Taunton manors of Somerset were characterised by very little assarting, and the soil there has been celebrated through the centuries for its high quality. The differences between Witney and Taunton were so marked that Titow used them to contrast the effects of the presence and absence of assarted land on the bishopric manors.[7] They nevertheless shared the characteristic of a busy land market. At

---

6.   Dyer, 'Changes in the size of peasant holdings', pp. 285, 294.

7.   Notably in Titow, 'Some differences', pp. 1–13.

Taunton this was made possible partly by the exceptionally advanced subdivision of virgates, which had progressed further here at an earlier date than almost anywhere else on the estate, but it also involved a large number of cottagers and smallholders. The South Hampshire group of manors was different again. The region was seemingly one of light population density, with no particular concentration of wealth except at Southampton. There were no assarts to speak of. The soil was of very mixed quality, deserving no particular commendation. The land market was appreciably less developed here than in the Woodland or the Taunton manors, and intrafamilial transfers were more prominent. The high turnover of property can be explained, at least in part, by the access of peasant families to trading activities that had encouraged the fragmentation of holdings, and so allowed a large number of tenants relative to the amount and value of the available land.

The second main conclusion to derive from analysis of our database is that the characteristics we have observed were vulnerable to changes affecting the country as a whole: changes to which different regions responded in different ways. The decline in land values was transformative for the Woodland manors. They experienced a steeper decline in the number of transactions than anywhere else on the estate — a decline of 66 per cent between 1263–1349 and 1350–1415. The South Hampshire manors also fared relatively badly in this respect, with a decline of 52 per cent. The Somerset manors, by contrast, with a decline of only 17 per cent, performed better than any other group (see Table 2.11). Not only did the high quality of land give some protection to land market activity on the Taunton manors, but there was an additional stimulus to demand from new sources of regional prosperity, notably the participation of Taunton in the development of England's woollen textile industry.

The Hampshire Chalk Plateau region is the best represented in our sample. Although its manors varied widely in some respects, it nevertheless had clearly defined regional characteristics. It was a region where pastoral husbandry was exceptionally important on the downs, so that much of the relevant resources of farmers lay in pasture rights. Despite the contrasts between manors, this region approximates to a norm for the whole estate, and perhaps for much of southern England. Its land market was relatively slow, and it had a high commitment to customary units, which defined the right to pasture sheep on common land.[8] Between 1263–1349 and 1350–1415 the decline in the number of transactions (46 per cent) corresponded to that of the estate as a whole (44 per cent). This region did not have land of particularly high quality. Although it contained Winchester, and was not lacking in smaller towns, it was not highly populated nor conspicuously industrial. It seems to be defined by the absence of any particularly strong stimuli to abandon traditional ways.

Intermanorial differences

Not surprisingly, given the number of manors on the estate, the possible range of contrasts between them is large. Some of these have already been embraced in the discussion of regional differences. Others, however, relate to differences that cut

---

8.   Vancouver, *General view*, p. 373.

across regional variation and may therefore contribute to differences of experience within individual regions, however small.

Perhaps the foremost of these is differences of size. From the time of Domesday Book onwards all our information about manors demonstrates that they were of very different dimensions, and that these differences had qualitative implications for the way in which they were settled and managed. Obviously there tended to be more transactions on large manors than on small ones. But, as observed in Chapter 2, large size was frequently accompanied by other attributes that provided a disproportionately large stimulus to the buying and selling of property. Large manors tended to have more land outside the structure of customary holdings, either in the form of forest and waste or as cultivated demesne land, either of which might be released into the peasant market in certain circumstances. Another feature of large manors, particularly relevant from the later twelfth century onwards, was the propensity of landlords to encourage commercial development there by establishing marketing centres. Even rural markets were often accompanied by increased settlement by smallholders and artisan cottagers but, particularly if lords were ambitious enough to found boroughs, population, wealth and access to cash could increase enough to make a difference to the demand for land. The bishops of Winchester were as active as their contemporaries in this respect, so that a number of their larger manors had markets and boroughs by 1263. There were boroughs at Alresford (New Alresford), Burghclere (Newtown), Fareham and Overton in Hampshire, Taunton in Somerset, Downton and Knoyle (Hindon) in Wiltshire, Wargrave in Berkshire, and Witney in Oxfordshire.[9] Not all these boroughs were equally active in the development of the market for agricultural land, although they implied a market in mills and urban properties. At Witney the burgesses significantly contributed to the buying and selling of assarted land, as we saw in Chapter 8.

Manors also differed in the intrinsic attractiveness of their tenancies. The size of the resident community was probably a relevant consideration in this respect, but the quality of the soil, access to pasture, ease of communications and proximity to markets were all additional features that might stimulate demand for land on some manors more than on others. Soil quality was an important issue, judging by the fact that the bishop suffered only slight losses of rent from the Taunton manors. There was barely a problem with lost rent at Adderbury in Oxfordshire, where the soil was 'an exceeding fine, deep, reddish-brown sand on a gritstone; some of the very finest soil in the county', producing exceptionally high yields.[10] Not all the reasons for variation between manors in this respect can be identified by our data, but the examination of family preferences in Chapter 6 nevertheless demonstrates great differences between manors with respect to the entry fines families would pay to retain their land. In general, the family bond weakened during the fourteenth century but, as we have observed, there were strong variations between manors in the same region. In the South Hampshire group, for example, the average family premium was very much higher at Gosport and Brockhampton than at Bitterne or Fareham. On the

---

9.   Letters, *Gazetteer*, I, pp. 58, 153, 155–6, 285; II, pp. 310, 369, 371. See also Beresford, 'The six new towns', pp. 187–215.

10.   A. Young, *General view of the agriculture of Oxfordshire* (London, 1813), pp. 111, 153.

Hampshire Chalk Plateau there were similar differences between Droxford, Marwell and Merdon, with high family premiums, and Overton and North Waltham, where they were exceptionally low (see Table 6.7). Other differences are apparent from Titow's estimates of rent income lost by the bishop between 1348 and 1383; there was no reduction at Morton or East Meon, and only a 9.7 per cent loss at Merdon, but rents were down by 27.9 per cent at Overton and by 66.6 per cent at nearby North Waltham. Tenancies on these last two manors, on the northern edge of the Chalk Plateau, were among the least attractive on the bishopric estates. Such differences inevitably affected the extent to which land passed by inheritance relative to their transfer between families, either *inter vivos* or *post mortem*. They shaped the extent to which different villages were deserted, which was very varied even within the chalkland region.[11] They also influenced the ease with which wealthier tenants could accumulate property.

Our evidence does not allow us to compare the topography of different manors, which would require close research in sources other than the Winchester pipe rolls. Nevertheless, it indicates that the land market was affected by features of the landscape such as field systems and farming units, which also differed from village to village. Observations on this point involve speculation, but it is difficult to imagine a cause other than one of a topographical nature that could explain why the exchange of properties should be so much more active on some manors – notably those of the Taunton group – than on others. It is likely that some topographical feature of the settlement at Farnham will account for the unusual addition of purprestures to customary tenures there between the 1280s and the 1330s.

Finally, we must also allow for difference in manorial custom that affected both inheritance and the willingness of manor courts to see tenures amalgamated and fragmented, since this too affected the level of land market activity to be expected from any given acreage of tenant land. Although these practices were influenced by broader economic and social trends, and to some extent followed regional patterns, each manor was to some extent autonomous. Table 3.2 shows the differences between manors within the manors of the Hampshire Chalk Plateau in the extent to which virgates were subdivided. The variation was extreme. At North Waltham 86 per cent of transactions involving customary units concerned whole virgates, but the proportion was only 6 per cent at Merdon. Only 2 per cent concerned quarter virgates at North Waltham, but 36 per cent did so at Merdon. Such contrasts, which ultimately affected the ease with which large properties could be accumulated, are difficult to explain by environmental reasoning, partly because their origins go back to time before record. It seems likely that in the history of the peasant land market there will always be some such variables that will have to remain unexplained, given the long prehistory of most of the properties under discussion.

---

11. Hare, 'Agriculture and rural settlement', p. 168.

Appendix

The number of recorded entry fines by manor, 1263–1349 and 1350–1415

Manor	1263–1349	1350–1415
Adderbury	522	403
Alresford	468	269
Alverstoke	433	34
Ashmansworth	224	111
Beauworth	100	47
Bentley	551	260
Bishops Fonthill	134	98
Bishopstoke	799	448
Bishopstone	260	161
Bishops Sutton	1029	609
Bishops Waltham	3211	1573
Bitterne	712	503
Brighstone	64	-
Brightwell	319	209
Brockhampton with Havant	1260	727
Burghclere	744	302
Calbourne	184	-
Cheriton	471	212
Corfe	35	-
Crawley	271	177
Culham	147	51
Downton	1394	763
Downton borough	12	8
Droxford	579	323
East Knoyle	249	172
East Meon	1999	1125
East Meon Church	227	160
Ecchinswell	403	212
Esher	178	106
Fareham	1385	488
Farnham	2439	1365
Fulford	25	-
Gosport	52	11
Hambledon	822	377

Harwell	320	142
Highclere	432	216
Holway	1961	1625
Ivinghoe	1028	544
Kingstone St Mary and Nailsbourne	781	689
Merdon	1412	710
Morton	123	58
Newtown	22	3
North Waltham	148	71
Otterford	111	127
Overton	441	211
Poundisford	1755	1304
Rimpton	168	152
Ringwood	40	-
Staplegrove	1368	1168
Taunton borough	68	91
Trull and Bishops Hull	1036	897
Twyford and Marwell	1151	635
Upton	18	16
Waltham St Lawrence	442	353
Warfield	442	377
Wargrave	1626	403
West Wycombe	726	337
Wield	132	89
Witney	4188	1598
Woodhay	857	439

Note: The list excludes places with fewer than twenty fines.

Bibliography

Primary sources

Babington, C. and Lumby, J.R. (eds), *Polychronicon Ranulphi Higden monachi Cestrensis*, 9 vols, Rolls Series, 41 (London, 1865–6)

Brooke, C.N.L. and Postan, M.M. (eds), *Carte nativorum: a Peterborough Abbey cartulary of the fourteenth century*, Northamptonshire Record Society, 20 (Northampton, 1960)

Fenwick, C. (ed.), *The poll taxes of 1377, 1379 and 1381*, 3 vols, Records of the Social and Economic History of England and Wales, new series, 27, 29, 37 (Oxford, 1998–2005)

Hall, H. (ed.), *The pipe roll of the bishopric of Winchester for the fourth year of the pontificate of Peter des Roches, 1208–1209* (London, 1903)

Harvey, P.D.A. (ed.), *Manorial records of Cuxham, Oxfordshire, circa 1200–1359*, Historical Manuscripts Commission Joint Publications, 23; Oxfordshire Record Society, 50 (London, 1976)

Holt, N.R. (ed.), *The pipe roll of the bishopric of Winchester 1210–1211* (Manchester, 1964)

Maitland, F.W. (ed.), *Select pleas in manorial and other seignorial courts*, Selden Society, 2 (London, 1889)

Oschinsky, D. (ed.), *Walter of Henley and other treatises on estate management and accounting* (Oxford, 1971)

Page, M. (ed.), *The pipe roll of the bishopric of Winchester 1301–2*, Hampshire Record Series, 14 (Winchester, 1996)

— (ed.), *The pipe roll of the bishop of Winchester 1409–10*, Hampshire Record Series, 16 (Winchester, 1999)

Poos, L.R. and Bonfield, L. (eds), *Select cases in manorial courts 1250–1550: property and family law*, Selden Society, 114 (London, 1998)

Riley, H.T. (ed.), *Chronica monasterii S, Albani*, 12 vols, Rolls Series, 26 (London, 1863–76)

Stenton, F.M. (ed.), *Documents illustrative of the social and economic history of the Danelaw*, Records of the Social and Economic History of England and Wales, 1st series, 5 (London, 1920)

Tait, J. (ed.), *Chronica Johannis de Reading et Anonymi Cantuariensis* (Manchester, 1914)

Secondary sources

Aston, M., 'Deserted settlements in the west of England', in M. Aston, D. Austin and C. Dyer (eds), *Tho rural settlements of medieval England: studies dedicated to Maurice Beresford and John Hurst* (Oxford, 1989), pp. 105 28

Bailey, M., 'Peasant welfare in England, 1290–1348', *Economic History Roview*, 51 (1998), pp. 223–51

—, *Medieval Suffolk: an economic and social history, 1200–1500* (Woodbridge, 2007)

Ballard, A., 'The manors of Witney, Brightwell and Downton', in P. Vinogradoff (ed.), *Oxford studies in social and legal history, V* (Oxford, 1916), pp. 181–217

Bean, W., 'Landlords', in E. Miller (ed.), *The agrarian history of England and Wales, III: 1348–1500* (Cambridge, 1991), pp. 526–86

Bennett, J.M., *Women in the medieval English countryside* (Oxford, 1987)

Beresford, M.W., 'The six new towns of the bishops of Winchester, 1200–55', *Medieval Archaeology*, 3 (1959), pp. 187–215

— and Finberg, H.P.R., *English medieval boroughs: a handlist* (Newton Abbot, 1973)

Beveridge, W.H., 'The yield and price of corn in the Middle Ages', *Economic History Review*, 1 (1927), pp. 155–67

—, 'The Winchester rolls and their dating', *Economic History Review*, 2 (1929), pp. 93–113

—, 'Wages in the Winchester manors', *Economic History Review*, 7 (1936–7), pp. 22–43

Billingsley, J., *General view of the agriculture of the county of Somerset* (Bath, 1798)

Bolton, J.L., *The medieval English economy 1150–1500* (London, 1980)

Bridbury, A.R., 'The Black Death', *Economic History Review*, 26 (1973), pp. 577–92, reprinted in *idem*, *The English economy from Bede to the Reformation* (Woodbridge, 1992), pp. 200–17

—, *Medieval English clothmaking: an economic survey* (London, 1982)

Briggs, C., 'Creditors and debtors and their relationships at Oakington, Cottenham and Dry Drayton (Cambridgeshire), 1291–1350', in P.R. Schofield and N.J. Mayhew (eds), *Credit and debt in medieval England, c.1180–c.1350* (Oxford, 2002), pp. 127–48

—, 'Manor court procedures, debt litigation levels, and rural credit provision in England, c.1290–c.1380', *Law and History Review*, 24 (2006), pp. 519–58

Britnell, R.H., *Growth and decline in Colchester, 1300–1525* (Cambridge, 1986)

—, 'Tenant farming and farmers: eastern England', in E. Miller (ed.), *The agrarian history of England and Wales, III: 1348–1500* (Cambridge, 1991), pp. 611–24

—, *The commercialisation of English society, 1000–1500*, 2nd edn (Manchester, 1996)

— (ed.), *The Winchester pipe rolls and medieval English society* (Woodbridge, 2003)

—, 'The Winchester pipe rolls and their historians', in *idem* (ed.), *The Winchester pipe rolls and medieval English society* (Woodbridge, 2003), pp. 1–19

—, 'English agricultural output and prices, 1350–1450: national trends and regional divergences', in B. Dodds and R.H. Britnell (eds), *Rural society and agriculture after the Black Death: common themes and regional variations* (Hertford, 2008), pp. 20–39

Burstall, E.B., 'A monastic agreement of the fourteenth century', *Norfolk Archaeology*, 31 (1957), pp. 211–18

Campbell, B.M.S., 'Population pressure, inheritance and the land market in a fourteenth-century peasant community', in R.M. Smith (ed.), *Land, kinship and life-cycle* (Cambridge, 1984), pp. 87–134

—, *English seigniorial agriculture, 1250–1450* (Cambridge, 2000)

—, 'A unique estate and a unique source: the Winchester pipe rolls in perspective', in R.H. Britnell (ed.), *The Winchester pipe rolls and medieval English society* (Woodbridge, 2003), pp. 21–43

— and Bartley, K., *England on the eve of the Black Death: an atlas of lay lordship, land and wealth, 1300–1349* (Manchester, 2006)

—, Galloway, J.A., Keene, D. and Murphy, M., *A medieval capital and its grain supply: agrarian production and distribution in the London region c. 1300* (London, 1993)

Carus-Wilson, E.M., 'An industrial revolution of the thirteenth century', *Economic History Review*, 1st series, 11 (1941), pp. 39–60, reprinted in *eadem*, *Medieval merchant venturers*, 2nd edn (London, 1967), pp. 183–210

Darby, H.C., *Domesday England* (Cambridge, 1977)

Davies, R.R., *Lordship and society in the March of Wales, 1284–1400* (Oxford, 1978)

Delille, G. and Levi, G. (eds), 'Il mercato della terra', *Quaderni storici*, new series, 65 (1987), pp. 351–659

DeWindt, E.B., *Land and people in Holywell-cum-Needingworth* (Toronto, 1971)

Dodds, B., *Peasants and production in the medieval North-East: the evidence from tithes, 1270–1536* (Woodbridge, 2007)

— and Britnell, R.H. (eds), *Rural society and agriculture after the Black Death: common themes and regional variations* (Hertford, 2008)

Doubleday, H.A. *et al.* (eds), *The Victoria history of Hampshire and the Isle of Wight*, 5 vols and index (London, 1900–14)

Du Boulay, F.R.H., *The lordship of Canterbury: an essay on medieval society* (London, 1966)

Dyer, A., 'Appendix: ranking lists of English medieval towns', in D.M. Palliser (ed.), *The Cambridge urban history of Britain, I: 600–1540* (Cambridge, 2000), pp. 747–70

Dyer, C., 'A redistribution of incomes in fifteenth-century England?' *Past and Present*, 39 (1968), pp. 11–33, reprinted in R.H. Hilton (ed.), *Peasants, knights and heretics: studies in medieval English social history* (Cambridge, 1976), pp. 192–215

—, *Lords and peasants in a changing society: the estates of the bishopric of Worcester, 680–1540* (Cambridge, 1980)

—, 'Changes in the size of peasant holdings in some west midland villages, 1400–1540', in R.M. Smith (ed.), *Land, kinship and life-cycle* (Cambridge, 1984), pp. 277–94

—, 'Changes in the link between families and land in the west midlands in the fourteenth and fifteenth centuries', in R.M. Smith (ed.), *Land, kinship and life-cycle* (Cambridge, 1984), pp. 305–11

—, 'Changes in diet in the late Middle Ages: the case of harvest workers', *AHR*, 36 (1988), pp. 21–37, reprinted in *idem, Everyday life in medieval England* (London and Rio Grande, 1994), pp. 77–99

—, 'The ineffectiveness of lordship in England, 1200–1400', in C. Dyer, P. Coss and C. Wickham (eds), *Rodney Hilton's Middle Ages: an exploration of historical themes*, Past and Present Supplement 2 (2007), pp. 69–86

—, 'Tenant farming and tenant farmers: the West Midlands', in E. Miller (ed.), *The agrarian history of England and Wales, III: 1348–1500* (Cambridge, 1991), pp. 624–35

—, 'Were there any capitalists in fifteenth-century England?', in J. Kermode (ed.), *Enterprise and individuals in fifteenth-century England* (Stroud, 1991), pp. 1–24

—, *Standards of living in the Middle Ages* (Cambridge, 1998)

—, *Making a living in the Middle Ages: the people of Britain, 850–1520* (New Haven, 2002)

Faith, R.J., 'Berkshire: fourteenth and fifteenth centuries', in P.D.A. Harvey (ed.), *The peasant land market in medieval England* (Oxford, 1984), pp. 106–77

—, 'Peasant families and inheritance customs in medieval England', *AHR*, 14 (1966), pp. 77–95

Farmer, D.L., 'Grain yields on the Winchester manors in the later Middle Ages', *Economic History Review*, 2nd series, 30 (1977), pp. 555–66

—, 'Prices and wages [1042–1350]', in H.E. Hallam (ed.), *The agrarian history of England and Wales, II: 1042–1350* (Cambridge, 1988), pp. 715–817

—, 'Marketing the produce of the countryside, 1200–1500', in E. Miller (ed.), *The agrarian history of England and Wales, III: 1348–1500* (Cambridge, 1991), pp. 324–430

—, 'Prices and wages, 1350–1500', in E. Miller (ed.), *The agrarian history of England and Wales, III: 1348–1500* (Cambridge, 1991), pp. 431–525

—, 'The *famuli* in the later Middle Ages', in R. Britnell and J. Hatcher (eds), *Progress and problems in medieval England: essays in honour of Edward Miller* (Cambridge, 1996), pp. 207–36

Feller, L. and Whickham, C. (eds), *Le marché de la terre au Moyen Âge* (Rome, 2005)

Fox, H.S.A., 'Servants, cottagers and tied cottages during the later Middle Ages: towards a regional dimension', *Rural History*, 6 (1995), pp. 125–54

Furió, A. and Mirar Jódar, A.J., 'Le marché de la terre dans le pays de Valence au bas Moyen Âge', in L. Feller and C. Whickham (eds), *Le marché de la terre au Moyen Âge* (Rome, 2005), pp. 573–623

Goldberg, P.J.P., *Women, work and life cycle in a medieval economy: women in York and Yorkshire, c. 1300–1520* (Oxford, 1992)

Gras, N.S.B. and Gras, E.C., *The economic and social history of an English village (Crawley, Hampshire), A.D. 909–1928* (Cambridge, Mass., 1930)

Gray H.L., *English field systems* (Cambridge, Mass., 1915)

Hampshire County Council, *Audit of Hampshire soils* (Winchester, 2004)

Hare, J., 'The demesne leases of fifteenth-century Wiltshire', *AHR*, 29 (1981), pp. 1–15

—, 'Agriculture and rural settlement in the chalklands of Wiltshire and Hampshire from *c. 1200–c. 1500'*, in M. Aston and C. Lewis (eds), *The medieval landscape of Wessex* (Oxford, 1994), pp. 159–69

—, 'The bishop and the prior: demesne agriculture in medieval Hampshire', *AHR*, 54 (2006), pp. 187–212

—, 'Lord, tenant and the market: some tithe evidence from the Wessex region', in B. Dodds and R.H. Britnell (eds), *Rural society and agriculture after the Black Death: common themes and regional variations* (Hertford, 2008), pp. 132–46

Harvey, B., *Westminster Abbey and its estates in the Middle Ages* (Oxford, 1977)

Harvey, P.D.A., 'A manuscript estate map by Christopher Saxton', *The British Museum Quarterly*, 23 (3) (1960–1), pp. 65–7

—, *A medieval Oxfordshire village: Cuxham, 1240–1400* (London, 1965)

— (ed.), *The peasant land market in medieval England* (Oxford, 1984)

—, 'Introduction' and 'Conclusion', in *idem* (ed.), *The peasant land market in medieval England* (Oxford, 1984), pp. 1–28, 328–56

—, 'The peasant land market in medieval England – and beyond', in Z. Razi and R.M. Smith (eds), *Medieval society and the manor court* (Oxford, 1996), pp. 392–407

—, *Manorial records*, 2nd edn (London, 1999)

Hatcher, J., *Rural economy and society in the duchy of Cornwall, 1300–1500* (Cambridge, 1970)

—, 'English serfdom and villeinage: towards a reassessment', *Past and Present*, 90 (1981), pp. 3–39

—, 'England in the aftermath of the Black Death', *Past and Present*, 144 (1994), pp. 3–35

Hewitt, E.M., 'Fisheries' and 'Salt', in W. Page (ed.), *The Victoria history of the county of Hampshire*, V (Oxford, 1912), pp. 466–74

Hilton, R.H., *The economic development of some Leicestershire estates in the 14th and 15th centuries* (Oxford, 1947)

—, 'Gloucester Abbey leases of the late thirteenth century', *University of Birmingham Historical Journal*, 4 (1953–4), pp. 1–17, reprinted in *idem*, *The English peasantry in the later Middle Ages* (Oxford, 1975), pp. 139–60

—, *The decline of serfdom in medieval England* (London, 1969)

—, *The English peasantry in the later Middle Ages* (Oxford, 1975)

—, *A medieval society: the West Midlands at the end of the thirteenth century*, 2nd edn (Cambridge, 1983)

Homans, G.C., *English villagers of the thirteenth century* (New York, 1960)

Hoskins, W.G., *The Midland peasant: the economic and social history of a Leicestershire village* (London, 1957)

Howell, C., *Land, family and inheritance in transition: Kibworth Harcourt, 1280–1700* (Cambridge, 1983)

Hyams, P.R., 'The origins of a peasant land market in England', *Economic History Review*, 2nd series, 23 (1970), pp. 18–31

Jones, A., 'Bedfordshire: fifteenth century', in P.D.A. Harvey (ed.), *The peasant land market in medieval England* (Oxford, 1984), pp. 179–251

Keen, M., *English society in the later Middle Ages, 1348–1500* (London, 1990)

Keene, D., 'The south-east of England', in D.M. Palliser (ed.), *The Cambridge urban history of Britain, I: 600–1540* (Cambridge, 2000), pp. 545–82

Kosminsky, E.A., *Studies in the agrarian history of England in the thirteenth century*, trans. R. Kisch, ed. R.H. Hilton (Oxford, 1956)

Kowaleski, M., *Local markets and regional trade in medieval Exeter* (Cambridge, 1995)

—, 'Fish production, trade and consumption, c1300–1530, 2: the western fisheries', in D.J. Starkey, C. Reid and N. Ashcroft (eds), *England's sea fisheries: the commercial sea fisheries of England and Wales since 1300* (London, 2000), pp. 23–8

Langdon, J., *Mills in the medieval economy: England 1300–1540* (Oxford, 2004)

Letters, S., *Gazetteer of markets and fairs in England and Wales to 1516*, 2 vols (London, 2003)

Levett, A.E., 'The Black Death on the estates of the see of Winchester', in P. Vinogradoff (ed.),
  Oxford studies in social and legal history, V (Oxford, 1916), pp. 1–180
McIntosh, M.K., *The royal manor of Havering, 1200–1500* (Cambridge, 1986)
Masschaele, J., *Peasants, merchants and markets: inland trade in medieval England, 1150–1350*
  (New York, 1997)
Mate, M.E., *Daughter, wives and widows after the Black Death: women in Sussex, 1350–1535*
  (Woodbridge, 1998)
Mayberry, T.W., *Estate records of the bishops of Winchester in the Hampshire Record Office*
  (Hampshire County Council, 1988)
Mayhew, N.J., 'Money and prices in England from Henry II to Edward III', *AHR*, 35 (1987), pp.
  121–32
Miller, E., *The abbey and bishopric of Ely: the social history of an ecclesiastical estate from the
  tenth century to the early fourteenth century* (Cambridge, 1951)
— (ed.), *The agrarian history of England and Wales, III: 1348–1500* (Cambridge, 1991)
—, 'The occupation of the land: the southern counties', in *idem* (ed.), *The agrarian history of
  England and Wales, III: 1348–1500* (Cambridge, 1991), pp. 136–51
—, 'Tenant farming and tenant farmers: the southern counties', in *idem* (ed.), *The agrarian
  history of England and Wales, III: 1348–1500* (Cambridge, 1991), pp. 703–22
— and Hatcher, J., *Medieval England: rural society and economic change, 1086–1348* (London,
  1978)
Mullan, J., 'The transfer of customary land on the estates of the bishop of Winchester between
  the Black Death and the plague of 1361', in R.H. Britnell (ed.), *The Winchester pipe rolls and
  medieval English society* (Woodbridge, 2003), pp. 81–107
—, 'The time and place of entry and marriage fines on the bishopric of Winchester estates:
  1350–1400', in M. Bourin and P. Martínez Sopena (eds), *Pour une anthropologie du
  prélèvement seigneurial dans les campagnes médiévales (XIe—XIVe siècles): Les mots, les
  temps, les lieux* (Paris, 2007), pp. 399—414
—, *Mortality, gender and the plague of 1361—2 on the estate of the bishop of Winchester*,
  Cardiff historical papers (Cardiff, 2007—8)
—, 'Accumulation and polarisation in two bailiwicks of Winchester bishopric estates,
  1350–1410: regional similarities and contrasts', in B. Dodds and R.H. Britnell (eds),
  Agriculture and rural society after the Black Death: common themes and regional variations
  (Hertford, 2008), pp. 179–98
Page, F.M., *The estates of Crowland Abbey, a study in manorial organisation* (Cambridge, 1934)
Page, M., 'Challenging custom: the auditors of the bishopric of Winchester, *c.*1300–*c.*1310', in
  M. Prestwich, R.H. Britnell and R. Frame (eds), *Thirteenth century England VI* (Woodbridge,
  1997), pp. 39–48
—, 'A note on the manor of Limerstone, Isle of Wight', *Hampshire Field Club & Archaeological
  Society Newsletter*, 29 (1998), pp. 25–7
—, *The medieval bishops of Winchester: estate, archive and administration*, Hampshire Papers,
  24 (Winchester, 2002)
—, 'The peasant land market on the bishop of Winchester's manor of Farnham, 1263–1349',
  Surrey Archaeological Collections, 90 (2003), pp. 163–79
—, 'The peasant land market on the estate of the bishopric of Winchester before the Black
  Death', in R.H. Britnell (ed.), *The Winchester pipe rolls and medieval English society*
  (Woodbridge, 2003), pp. 61–80
—, 'The peasant land market in southern England: the estate of the bishops of Winchester,
  1260–1350', in L. Feller and C. Whickham (eds), *Le marché de la terre au Moyen Âge* (Rome,
  2005), pp. 315–40
—, 'Lords, peasants and property: the effect of the Black Death on the bishop of Winchester's
  estate' (unpublished)
Palliser, D.M. (ed.), *The Cambridge urban history of Britain, I: 600–1540* (Cambridge, 2000)

Plucknett, T.F.T., *Legislation of Edward I* (Oxford, 1949)

Postan, M.M., 'Some agrarian evidence of a declining population in the later Middle Ages', *Economic History Review*, 2nd series, 2 (1950), pp. 221–46, reprinted in *idem, Essays on medieval agriculture and general problems of the medieval economy* (Cambridge, 1973), pp. 186–213

—, *The famulus: the estate labourer in the XIIth and XIIIth centuries*, Economic History Review Supplement II (Cambridge, 1954)

—, 'The charters of the villeins', in C.N.L. Brooke and M.M. Postan (eds), *Carte nativorum: a Peterborough Abbey cartulary of the fourteenth century*, Northamptonshire Record Society, 20 (Northampton, 1960), pp. xxviii–lxv, reprinted in *idem, Essays on medieval agriculture and general problems of the medieval economy* (Cambridge, 1973), pp. 107–49

—, 'Subtenants on some manors of the bishops of Winchester', in C.N.L. Brooke and M.M. Postan (eds), *Carte nativorum: a Peterborough Abbey cartulary of the fourteenth century*, Northamptonshire Record Society, 20 (Northampton, 1960), p. lxiii

—, 'Village livestock in the thirteenth century', *Economic History Review*, 2nd series, 15 (1962), pp. 219–49, reprinted in *idem, Essays on medieval agriculture and general problems of the medieval economy* (Cambridge, 1973), pp. 214–48

—, 'Medieval agrarian society in its prime: England', in *idem* (ed.), *The Cambridge economic history of Europe, I: The agrarian life of the Middle Ages* (Cambridge, 1966), pp. 548–632

—, *The medieval economy and society* (London, 1972)

—, *Essays on medieval agriculture and general problems of the medieval economy* (Cambridge, 1973)

—, 'The chronology of labour services', *Transactions of the Royal Historical Society*, 4th series, 20 (1937), pp. 169–93, reprinted in *idem, Essays on medieval agriculture and general problems of the medieval economy* (Cambridge, 1973), pp. 89–106

— and Titow, J.Z., 'Heriots and prices on Winchester manors', *Economic History Review*, 2nd series, 11 (1959), pp. 392–411, reprinted in M.M. Postan, *Essays on medieval agriculture and general problems of the medieval economy* (Cambridge, 1973), pp. 150–85

Powicke, F.M., 'Observations on the English freeholder in the thirteenth century', in *Wirtschaft und Kultur: Festschrift zum 70. Geburtstag von Alfons Dopsch* (Baden bei Wien, 1938), pp. 382–93

Prestwich, M.C., 'Currency and the economy of early fourteenth century England', in N.J. Mayhew (ed.), *Edwardian monetary affairs (1279–1344)*, British Archaeological Reports, 36 (Oxford, 1977), pp. 45–58

Raftis, J.A., *Tenure and mobility*, Pontifical Institute of Medieval Studies, Studies and Texts, 8 (Toronto, 1964)

—, *Peasant economic development within the English manorial system* (Stroud, 1996)

Ravensdale, J., 'The transfer of customary land on a Cambridgeshire manor', in R.M. Smith (ed.), *Land, kinship and life-cycle* (Cambridge, 1984), pp. 197–225

Razi, Z., 'The Toronto school's reconstitution of medieval peasant society: a critical view', *Past and Present*, 85 (1979), pp. 141–57

—, *Life, marriage and death in a medieval parish: economy, society and demography in Halesowen 1270–1400* (Cambridge, 1980)

—, 'Family, land and the village community in later medieval England', *Past and Present*, 93 (1981), pp. 3–36

—, 'The erosion of the family-land bond in the late fourteenth and fifteenth centuries: a methodological note', in R.M. Smith (ed.), *Land, kinship and life-cycle* (Cambridge, 1984), pp. 295–304

—, 'Intrafamilial ties and relationships in the medieval village: a quantitative approach employing manor-court rolls', in Z. Razi and R.M. Smith (eds), *Medieval society and the manor court* (Oxford, 1996), pp. 369–91

— and Smith, R.M. (eds), *Medieval society and the manor court* (Oxford, 1996)

Robo, E., *Medieval Farnham: everyday life in an episcopal manor* (Farnham, 1939)

Roden, D., 'Fragmentation of farms and fields in the Chiltern Hills: thirteenth century and later', *Mediaeval Studies*, 31 (1969), pp. 225–38

—, 'Field systems of the Chiltern Hills and their environs', in A.R.H. Baker and R.A. Butlin (eds), *Studies of field systems in the British Isles* (Cambridge, 1973), pp. 325–76

Rogers, J.E.T., *A history of agriculture and prices in England, 1259–1793*, 7 vols (Oxford 1866–1902)

Schofield, P.R., 'Tenurial developments and the availability of customary land in a later medieval community', *Economic History Review*, 49 (1996), pp. 250–67

—, 'Dearth, debt and the local land market in a late thirteenth-century village community', *AHR*, 45 (1997), pp. 1–17

—, *Peasant and community in medieval England, 1200–1500* (Basingstoke, 2003)

Schofield, R.S., 'The geographical distribution of wealth in England, 1334–1649', *Economic History Review*, 2nd series, 18 (1965), pp. 483–510

Searle, E., *Lordship and community: Battle Abbey and its banlieu, 1066–1538* (Toronto, 1974)

Slota, L.A., 'Law, land transfer, and lordship on the estates of St Albans Abbey in the thirteenth and fourteenth centuries', *Law and History Review*, 6 (1988), pp. 119–38

Smith, R.M. (ed.), *Land, kinship and life-cycle* (Cambridge, 1984)

—, 'Some issues concerning families and their property in England, 1250–1800', in *idem* (ed.), *Land, kinship and life-cycle* (Cambridge, 1984), pp. 1–86

—, 'Families and their land in an area of partible inheritance: Redgrave, Suffolk, 1260–1320', in *idem* (ed.), *Land, kinship and life-cycle* (Cambridge, 1984), pp. 135–95

—, (ed.), 'Human resources', in G. Astill and A. Grant (eds), *The countryside of medieval England* (Oxford, 1988), pp. 188–212

—, 'Plagues and peoples: the long demographic cycle, 1250–1670', in P. Slack and R. Ward (eds), *The peopling of Britain: the shaping of a human landscape* (Oxford, 2002), pp. 177–210

—, 'Women's property rights under customary law: some developments in the thirteenth and fourteenth centuries', *Transactions of the Royal Historical Society*, 5th series, 36 (1986), pp. 165–94

Stocks, K., 'Manorial courts in England before 1250' (unpublished PhD thesis, University of Durham, 1998)

—, 'Payments to manorial courts in the early Winchester accounts', in R.H. Britnell (ed.), *The Winchester pipe rolls and medieval English society* (Woodbridge, 2003), pp. 45–59

Stone, D., *Decision-making in medieval agriculture* (Oxford, 2005)

—, 'The consumption of field crops in late medieval England', in C.M. Woolgar, D. Serjeantson and T. Waldron (eds), *Food in medieval England: diet and nutrition* (Oxford, 2006), pp. 11–26

Thornton, C.C., 'The determinants of land productivity on the bishop of Winchester's demesne of Rimpton, 1208 to 1403', in B.M.S. Campbell and M. Overton (eds), *Land, labour and livestock: historical studies in European agricultural productivity* (Manchester, 1991), pp. 183–210

—, 'The level of arable productivity on the bishopric of Winchester's manor of Taunton, 1283–1348', in R.H. Britnell (ed.), *The Winchester pipe rolls and medieval English society* (Woodbridge, 2003), pp. 109–37

Titow, J.Z., 'Evidence of weather in the pipe rolls of the bishopric of Winchester, 1209–1350', *Economic History Review*, 2nd series, 12 (1959–60), pp. 360–407

—, 'Land and population on the bishop of Winchester's estates 1209–1350' (unpublished PhD thesis, University of Cambridge, 1962)

—, 'Some differences between manors and their effects on the conditions of the peasantry in the thirteenth century', *AHR*, 10 (1962), pp. 1–13, reprinted in W. Minchinton (ed.), *Essays in agrarian history*, 2 vols (Newton Abbot, 1968), i, pp. 37–52

—, *English rural society, 1200–1350* (London, 1969)

—, *Winchester yields: a study in medieval agricultural productivity* (Cambridge, 1972)

—, 'Lost rents, vacant holdings and the contraction of peasant cultivation after the Black Death', *AHR*, 42 (1994), pp. 97–114

—, 'Labour problems and policies on the Winchester estates, 1208–1275' (unpublished paper presented to the British Agricultural History Society in 1995)

Toulmin, J., *The history of Taunton in the county of Somerset*, new edn enlarged by J. Savage (Taunton, 1822)

Vancouver, C., *General view of the agriculture of Hampshire and the Isle of Wight* (London, 1810)

Waugh, S.L., *England in the reign of Edward III* (Cambridge, 1991)

Whittle, J., 'Individualism and the family-land bond: a reassessment of land transfer patterns among the English peasantry *c.*1270–1580', *Past and Present*, 160 (1998), pp. 25–63

Whitty, R.G.H., *The court of Taunton in the sixteenth and seventeenth centuries* (Taunton, 1934)

Williamson, J., 'Norfolk: thirteenth century', in P.D.A. Harvey (ed.), *The peasant land market in medieval England* (Oxford, 1984), pp. 30–105

Yates, M., *Town and countryside in western Berkshire, c.1327–c.1600: social and economic change* (Woodbridge, 2007)

Young, A., *General view of the agriculture of Oxfordshire* (London, 1813)

Index

accumulation of holdings, 132–51, 153; across manors, 121, 141; after the Black Death, 62–4, 67–70, 122, 132, 136–42, 150–1; before the Black Death, 42–4, 132–6, 146, 150; and characteristics of major accumulators, 144–8, 151; and entry fines, 77; hindrances to before 1349, 135–6; large, 142–51; opposition to, 42–4, 132, 150, 153; scattered units in, 121, 131–3, 141, 144–5; size of manor affecting, 135, 156

acre, measured, 39–40, 48.

Adderbury (Oxon.), assarts at, 24; *gabulum* from, 20; demesne at, 21–3, 58n; high proportion of extrafamilial transfers at, 93; labour services at, 58; level of fines at, 94–5; number of fines at, 159; peasant leases at, 129–30; soils at, 156; tenures at, 47; virgates at, 39; widows' rights at, 108

Alresford (Hants.), 15; borough at, 28, 54, 156; demesne at, 21–3, 66; fulling mill at, 54 *gabulum* from, 20; labour services at, 59–60; manorial customs at, 45; number of fines at, 73, 159; weak family attachment to, 93, 96; widow at, 106

Alverstoke (Hants.), 29, 152; above average turnover of land at, 31–2; communications from, 33; fragmentation of holdings at, 46; free land at, 38; number of fines at, 159; soils at, 33; tenures at, 46; virgates at, 40; *see also* Gosport

Arlesey Bury (Beds.), 87

Ashmansworth (Hants.), above average turnover of land at, 35; actions of recovery at, 97; assarts at, 24; cotlands at, 52; demesne at, 21–3; *gabulum* from, 20; high proportion of extrafamilial transfers at, 93; labour services at, 60; number of fines at, 159; weak family attachment to, 93, 96

assarts, 19, 22–5, 30, 37, 41, 48–51, 56, 64, 68, 70, 80–1, 96, 103, 121, 123, 133–6, 140, 150–1, 153; defined, 22, 37

Assier, Rigaud of, bishop of Winchester (1319–23), 15

bailiwicks, 13–14

bastardy, 86, 98

Beauworth (Hants.), 15; accumulation at, 135; demesne at, 21–3; *gabulum* from, 20; labour services at, 61; number of fines at, 28, 159; weak family attachment to, 93, 96

Bentley (Hants.), 154; accumulation at, 133; assarts at, 24; demesne at, 21–3, 66; forfeiture of property at, 85; number of fines at, 159; smallholdings at, 53; virgates at, 39

Beveridge, W.H., 13

Billingsley, J., 30

bishops of Winchester, and compliance with manorial custom, 42–4, 46, 56, 152; and depression of wages, 74; flexibility of policy of, 61, 96; income of, 12, 75, 77; income from fines of, 75, 77; licensing breach of custom by, 53; negotiation for entry fines by, 74–5; pressure on tenants to take up vacant land by, 60, 84; *see also* Rigaud of Assier, William of

Edington, Nicholas of Ely, John Gervais, Adam Orleton, John of Pontoise, John Sandale, John Stratford, Henry Woodlock, William of Wykeham

Bishops Fonthill (Wilts.), accumulation at, 135–6; demesne at, 21–3; forfeiture of property at, 85; high proportion of extrafamilial transfers at, 96; number of fines at, 72, 159; tenures at, 46; ultimogeniture at, 106, 108; widows and widows' rights at, 106, 108

Bishops Sutton (Hants.), 126–7; accumulation at, 135–6; bailiwick of, 14; cotlands at, 112; demesne at, 20–3; elections to holdings in, 127; fulling mill at, 54; *gabulum* from, 20; intrafamilial grants to sons at, 113; labour services at, 61; low yields of grain at, 127; number of fines at, 73, 159; purpresture at, 48–9; smallholdings at, 53; widow at, 112; woodland at, 50

Bishopstoke (Hants.), 16; above average turnover of land at, 31–2; absence of defaults of rent after the Black Death, at 142; buyers of land at, 119–20; communications from, 33–4; demesne at, 21–3, 58n; extrafamilial transfers at, 90; *gabulum* from, 20; labour services at, 58; leased, 67–8; level of fines at, 76, 79; little accumulation at, 135, 141–2; number of fines at, 73, 142, 159; soils at, 33; tenures at, 48; transfers by inheritance at, 95; ultimogeniture at, 33, 108, 113; virgates at, 39, 52; widows at, 107–8, 142

Bishopstone (Wilts.), accumulation at, 135; avoidance of manorial office at, 148; bordland at, 37; demesne at, 21–3; maintenance agreement at, 124; near Salisbury, 27; number of fines at, 159; smallholdings at, 53; tenures at, 46; weak family attachment to, 93, 96

Bishops Waltham (Hants.), 11, 119, 121, 126; above average turnover of land at, 31, 126; accumulation at, 42, 132–3, 135, 137–9, 142–3, 146, 150; actions of recovery at, 97–8; avoidance of manorial office at, 148; bailiwick of, 14; below average proportion of transfers *post mortem* at, 93; cottages and cotlands at, 52, 123, 149; communications from, 33–4; demesne at, 20–3, 58; devices to protect title to property at, 98, 100–1; distribution of land at, 53, 137; extrafamilial transfers at, 90, 95, 100, 109; ferlings at, 140; forfeiture of property at, 85; fragmentation of customary units at, 56, 109; fulling mill at, 54; *gabulum* from, 20; labour services at, 58; level of fines at, 76, 79–80, 95; number of fines at, 28, 159; peasant leases at, 129; purprestures at, 22; manorial customs at, 42, 45; marsh at, 22; quasi-burghal development at, 27–8; rental of c.1332 for, 17–18, 55, 132–3, 137, 146; shops at, 55; smallholdings at, 51–3, 55, 95, 137, 150; soils at, 32–3; tenures at, 33; tithings of, 13; transfers by inheritance at, 95; ultimogeniture at, 33, 108–9; virgates at, 39–40, 52; widow at, 112

Bitterne (Hants.), above average turnover of land at,